BEEN SO LONG

BEEN SO LONG

My Life and Music

JORMA KAUKONEN

St. Martin's Press
New York

www.stmartins.com

The Library of Congress Cataloging-in-Publication Data is available upon request.

ISBN 978-1-250-12548-4 (hardcover)
ISBN 978-1-250-20272-7 (signed edition)
ISBN 978-1-250-12549-1 (ebook)

First Edition: August 2018

10   9   8   7   6   5   4   3   2   1

Contents

Acknowledgments

My story is my story. I've told bits and pieces of it over my lifetime to a treasured few, but it was time to tell all to a bigger audience, and nothing is ever accomplished alone. There are a number of people without whom this project would not have come to be. I'd like to thank and acknowledge as many of them as I can—mea culpa for not being able to name them all.

To Kevin Haworth, whose editing skills from start to finish helped forge my loosely told tales into a book. He guided me to speak my truth and present it through my eyes without "punching down" on others. Peter Wolverton from St. Martin's Press held my nose to the grindstone in a relentless, honest, and creative way. Lena Margareta Pettersson, whose life I had to tell in order to tell my own. We were like opposite ends of magnets, and though I chose to stay in that space until I was ready to jump in front of the fear, Margareta helped shape who I am today. Jack Casady, who has been by my side since we were kids. As each other's oldest friends we lit the way for each other throughout our friendship. Grace, Paul, Marty, Spencer, Signe . . . it has been my honor to have played with you and to have been a part of the magic of Jefferson Airplane. The exciting exchange between us as friends and colleagues cannot be measured. To my many musical friends who have left this Earth: Pigpen, Janis, Jerry Garcia, Skip Spence, Ian Buchanan, Mike Bloomfield, Larry Coryell, and too many to name. We came up together musically and the things I learned from you about the love of song has stayed with me all these years. Today, when I play some of the songs that we enjoyed together as young men and women, it's like having you onstage with me.

To my Fur Peace Ranch and Hot Tuna family: John Hurlbut, Kelly Stewart, Justin Berry, Jerry Sullivan, Brenda Bolin, David Wolff, Treva, Smiles, Michael, Shannon, Wendy, Sara, Joe, Phil Jacobs, Michael and Claudia Falzarano, Barry Mitterhoff, Justin Guip, and Myron Hart. You all made it possible for the two entities to cross-pollinate, which allows us to give back the way we do. To Cash Edwards, thank you for your tireless efforts and your commitment to excellence. To Steve Martin and Seth Rappaport, who are the Gatekeepers of my life on the road. They have made it possible for me to travel the world and find my way to the best audiences ever. To Marc Schechter, my good friend and Gladiator at Law who makes sure the perimeter is always secure . . . many, many thanks!

To my son, Zachary, and my daughter, Izze, whose collective existence is just shy of a miracle. Had I not made that choice, it would have left me not knowing how amazing it is to find the kind of love I have found because of the both of you. You keep me honest and living in the moment. And last but not least, my beautiful and absurdly funny wife, Vanessa, whose mind is always filled with goals that must be met. She has been my muse for almost thirty years. Without her loving encouragement and commitment to authentic excellence I would probably be sitting in a log cabin on a mountaintop somewhere watching the sun rise and set.

Foreword

If I think I know someone, I ought to think again.

I never knew that Jorma was often walking Winston Churchill's "Black Dog." What I saw was a bright, funny, superb guitar player who incidentally wrote one of my all-time favorite songs, "Embryonic Journey." Just today, my daughter, China, and I listened to his song "Genesis" and broke out into a bawling fest. It's such a beautiful piece of work.

Having cleared some fog more than twenty years ago, he has opened up and brought out the often poignant feelings of a man looking for a new morning.

He has been all over the map—literally and figuratively. He moved on a regular basis among several continents. He has a love of driving (almost any vehicle), crossing countries countless times and just appreciating the people, the scenery, and the sense of freedom. On a constant ride, I'm surprised he didn't just explode at some point.

His ability to talk honestly about fear and confusion without sounding maudlin is a finely tuned process. Even if you know nothing of the man, it is a moving story of the extremes in a life pushed to the limits.

A good read, a modern parable.

—Grace Slick

Into the Light

What is it that makes us who and what we are? If I truly knew, I wouldn't have to write this book. I've got some suspicions though. Our first moments of existence grow in the darkness of our mothers' wombs. At some point the moment comes when we venture from darkness to the light of the world. It seems that we have been waiting for a long time. My first memories of light in the world seem to be about two or three years of age, and I remember this because that light came to me in the form of my mother's song. When Mom was at home doing whatever chores awaited her, she would always sing, and if she wasn't singing, the radio was on and song would fill the room. Music seemed to me to be the reward for being alive. To me, nothing has the power to evoke a place in time like music. It stirs memory in a singular way that is unmatched.

Indeed, in my small world back then, light came to me in the form of song. I learned to read in preschool, and some of the first words that called to me from a printed page were song lyrics. As I grew older it was important that most of my friends liked reading, listening, and singing. As years began to slide into the past, the music that flowed to us from the airwaves began to define a soundtrack in our lives; coupled with adolescence, this opened a door into a room filled with possibilities and sound. This room was always filled with light, and whatever else might be happening in my life, it was always a summer day there.

The light waited for me in the brief moments I played violin in the junior high school orchestra and later when I took piano lessons. It bathed me when I practiced and illuminated me when I played at recitals. Now, I wasn't a prodigy, but I loved performing. People sometimes ask me if I ever had stage fright. I was nervous and excited, but not afraid. For someone who was as intrinsically shy as I was, this gave me a way to communicate on a primal level.

The first time I played an open mike on a real stage, the light waited for me and invited me in. I walked into that light knowing that was where I belonged. All my close friends lived in the same world. Jerry Garcia, Janis Joplin . . . these are names most people recognize these days, but there are many you will never hear about because their light was not quite so public. Awareness of this affinity really hit me four or five years ago when I was on a tour with David Bromberg. We each took turns opening the show and got together to finish each set. One night David was playing his part of the show and I was backstage right, waiting for him to call on me. He was illuminated by spots, and it occurred to me that as always I was waiting to be called into light, and that in one way or another I have spent my life doing this.

The dance with darkness is always with us, but the light is there too. For more better than worse, the music has always been my beacon and I have followed it most of the time. The sounds of music in general and the guitar in particular have always pierced my night with a welcome glow. The feeling of a guitar on my lap and my hand on the neck has always surrounded me in a protective armor of tranquility. After all these years, the feeling is stronger than ever. The light brought me out of darkness and into the world, and at some point I will follow the last light and it will take me home. I'm definitely not in a hurry for that journey. In the meantime, let's get on with the story.

Introduction

It's a lovely day here in Southeast Ohio as I begin this journey across the page. I know there is a big difference between blogging and writing a book and that there are two kinds of people. There are those who talk about writing books and those who actually do it. I guess this is my chance to jump from one camp to the other.

I need to issue a comprehensive disclaimer here. Sometimes the "truth" of history is written by those who take the time to write it. Winners and survivors tend to be these writers. I must caution my readers to realize that this history—my history—is drawn from my subjective memory. These will be the stories that shaped my life as I remember them. As the tell reveals facts that might conflict with my recollections, I will make note of these. All that said, this is my story as I remember it, as seen through the prism of my mind's eye.

I can do no better than that.

I think about the unseen forces that conspired to cause my forebears to leave the home places where their ancestors had always lived to come to America. Why would you want to leave a place where your family had always lived, where your DNA was imprinted on the trees, on the rocks, in the rivers and fields? Frankly, I don't know. I could not imagine leaving the United States of America or even the little corner of the universe I have inhabited here in Ohio for more than a quarter of a century. My life has not always been kind or gentle, but most of my crises have been self-inflicted. I have not been singled out because of my religion or lack of it, because of my race or because of my status in society. These days I am always trying to make my world a better place, but I want to be able to do it here . . . in my world.

As a second-generation American, I know my grandparents on both sides of my family came here to seek a better life for themselves and their children. Did they believe in the American Dream? Was there ever such a thing to them, or was finding a home in America just better than hunger, persecution, or death in their respective home places?

Sad to say, the old ones who could answer these questions are now all gone. The cards and letters from my grandparents lie in the boxes my parents left me when they passed. They are still wrapped in the ribbon and twine they were wrapped in when my grandparents said good-bye to the old country almost a hundred years ago. These little notes stare up at me from their resting places like hieroglyphics. Along with their lives, their joys and dreams, sorrows and longings have been dust for a very long time. Those of the generation before me who could have seen through this glass darkly and brought the pictures into the light are now gone too.

Perhaps there was some disaffection in my family with living "the way things were." Their diaspora led them across the Atlantic Ocean; mine led me away from a 9-to-5 bureaucracy and into a world of creative freedom that had very long legs indeed. From rehearsals and jams in small apartments and tiny back rooms to Monterey, Woodstock, Altamont, the Rock & Roll Hall of Fame, the world of the Grammys, and beyond—this was the road I lived on. Indeed, this was my embryonic journey and much, much more!

1

Land of Heroes

Jaako Kaukonen, my grandfather, came over in the days just prior to the twentieth century. He came from a little town in Finland near the Bay of Bothnia called Ylistaro. There are still Kaukonens there, and Kaukallas and all sorts of Kaukas. What possessed him to make such a journey? I never had the opportunity to meet Jack, as he would call himself in America. He passed in Los Angeles in the mid-1950s. He now rests in Inglewood Cemetery near my grandmother Ida, my uncle Pentti, my dad, Jorma, and my mom, Beatrice. Tarmo, my other uncle, whom I never met, is buried in a military cemetery, also in LA. He died while he was still in the service, but we shall get to that.

My father told me that Jaako landed in Ellis Island and his brother, whose name I do not know, landed in Boston. The two Kaukonen brothers never saw each other again in America . . . ever. Dad told me that they wrote and would occasionally call, but that was it. Finns are a stoic lot.

At the dawn of the twentieth century it became profitable to extract copper ore from the deep pit mines of Gogebic County in the Upper Peninsula of Michigan. The workers came mainly from Sweden, Germany, England, Italy, Poland, and Finland. The Brits were mostly from Cornwall. My dad and his Finnish buddies affectionately called them Cousin Jacks. The Cousin Jacks brought pasties with them . . . one of the great culinary inventions of all time. When the men headed down into the pits, their tiffin carriers would be filled with, among other things, pasties, which in addition to being really tasty stay hot for a long time. There is nothing like a hot lunch when you're a mile beneath the surface of the Earth.

Ida Palmquist, my grandmother, was from Hanko, Finland, a little seaport town just north of Helsinki. Finland was the eternal battleground between the Swedes and the Russians. Kaukonen is very definitely a Finnish name, whereas Palmquist is from the Swedish heritage that was present then in Finland and still is. Ida came to Ironwood, Michigan, as did Jaako. There was work in the mines and languages they all knew. I don't know where she first landed in America— somewhere, obviously, because there she was.

Did she and Jaako meet immediately? I don't know and I wouldn't know who to ask. I do know that at some point before she was married, she worked in Montana for a couple of years as a domestic. Yep, Grandma Ida was a maid on a ranch. I've got all the postcards she wrote back to her friends in Ironwood when she was working there. Finland to Michigan to Montana and back to Michigan was like crossing galaxies in the early 1900s. She was obviously not afraid to travel great distances to find work and her place in the world.

In any case, Ida returned to Gogebic County and she and Jaako got married. My dad, Jorma Sr., was born on October 24, 1910. His brother Tarmo was born in 1912 and his brother Pentti in 1914. Jaako realized that there had to be a better way to make a living than breaking rocks looking for copper ore in the depths of the Earth. He became a tailor. He set up shop on East Aurora Street in Ironwood across from the Carnegie Library. My father learned to speak English at that library. My grandfather Jaako wound up owning much of the city block across the street.

Much more recently, in 1993, as my dad was becoming mobile again after his first stroke, I was blessed to be able to go on a "roots" trip with him to his old home place. Many of his old friends were still alive then, and to see my father reconnect with them brought the past right up to the present moment. There was Robert Lee the Norwegian. When he was young Robert was a ski flyer, a particularly Norwegian version of ski jumping. "Do you want to see the big jump at Copper Mountain?" he asked. Of course I did. This was a ski flying hill, one of the largest in America. Bob knew a shortcut through the woods. He had a large 4×4 and planned on going off road. "Do you want me to drive?" I asked the old man. "NO! You will go too slow!" Da Yoopers are a tough lot. I also got to meet Francis Ann, who was my dad's girlfriend when he was thirteen before the Kaukonens left for LA.

I'm going to pause for a moment here and introduce you to another Jorma oddity. I've been journaling for a number of years and any time you see passages in italics, they will be from my diary. I'm glad that I kept all this stuff; it's hard to re-create these kind of fresh insights.

Saturday, February 19, 2005, Hillside Farm, Meigs County

I spend lots of time writing about recollections of the past. The journey is not always pleasant, but it is my journey. The road to enlightenment is slow and incomplete at best, but at least I'm making progress. My life today is rich beyond belief. That is not to say that the road is without bumps or that I don't just frigging lose it sometimes. I do . . . but not often . . . not like I used to. Today is a great day . . . cleaning the barn . . . looking at old family memorabilia . . . throwing much away . . . saving some. Dad looks at me in a picture from Hancock, Michigan. His face is twisted from his stroke . . . he is not smiling . . . the trip to the UP has stirred deep memories in him I can only imagine. Behind that thoughtful look lies a latent twinkle that would say sarcastically, "What's it to you?"

As it turns out, Dad, it all meant a lot to me . . . and still does.

There was the old Finn Hall where Dad learned to play the mandolin and the violin; there were the black agate beaches where he played as a kid; there was the old Kaukonen family home on Garfield Street.

I wouldn't have missed it for anything.

What the heyho was going on? Lots, obviously. The Kaukonens were trying to find their way in America, and it took them from Ironwood, Michigan, to Tucson, Arizona. I don't know much about this time except that it didn't work out. They went back to Ironwood again, all five of them, and they remained there until 1923 when they moved to Lincoln Heights in East LA.

The Kaukonen family was on their way to San Francisco—at least at first. In those days, a transcontinental trip was a major undertaking. I have no idea what kind of car they would have owned that could hold five people and all their earthly possessions. In any case, they set out for San Francisco. In an era before interstate highways (and paved roads in general) this was a heck of a project.

Now I love to travel, always have. I guess I came by it naturally. When I'm driving somewhere it is always an existential adventure. Time can stand on its own when you're on the road. I always felt that whether riding a motorcycle or driving a car, you are the captain of your fate seeking the far places.

But automobile travel in the 1920s was way beyond seeking a far place of great adventure. This was a momentous voyage! In that spirit, Jaako, the skipper of that little four-wheeled ship, ran into some difficulties. Was it weather by the Front Range in Colorado? Lack of roads in the Rockies? I do know that they headed southwest and wound up in Lincoln Heights, East LA, instead of San Francisco and that was that. My dad and his brothers grew up to be Angelenos in what is considered to be the oldest neighborhood in LA outside of downtown.

Wow! So here are these Finns. In East LA. Jaako started another custom tailoring business. He wound up making clothes for movie stars such as Douglas Fairbanks. The Kaukonens may not have been rich, but they were comfortable and the three kids always had cool clothes.

Jaako became Jack, Tarmo became Leonard, and Pentti became Pen. My dad was still Jorma, but it was important for the boys to be Americans, and if this meant mostly shedding Finnish names, so be it. It wouldn't be until the 1950s that Dad really started to rediscover his Finnish roots.

The Great Depression came and Dad and his two brothers went to Trona, California, to mine borax. Ironic. The Finnish family left Ironwood, Michigan, and the mines, moved to Southern California, and the kids wound up working in mines.

The climate, though, was the antithesis of the Upper Peninsula. Trona in the Mojave Desert is a long way from Gogebic County and Lake Superior. The boys worked for the American Potash Company on scaffolds on the desert and in Lake Searles. Mining doesn't seem like a lot of fun no matter where you find it, but there's nothing wrong with a gig. According to family legend, Dad fell off a scaffold and broke his hip, which ended his borax mining career.

My dad went to UCLA, and in 1932 he was an usher at the Summer Olympics. Tarmo and Pentti were both talented artists. Tarmo was also a figure skater of some accomplishment and at some point had a hand in the training and handling of Leo, the MGM lion. At least that's how family lore has it.

On July 14, 1936, Jorma Ludwig Kaukonen met Beatrice Love Levine at a Bastille Day party somewhere in southern Maryland. Dad always loved to play tennis and I guess he cut a dashing figure that day in his tennis whites with his racket in his hand. That's what I heard, anyway, and it helped their marriage last more than sixty years. I was born four years after they were married, but we'll get to that anon.

Beatrice Love Levine's parents were Vera and Ben. My grandmother's family was from the St. Petersburg area in Russia. As I was writing this, I remembered that I knew of some distant relatives in Ellington, Connecticut, where that part of the family took root in America. I went to the Internet, of course, to find a cousin named Rose Rychling. Sad to say, I found that she passed at eighty-three on December 6, 2015. I guess we won't be talking for a while. When my mom died on May 8, 1998, there were a flurry of connections with relations who were distant to me . . . and then they were gone. My life went on and I lost track. I know there are only so many hours in the day, but this one is on me.

So Vera landed at Ellis Island like so many. I don't know when. The name Haskevitch was just too much for the immigrations officer to deal with, so she became a Joseph. Easier to spell, I would assume. Some of her family became Haskells—again, easier to spell. What prompted my grandparents to come to this country? I have no idea. When I was younger and could have had this discussion with them I simply accepted their quaint old world qualities as their norm and focused only on my place in the world.

There are stories though. In the St. Petersburg area, Jews were not allowed to own property in the time of the czars. But somehow Vera's father had an "arrangement" with a wealthy Gentile nobleman and they owned thousands of acres of timberland in what we know as Karelia. It seems she lived a life of some privilege. That said, she somehow ran afoul of the authorities and wound up in a gulag. It is said that one of the family's servants took her place and she escaped. Upon returning home, she found that Cossacks had trampled her brother and killed much of the family. Keep in mind, this is before the Russian Revolution. On her way out of Russia—so the story goes—she dynamited the home of the headman of the shtetl, escaped Russia, and found her way to America. "When you are young it is good to be audacious," she would say with a wry smile.

My grandfather Benjamin S. Levine's family came from a shtetl on the Dnieper River. His father, Shmuel, was a patriarch of some note and had already brought much of the family over to Ellington, Connecticut.

In 1897, Jacob and Shifra Rosenberg, a Russian-Jewish immigrant couple newly arrived in the United States, bought a piece of land near Crystal Lake, approximately fifteen miles northeast of Hartford, Connecticut. The Rosenbergs were the first Jewish farmers in the Connecticut rural area known as Rockville-Vernon Ellington. According to the *Ledger of the Jeshurun Society of Russian Refugees Who Settled on Farms in the Rockville-Vernon Ellington Area* (a Hebrew document written in 1905 by Shmuel Levine, my great-grandfather), the Rosenbergs created their homestead "through the labor of their own hands and by the sweat of their brow!" In the next few years, the Levines and other Russian-Jewish immigrant families followed the Rosenbergs. "Armed with few belongings but with a strong will and a determined spirit, we searched for a place to settle and through the righteousness of the Lord [we] chose this place . . . the Connecticut valley . . . in the area of Rockville-Vernon Ellington."

My grandfather Ben was not a farmer, but he was one of many children and they all worked on the tobacco farm. There is a little Torah in the shul by the Orthodox graveyard in Ellington scribed by my great-grandfather Shmuel.

How interesting that Shmuel is only three generations back yet I, Jorma, know so little about his life. The ripples of memory dissipate so quickly and a hundred years can swallow it all. My son, Zach, will never really know anything about my parents, nor will my daughter, Izze. Izze is fortunate to have a relationship with my wife Vanessa's mother, Virginia. As a result Izze will always have that grandma in her life and in her memory.

Monday, May 2, 2005, Hillside Farm, Meigs County
Ellington, Connecticut, and more

Life and all the things you've left unsaid. That covers a lot of ground even if you limit the experience to this metaphor. I'm always talking about living in the moment, drinking in the joy of life each day and I believe these things. But there is more for me. It is true that I am comfortable in the world of wistful metaphors. I like feelings of loss and longing, but I don't live there. So I'm thinking today that life is indeed all the things that you've left unsaid . . . It is also all the things that you did say, good and bad, as well as all the things you need to say. If I were a wordsmith and my livelihood depended completely on writing and selling songs I would always be looking for subjects that people could relate to without knowing my situation or me. Now my situation is actually quite sunny. Vanessa and I had a little time off so we went to New York to celebrate Passover with some dear friends. They welcomed us, the Novice Jews, into their home and allowed us to share their

Pesach experience. In the morning we went to Temple at B'nai Jeshurun on the upper west side where the music and the service were simply stunning. Friends are asking me if I am rediscovering my roots because I'm getting old, or what. Well, I am who I am today for sure, but faith and comfort are not predicated upon dogma of any religion, but that dogma may give structure for a meditative space. Anyway, with all due respect, wrapping myself in the tallit of belief gives me a serene space in which to center myself.

We went to Connecticut. My mother was born in East Windsor, up near Hartford. Vanessa is from Southington. It is a home place for us both. I had talked to Cousin Audrey for years about coming up there and it was always, "One of these days when we get time." Well, I realized if I waited for that to happen, we'd never go, so we just did it.

My mother told me, "Your grandfather is buried in the oldest Jewish cemetery in the United States." As with many things buried in memory, this proved to be not quite the case. In the latter part of the 19th century, my grandfather's people came to Connecticut from Russia and began to grow Connecticut broadleaf tobacco. Even though the climate in the United States at the time was fraught with anti-Semitic behavior it was better than the shtetls of Eastern Europe. The Jews have been in America for a very long time. It would be hard to find the oldest Jewish anything. However, the cemetery in Ellington is one hundred years old this year, and that is good enough for me.

My second cousins, Audrey and Isabel, took Vanessa and me from Manchester to Ellington, and as we drove through that little town we passed through developments that had been farm country but now were filled with houses. As the road shrank there were fewer houses and then we were there at the graveyard, still surrounded by fields. The first stop was at Samuel and Gittel's grave. My great-grandfather and great-grandmother. The Patriarch of the family, it seemed to me that it all started with him. Almost immediately thereafter I rush to Ben, my grandfather's stone. He meant so much to me, he and Vera. He taught me so much in spite of myself. There are many things left unsaid between Ben, Vera, and myself, but I no longer need a phone to communicate with them.

Ah, the old family photographs, everyone sitting as if frozen so as not to blur the photos. These Orthodox Jews are looking stern, but from the stories I've been hearing, there was lots of fun-loving camaraderie. Strength in family, tradition, love of education, and of course guilt and narrow-minded traditionalism. Wow, what stuff! How did they all survive? So much has changed in the last one hundred and fifty years that if Shmuel and I were to meet, we would be different species from a different galaxy, maybe.

And here I am, an aging musician so far in some ways from the root, and so close in others. I touch my grandfather's stone and I tell him, "You gave me keys, Ben, and in my life I have opened many doors!" Vera would drag my face down to her and give me a kiss when I would leave the house. She always smoked so she always smelled of cigarettes. Being a teenager, I didn't like being woman-handled by my grandmother; I needed to be so grown up, you know. Today it would be nice to kiss her cheek and tell her I love her, but that's how it goes. I can only presume that she knows and no longer needs to be told.

At the little shul not far from the cemetery there is evidence of the little Orthodox community in Ellington. It is rumored that Shmuel himself scribed one of the Torahs. The tracks are everywhere. I am deeply touched, and I feel as if I belong.

We have dinner with Audrey and Isabel and we talk and talk.

The tobacco farms in the East Windsor area of Connecticut . . . what a concept. It was a successful collective effort that seemed to work for everyone involved. Ben would go to Brown University and receive a PhD. He was always so proud of this and would never omit that suffix when he wrote his name. Vera graduated from Trinity College but I never remember her having a job. The story goes that Vera was pregnant with my mom before she and Ben were married. I heard that from cousin Audrey Brett. Audrey would say, "And that is what happens when you walk together in the cornfields under the moonlight."

Vera was always a contentious sort. She was short with everyone, always acerbic. She always seemed unfulfilled to me. Ben worked relentlessly until the day he died. I can still see him at his typewriter writing late into the night . . . or in his gardens in the yard . . . or in the basement crafting some project. Busy doesn't even begin to describe where he was coming from.

I remember watching Vera playing solitaire and chain-smoking Kents. When they got a TV, she would watch *Perry Mason*. "You're a clever devil, Perry," she would say to the TV. She was tough on her friends, and really tough on her daughter, my mom. Ben watched professional wrestling, which he loved, and released his tensions by yelling at the TV.

Being a girl child in that Levine household had to be really difficult. I don't know where Mom went to school when she was young, but she went to college at the University of Wisconsin at Waukesha. It is said that she had an Indian Scout motorcycle. Perhaps that's why she never took issue with my love of motorcycles. It is also said that she wore a backless bathing suit on a beach in Delaware, causing some consternation.

Mom got her teaching certificate and became a teacher. Enter Dad at that Bastille Day party in 1936. How did Jorma Sr. find his way to a party that was probably filled with Jewish intellectuals of questionable political bent? I will probably never know, but there he was—and there she was.

Well, one thing led to another and they got married. They were both employees of the federal government in the District of Columbia, and in those days federal employees in DC could not marry, so they drove to Mount Vernon, New York, where the then youngest mayor in the United States performed the ceremony. Mom and Dad, early rebels, somehow managed to circumvent the proscriptions of the feds. I wasn't born until 1940, so for four years Mom and Dad had only each other—and of course the massive Levine/Joseph clans.

Dad always seemed to profess that he wasn't interested in children, that he wanted to roam the world doing this and that. Had it been up to Mom, I would have had a dozen brothers and sisters. Mom was a teacher and Dad had started out as a fingerprint clerk for the FBI. Back in those days it was illegal for government employees to have unions. Dad and some of his pals tried to start a union for fingerprint clerks and until he retired from his long career in the State Department, over thirty years later, he was always flagged for this seditious act.

March 26, 2001, Sarasota, Florida

A seven hundred and fifty eight mile drive from Nashville and here we are. I was thinking about this place earlier on the trip. Siesta Key is right down the road from us and I recall that in 1948 when my mom was separated from my dad she took my brother and I down here to live for a year or so. We drove down from Washington, DC, in our 1940 Studebaker two-door sedan and when we got to Siesta Key Mom found a stilt house on the beach. It's a long time ago but I recall Siesta Key being sparsely populated and generally speaking heaven to me at the time. I wore my Roy Rogers pearl-handled two-gun rig around and tipped my cowboy hat back on my head. Yee haw! I went to school in Sarasota with the kids from the circuses who were wintering there. I learned how to swim in the gentle surf of the Gulf and I scavenged on the beach. When a hurricane came we took refuge with a friend of Mom's who lived inland. We returned to our house and found the stilts had almost disappeared with the storm surge. I didn't know about storm surges then, I just marveled. Mom taught me to swim and body surf. She told me about the marvelous things I picked up on the beach, from egg cases to sharks teeth and conch shells. I wish I had more memories of my brother, but we didn't interact much . . . not then, and not now. I regret that but cannot change it.

When Mom was ready to return to DC and to Dad, we packed up what little we had into the Studebaker and headed north. Somewhere on the trip back up the Coast, we were rear-ended and had to spend a week or so in some Southern town I don't remember while the car was repaired. The Studie was red when we went South, but blue when we came home. Mom had just bought a house in Chevy Chase across the street from Lafayette Elementary School where I wound up going. Dad came home from Korea and the Far East. The time in Siesta Key faded like a dream but that tropical smell of the sea and its attendant sounds still touch my face with tendrils of memory . . . faded like a dream.

2

A New Song

"Don't you want to find out who you really are?" That's what Vanessa asked me the other day when we were talking about this memoir. I have to say the answer is yes. Good or bad, it truly is what it is . . . but the landscape of my forebears has certainly helped to guide my footsteps.

Yesterday was one of those beautiful days, truly perfect in every way. Blue sky, fluffy clouds, not too hot, not too cool—a great day for a motorcycle ride. At this moment I am motorcycle-less, but Vanessa isn't and she lets me take her Dyna for a putt. It's a bare-bones bike, its only amenity a windshield. Truly old school in every way, and just what I needed.

For whatever reason, two wheels have always meant freedom to me. I remember the first time I was able to ride a bicycle without the Old Man running next to me. It was on the Lafayette Elementary School playground across the street from our house at 3312 Northampton Street in northwest DC. There was a large blacktop then. It's gone now, school buildings everywhere. Just saw it last week when Izze and Vanessa took a trip with me to rekindle these memories.

I was on my mom's bicycle. It was a Schwinn "girls'" bike. The cross tube dipped down so a woman could ride the bike in a skirt. (Do such things still exist?) Anyway, because there was no cross tube, even though I couldn't reach the pedals from the seat, I could stand up . . . and there I was, riding. I began to pick up speed and I left Dad behind as I sailed around that old blacktop.

Pedaling up what seemed like a big hill, flying down it with gravity as my guide. It was magical. The next thing I remember was my first bicycle. It was a twenty-four-inch Dayton Rollfast and it was the most beautiful thing I had ever seen. In those days, parents released their children into the world with the only limit being "Be home for dinner."

I rode the Lafayette playground and, as I became more adventuresome, through the neighborhood until I was daring enough to ride down Military Road into Rock Creek Park itself.

I was free.

My parents loved their kids, and I guess each other, in a contentious way. The landscape in the Kaukonen household was dotted with minefields and you just never knew when you were going to step on one, so out of the house was always a good thing.

I'm not sure I had really been made conscious of the existence of motorcycles yet, but with that nascent spirit in mind I bobbed my Rollfast and took not only the fenders off, but also everything I deemed unnecessary, from the stand to the bell to the chain guard. Bare bones: old school in a time when old school was still new school.

In late 1952 or early 1953 Dad got a job as director of the Asia Foundation in Karachi, Pakistan. We sold the Dayton Rollfast, said goodbye to our dog Toby, and I took my first plane ride, on a Lockheed Constellation, to New York City. Even after all these years I remember the thrill of seeing those four piston engines fire up. A cough of black smoke as the oil blew out of the jugs and then the blue engine fire pulsing out of the visible exhausts. Modern jets are cool, but they're just not the same.

In New York, we cabbed over to the docks where the Kaukonen family had passage booked on the SS *United States*. The ship was built to capture the transatlantic speed record and I remember a card that said the only wood on the ship was the pencils. Any time you're out of sight of land and in deep water, you realize immediately, "Oh G-d, Thy sea is so great, and my ship is so small." We anchored for a bit in the Straits of Gibraltar and folks came out from the shore in small boats to sell trinkets. Bumboats, they called them. "*Nizastoffa, nizastoffa*," the merchants would shout. "Nice stuff, nice stuff!" They threw trinkets up on weighted lines and the money came down the same way. Welcome to the Mediterranean Sea! This was pretty earthshaking stuff for American kids.

Next port of call: Greece. We took a walk around the Parthenon in Athens and saw the feet of the Colossus in Rhodes. Not quite done with ancient culture, the SS *United States*' final port was in Alexandria, Egypt. The Kaukonens disembarked with all their collective junk and made their way to Cairo.

What to remember here? I remember the trip to the Great Pyramids on a camel. I remember climbing up the pyramids. I remember flying from Cairo to Basra, Iraq, and from Basra to Karachi, Pakistan, which would be our home for the next three years.

My nickname since I was four years old was Jerry. Back in 1944, in the closing years of World War II, my dad was at the Navy Language School in Ann Arbor learning Japanese. Mom and Dad and I lived in some sort of military housing complex. Some of the base kids grabbed me on the way home from preschool (or whatever they called it back then) and tried to hang me with a coat hanger from the bucket of a backhoe. Jorma was so foreign-sounding to these little patriots that they took it upon themselves to identify me as a Nazi spy and were proceeding with the execution. Mom happened by in the nick of time and saved the day. As an upshot of this little event, I took Dad's nickname, which was Jerry. I guess Jorma was too much to deal with. Perhaps in the good old US of A of the time, a man's name that ended in a vowel was an upsetting thing.

Well, this American kid Jerry lands in Karachi with his mom and dad and brother Peter. Pakistan was like a sensory vision from another universe. I knew nothing about the British Raj, or the unbelievably complex issues that surrounded Partition in 1947 that plague the Indian subcontinent to this day.

The East India Company, the Raj, the Indian Civil Service, and the waning British Empire meant truly a new reality. Even though as a kid my mom dragged my brother and me around the US while Dad was in the service, that was a far cry from my first international experience. When we first landed, we lived at one of the Asia Foundation's houses in a Karachi suburb called Clifton. There were ceiling fans, no air-conditioning. There was mosquito netting but I still got malaria. We boiled drinking water but I got amoebic dysentery. There was an in-house parrot named Dilbert.

Yeah . . . there I was in Pakistan. Looking back on it all, my mom and dad always had what I can only call an alienated relationship. I was never abused physically but my parents relentlessly took emotional hostages. I never knew when a seemingly harmless conversation might take a left turn and become an arc light of emotional dissatisfaction. It was always thus in my memory, and the new life on the Indian subcontinent was no different. Dad was the big dog at the Asia Foundation. We had servants, lots of them. Each was obedient to the caste system they were born into. There was the guard, the gardener, the sweeper, the cook, the house servants, and the drivers. A sweeper would always be a sweeper, as would everyone in his or her family. There was no mobility, upward, lateral, or otherwise.

Shanawaz and Mir Khan were our drivers. Shanawaz allowed me to log driving time in the company vehicles. We had a 1953 Chevy four-door, a 1955 Chevy four-door, and a 1950 Jeep Station Wagon. All manual transmissions, all right-hand drive. That was one of the best parts, driving amidst the rickshaws and camel carts.

I drove the twenty or so kilometers from Karachi to Hawke's Bay where there was a company beach house. Between the Gymkhana Club and the beach house, the backwash of the British Empire and the Raj was good to us Americans. That road from Karachi seemed much longer than it probably was, especially with me driving at twelve or thirteen years old. But I felt in control in a way the rest of my life did not allow.

So I'm driving this Jeep Station Wagon, sort of an SUV before there were such things. Four-speed tranny with a four-wheel drive and a transfer case with high and low range. I thought there was no place I could not go. I loved it, but I have come to learn that four-wheel drive gets you into lots of places but won't necessarily get you back out of them.

Somewhere between Drigh Road, where we lived, and the beach at Hawke's Bay was a refugee camp with about half a million people in it. Left over from the furies of Partition in 1947, they had no running water, no sanitation, and their only food depended on some fragile government organization. Even after more than a half a century, I can remember the smell of that camp, which permeated the countryside for miles around.

No air-conditioning in any of our vehicles, windows open always to the rough smells of the subcontinent. The air cleared as we approached the beach. There was the ocean. There was the beach house. Surf's up! Let's get to it, but first, let's drive the Jeep through the dunes. Before I knew it, I buried all four wheels in the sand and stuck that thing up to the floorboards. Dad was not pleased. Mom, ever practical, got some passing camel walla to pull us out with his camel. Rupees well spent and a family tragedy averted!

room doors that sometimes spilled out into the living room. I think I just accepted that relationships were inherently volatile. That's the way it seemed to be; why should it ever be different?

I spent lots of time riding my bicycle everywhere through the desert that surrounded our Drigh Road residence. Two wheels: my freedom machine. One of the kids whose parents were either military or diplomatic had been given a motorcycle. Since American government officials were involved, the fact that no one was old enough for a driver's license was not an issue. The bike in question was a BSA Bantam Major, with a 150 cc two-stroke engine. It was the coolest thing I had ever seen.

The owner was proudly putting around and the rest of us kids were marveling at his majesty. I was aware of manual transmissions. The cars I had been "driving" were all manual transmissions. I studied the workings of the little motorcycle. I saw where the clutch was: the lever on the handlebar, left-hand side. The lever on the right handlebar was the front brake. I figured that out by process of elimination. The right grip twisted—had to be the throttle.

Got it.

Left foot brake, right foot shifting lever. A three-speed tranny, the lever actuated a ratchet. One down for first, up for second, up for third. Neutral between first and second.

Got it.

My hunger was palpable. "Do you want to take it for a ride?" the owner asked. "Of course," I said. "Do you know how to ride?" Having ridden a bicycle for a number of years, and having studied the sequence of motorcycle operations for about five minutes, I told the owner, "You bet!"

I got in the saddle, took it off the side stand, pulled in the clutch, and kicked it down into first. I twisted the throttle a little and started to let the clutch out. The bike was in a driveway with the street behind me. About fifty feet ahead was a garage with the door closed. Not the best place to start a ride.

OK . . . throttle . . . left hand relaxing as the clutch engaged, bike moving forward and picking up speed. The garage door started to get larger. Panic set in and the reflex of bicycle riding kicked in. That reflex was to put the brakes on. How do you put the brakes on? With the levers on the handlebars, of course. My right hand was engaged in shutting down the throttle so the front brake was out of the question. The rear brake, being foot-actuated, wasn't part of the picture. My left hand was used to that lever being a brake so I pulled it. Now the bike was freewheeling. No matter how hard I pulled that clutch lever, no braking action happened because it wasn't a brake.

I collided with the garage door and the bike and I fell over on our sides. Now, it was almost no harm no foul, but not quite. The forks had twisted a little bit, but in those days the way to straighten twisted forks was to straddle the front wheel facing the bike, hold the handlebars, and twist them until the forks were straight. Mission accomplished. Not much was said between us kids about this mishap. No one wanted parents to hear what was going on and get involved.

I never got to ride that bike again, but in those fifty feet, I had tasted freedom. From that moment on every time I rode my bicycle I simulated the riding of a motorcycle, imagining throttle, clutch, and appropriate brakes. It was the beginning of a beautiful romance.

Another activity was serving as a butler at the big parties that all parents had frequently. Sure there were servants everywhere, but the folks liked having the kids involved so we helped serve drinks. And when all was said and done at the end of the evening, we helped ourselves to what was left over . . . and there was always a lot left over. We'd mix that crap together and drink it. It didn't taste good to begin with, so mixing it didn't change much.

Drinking did something to me.

The edge was off my loneliness . . . I felt empowered . . . all that stuff. I liked it.

I didn't drink all the time. But I looked forward to that release when the opportunity afforded itself. Thinking back today I feel the wisps of a chill wind out of my memory. What causes one to hurt? What gives one that dull ache of an enduring pain—one you just can't put your finger on, but you'll do anything to make it stop? It's not the pain of a wound or a disease; it just afflicts the soul in a way that is hard to address because it's so hard to define.

Sometimes, if you're lucky, you will be wrapped in a thread that will hold you together when everything else you do scatters you like dust.

That something was music.

Music was everywhere in our house. Mom loved to sing, but my recollection is that Dad always made fun of her when she did . . . so she did it less and less. That said, we had a Steinway upright in our house for as long as I could remember. Dad took lessons, and Mom played too. One day sometime in the late forties, before Pakistan, they had decided that I should take lessons, and so I did. My teacher was a gentleman named Everett Stevens. He was a patient man; he tolerated my dilatory attitudes. I wish I had stuck with it longer, in retrospect, of course. Almost everything I know about the "technical" aspects of music, I learned in those early piano lessons. I tried Dad's violin later on. I was not encouraged to continue. I was not in love with classical music, but since the music I would come to love was yet to be discovered, it had to do.

I preferred playing to studying theory. It would be years before I appreciated the important relationship between the two. I was not fond of reading music but I had a good ear, so when Mr. Stevens played a piece for me, the relationships between the sound of his piano and the written notes on the page became apparent. In any case, my piano lessons continued until Dad got posted to Pakistan in the early 1950s. During that time rock and roll would emerge and everything would change!

"Why doesn't your story follow a strict time line?" one might ask. I guess the answer is simply that I don't think that way. My memories slip in and out of time like Billy Pilgrim in *Slaughterhouse Five* . . . but to me the sequence makes perfect sense. As I write these pages, it is

September. Our daughter, Izze, walks through the hall on the way to her bathroom and she notices nothing today . . . as I would have noticed nothing when I was her age, or even older. Someday perhaps she will look, and the memory will wrap her gently. In the meantime, it is just a hallway in her parents' house and the people in the photos are just faces from another time. She goes to the kitchen and pops popcorn, something to nibble while she begins her homeschooled lessons. The ancestral faces cannot compete with a freshly popped kernel.

Saturday, April 14, 2007, Hillside Farm, Meigs County

I was saddened to hear of the death of Kurt Vonnegut even though it has been decades since I read any of his work. I remember reading Player Piano *and* The Sirens of Titan *back in the early fifties. A paperback cost a quarter in those days and I spent my whole allowance as well as the money from my paper route on science fiction novels and model airplanes. (I don't read science fiction any more, but I still build model airplanes.) When* Slaughterhouse-Five *came out in the sixties I read it, loved it and empathized with the characters. I also read* Catch-22 *by Joseph Heller and* V *by Thomas Pynchon. I loved them also. These books seemed to touch the temper of my heart. I was thinking music, and Beatnik Thoughts . . . ready to hit the road . . . ready to be snatched by aliens . . . ready for anything outside my limited experience.*

Many things have happened to me since then. The road has been my life and life is far stranger sometimes than being snatched by aliens. These books were like an old watershed . . . a benchmark of where I was back then. One of the obits for Kurt said that by the seventies his work, brilliant as it was, had become irrelevant. Musicians have it easy compared to writers. We can play and rework old songs as well as write new ones. Our show can comprise everything from the erection to the resurrection, so to speak, and if we are lucky, people will still take us seriously as artists. Kurt hadn't become irrelevant . . . time and his audience had just moved on and language had begun to change.

People tell me that I was part of something big in the sixties along with a bunch of the rest of us. I don't see it. Life is, quite simply, just life. Mine is probably not much more interesting than one of my peasant ancestors in north-

ern Finland. There is no royalty anywhere in my veins and that's fine with me.

Anyway, whether I kept up with Kurt's later years or not, his passing sounds the knell for all of us as the bell continues to toll. In his work were the reflections of a time when I was young. You can't bottle that; you just have to remember it. I do remember, but you know . . . I am so glad to be where I am today.

When my dad passed away and my brother was getting rid of stuff, I wanted the Thomas Wolfe books that he and Mom had on their bookshelves all my life. Of Time and the River, Look Homeward, Angel, You Can't Go Home Again. *I read them all when I was a kid because they were important to Mom and Dad. Their place on the shelf was like wallpaper that never changed. Mom and Dad never, to my knowledge, read them again and you know, neither did I . . . but I still have them.*

I still have my old paperback of Cat's Cradle *as well as* Slaughterhouse-Five. *Will I read them again? I doubt it . . . but who knows. Hey Kurt, say hello to my mother and father if you see them. Like them, you were a part of my life that will stay with me. Rest well!*

When the Pakistan posting was over we flew to Italy and wound up in Torino, and Dad bought a brand-new 1955 Fiat 1100 Turismo Veloce, a little four-door. It had a liter-plus engine with a two-throat Weber carburetor. All four of the Kaukonens—Mom, Dad, Pete, and myself—climbed in this little thing, got a roof rack for our luggage, and after spending a little time looking around Italy, headed north, where Dad was to connect for the first time with some of our family in Finland. Before we started north to Finland, we went south to Naples, to the Amalfi Drive, Pompeii, and Herculaneum. The Kaukonen family undertook a hike up Mount Vesuvius. After marveling at the view from the summit, I thought it would be fun to gallop down the slope. In the blink of an eye gravity controlled my destiny and I lost control of my body and flew off the path, bouncing down the side of the mountain for about a hundred and fifty feet, and plowing through volcanic ash before coming to a stop. I remember hearing Mom's screams as I contemplated the end of my teenage life on the side of a volcano in Italy. After all was said and done there was not an inch of my body that was not uniformly gray with ash. My parents were not pleased. I had to change my clothes and do a cursory body wash with an outdoor faucet before they would let me get back in the car.

In 1955, World War II was only a decade in the past. Italy still bore the very fresh scars that the war left behind. When we drove through Italy, buildings were still pockmarked by bullets. The same could be seen further north throughout Europe. We took a ferry from Denmark to Sweden and from Sweden to Finland and there we were, in the land of my ancestors. Helsinki was a gray city, but the roads there were paved. Heading north to Oulu, where my dad's cousin Jorma Rasi lived, the roads were still mostly dirt and gravel.

The pine and birch forests of Scandinavia have a distinct smell all their own. There is no place in the world for me that has a scented memory like that, in Finland even more so than Sweden or Norway. One really had to plan ahead for a trip. Fuel stops were few and far between, and nothing like a convenience store existed.

Hanging in northern Finland with cousins Jorma and Helvi Rasi and their three daughters—Tuula, Laina, and Taina—gave me a family connection I never had before. I have no first cousins, so that extended family thing that all my friends took for granted was new to me and I liked it.

We spent some weeks there in Oulu and then went to Hanko. My dad's mom, Ida, had flown from Los Angeles to visit her sister and other family members. Jaako was back in California. We went to Hanko and spent time with Ida's family and after a few days she'd had enough and booked a flight back to the States. I said goodbye to her. In her heavily accented English, she said, "This is not my home. I'm going back to Los Angeles." She walked to the plane and never looked back. That's how Grandma Kaukonen was: matter-of-fact and outwardly unsentimental. She knew her place in the universe and was in sync with it.

4

Living in the Moment

The time spent that summer of 1956 with our Finnish family was pivotal in so many ways. How to describe the transition into and through adolescence? I remember that it was crucial for me to become an adult and enter the world. What was my goal in adulthood? In my rearview mirror the memory is so shallow I want to slap myself in the face and say, "Is this all you have?" I thought about being able to drink, to have a car, to be married, and maybe even to have a job, although I had no idea what that job might entail.

By the time we were heading south out of Scandinavia in our little Fiat with the port of Genoa as our destination, the next milestone of my life was to return to the States, reconnect with my pals, turn sixteen, and get a driver's license and a car.

In Genoa we were booked on the *Giulio Cesare*. We followed the sea route where not long before the *Andrea Doria* had gone down in a collision with the liner *Stockholm*. Pretty fancy stuff for the kid from DC. First-class on a luxury liner, there I am, a middle-class lad hanging out with folks that were much richer than I—and what was happening on board every night on the dance floor? Elvis and rock and roll. Wow! What's not to like? Kids my age and parents who didn't care if we stayed up all night as long as we stayed out of their way. From the third world of Pakistan to the one percent in first class of the *Giulio Cesare* en route to America of the 1950s. You can't make this up!

What a time for a teenage boy. First airplane flight, first ocean liner in the heyday of ocean liners . . . a journey to and through exotic countries . . . a handful of years in Pakistan . . . road trip back through Europe . . . drive to Finland, meet family . . . back to Italy and on another liner for home. To this hearty stew, add adolescence and all that goes along with that. Yeah, that's what I'm talking about.

When we landed in New York, we got our little Fiat off the boat along with our luggage and started to drive home. The glory of the I-95 corridor had yet to blossom. The New Jersey Turnpike was only five years old at the time. The dusty, partially paved roads of the Indian subcontinent were a thing of the past. The high-speed motorways of Europe were awesome, but most of the roads there were narrow channels in towns where only small cars could navigate. America! We were driving big roads with radio stations in English. We were back in the US of A!

Somewhere on the Baltimore-Washington Parkway on the way south toward the District of Columbia, the little Fiat blew a head gasket. This could have had something to do with us having been crunched between two trucks somewhere north of Torino. Who knows? In any case, there we were, first day back in the States, standing by the side of the road with a foreign car that had ceased to run. In 1956, there were very few foreign cars in the States. There were no Fiat dealers. Few people even knew what a Fiat was. Dad called some service station and they sent a tow truck. "Head gasket," the driver said. "We'll make one for you." A guy from the garage packed us all into his 1956 Ford Fairlane Victoria hardtop along with all our luggage and drove us the rest of the way to 3312 Northampton Street.

On one hand, this was an inconvenience and a minor tragedy. On the other hand, I was riding shotgun in the coolest car I had even seen. The dual glasspacks were rumbling with a sound I had never heard before, and on the radio, in English, was a rock-and-roll station.

What a triumphant return! But this was only the beginning. I immediately started calling my friends to tell them I was back. There had been a lot of changes since I had been gone. They all had driver's licenses and cars and girlfriends. I was really out of the loop.

I dropped by my old pal Mike Oliveri's place, and he had this beautiful Gibson J-45 and was picking music. I was enthralled. Mike was playing a Flatt and Scruggs song as I recall, "Jimmy Brown the Newsboy." Then he played "Worried Man Blues." This reunion would profoundly change my life. This was the shit! I rushed home and told my dad I wanted a guitar and lessons.

The Old Man had some conditions before a guitar would come my way. He said that I needed to learn two songs and be able to perform them for him.

I picked the first songs Mike played for me. I started with "Jimmy Brown the Newsboy."

I sell the morning paper sir, my name is Jimmy Brown
Everybody knows that I'm the newsboy of the town
—W. S. Hays. First recorded by the Carter Family in 1931.

Yeah, that was the dang deal! It had cool guitar parts that were accessible even to me at the time. Then I learned "Worried Man Blues," attributed to A. P. Carter.

It takes a worried man to sing a worried song
I'm worried now, but I won't be worried long

These tunes did not reflect the "cool sounds" of the time. They were definitely outré by teenage standards. I didn't know this at the time, but in 1956 on Nebraska Avenue, across the street from Woodrow Wilson High School, Mike Oliveri opened the door for me to the Great Folk Scare the rest of the country would come to know in about four or five years.

With Mike showing me the way, I laboriously learned to play and sing those two songs on his Gibson J-45. Mike lent me the guitar and later that day, after dinner, I corralled the Old Man and played the two songs for him. It was hard to say what Big Jorma really thought. He wasn't shy about being sarcastic or critical, but he kept a lot of shade on himself when it came to positive observations. What he said was "What do you know about being worried?" What I wanted to say was "I'm a teenager, I know a lot about being worried." But I kept my mouth shut and let that one go.

A couple of days later, he took me down to 1216 Connecticut Avenue NW, to the Guitar Shop. My best recollection is that at that time the guitar was not the cool instrument we all consider it to be today. Hillbillies played the guitar. The saxophone, drums, and piano were considered cool. The Guitar Shop was the exception that proved the rule. Guitars of all sorts filled the walls and floors of this small second-floor store. There were two teachers at the shop when we walked in: Bill Harris, the great jazz guitarist, and Sophocles Papas, a renowned classical guitarist and a contemporary of Andrés Segovia. Harris had been an accompanist for the Clovers, a rhythm and blues group, so that tainted him in my dad's eyes. Mr. Papas was a classical guitarist, and he owned the shop.

Sophocles Papas it was. We wandered around the shop looking for a guitar that would be mine. I picked out a new Gibson Sunburst J-45 just like Mike's. "What kind of music do you want to play?" Mr. Papas asked me. I showed him the two songs I had learned. He wasn't impressed. "We're going to start from the beginning," he said.

The first books had songs like "Red River Valley" and "This Old Man"; I practiced relentlessly whether the music set me on fire or not. I sang the words, silly or not, if that's what the tune required.

Part of the learning process involved tuning. The last music lessons I took had been on the piano some years before. You don't have to tune a piano. Someone else comes to your house every year or so and does it for you. I wondered why, as the week went on, my guitar sounded worse and worse. "You need to tune your guitar," Mr. Papas said. I guess I wasn't paying attention. He showed me. I got it. It was another great moment in early guitar playing. When I broke a string, which I did from time to time, I would go to Sears and buy the one string I needed. Black Diamond, of course; those were all they had. I would replace the string and then wonder why all the other strings sounded shitty. Important lesson: it is possible to buy a set of strings and change them all at the same time, and then they will all sound the same, equally bright.

Lesson learned.

When I was home alone in the Northampton house, I practiced in the bathroom. The tiles bounced my voice as well as the guitar, and it sounded great. I didn't know it yet, but I was truly home.

I turned sixteen on December 23, 1956, and immediately went down to the Department of Motor Vehicles with my first car (which I had gotten before the license) and passed my driving test. My first ride was a 1950 Studebaker Starlight coupe. It was a bullet-nose, two-door sedan with wraparound starlight windows in the back. Each armrest in the backseat opened and could hold two six-packs of beer.

I continued my lessons with Mr. Papas, and after a while I felt like I was ready to strike out on my own. At some point in 1956 I quit taking lessons and focused on building a repertoire. Interestingly enough, I never really considered myself a guitar player. I merely accompanied myself so I could sing the songs. A couple of years later at Antioch College, Ian Buchanan would take my hand and lead me into the world of fingerpicking guitar. I would become a guitar player in spite of myself.

Toward the end of my sophomore year at Woodrow Wilson High School it became apparent that my dad was going to take a State Department posting to Manila in the Philippines as labor attaché and first secretary. My days in my hometown were numbered again.

I tried to pack as much teenage living as I could into the remaining months. Mom and Dad cleared me to take my car, guitar, and a couple of friends on a Presbyterian teenage retreat somewhere down in Virginia.

Our family was a group of nonobservant Jews with a nonobservant Lutheran dad. I started hanging out in the basement of that church on Chevy Chase Circle when I was in Boy Scouts. I got to know a bunch of the kids, and when we had a chance to go to a coed sleepover retreat in the country . . . yeah, let's go!

I don't remember much about the actual Presbyterian goings-on of the retreat, but they had a talent show and I signed up for it. This was the first time that I ever played in public. I selected "Worried Man Blues" and I brought down the house. I got so excited that even though we were only supposed to play one song, I broke into Champion Jack Dupree's "Dirty Woman."

You is one dirty woman, someday Imma find your trail
When I find your trail, I'm gonna wind right up in jail

I got through the opening chorus and half the first verse before I got the hook. Censorship at the Christian camp got me and I realized that salacious lyrics would sell. The kids loved it. The adults hated it. Good times! Except for my foray into suggestive lyrics, the weekend was sadly innocent.

Yeah, that Champion Jack Dupree album, *Blues from the Gutter,* was a crowd-pleaser with the boys. I'm not so sure about the girls. In any case, so it went.

That summer and the things that went along with it has stayed in my memory all these years. Sometimes my memories are like jagged pieces of shrapnel and sometimes they are seen through a gentle veil. That adolescent summer of 1956 with guitar, first car, and a year at "home" in the States was seminal in so many ways.

Then there was the "Traipsin' Woman" incident at the Kaukonen household on Northampton Street. At some point, you all need to look up Jean Bell Thomas, the Traipsin' Woman. I have a story that involves Jean, but I did not know how deep her Americana tradition was until I looked up her name as I was writing this. It was in early June 1956.

My sophomore year at Woodrow Wilson High School was over. I learned to play the guitar and got a car and a driver's license. There was a lot going on. Mom loved a lot of different things, all of which needed to have "cultural relevance," so rock and roll wasn't in her ken yet, and blues was marginal. That said, she loved folk traditions, especially American ones. Jean Thomas had been holding one of the most amazing festivals in Ashland, Kentucky, for many years. Starting in the early thirties, the American Folk Song Festival lasted until the early seventies.

If this were today, I wouldn't miss this event for anything. But it wasn't today, and I was looking to explore different paths. My mom, dad, and brother Peter set out to Ashland, Kentucky. I was invited, of course, but I had other plans and those plans involved having a party at our house on Northampton Street that would certainly involve underage drinking and maybe even sex. Who could refuse this exacta? Not I. So I missed my chance to go to one of the last old-school folk festivals and I never got to see Jean Thomas. I don't even remember what we did. Probably drove around in my old Studebaker Starlight coupe, went to Maggie's Bar and Grill on Wisconsin Avenue for a pizza . . . who knows? I had calculated the surprise factor with regards to Mom and Dad coming home. I figured they would be gone at least four days.

I was wrong.

Some friends of mine—a girl named Loyes (my dog-washing partner from the neighborhood when we were nine or ten), Jack Casady, and his older brother Chick were hanging out downstairs on the couch. I was upstairs brushing my teeth when I heard the front door open. The next thing I hear was my mother screaming, "Fucking! Fucking on my couch!" Now I'm sure that fucking was what Chick had in mind. Hope sprang eternal in the mind of a teenage boy. I'm also sure that wasn't what was happening. Making out probably . . . heck, Jack was sitting on the couch next to them. Anyway, what Mom saw was fucking, and it was burning the retinas of her eyes. I finished brushing my teeth and came downstairs. What I saw was my mom in the hallway holding her hand over my little brother's eyes. My dad was behind them looking nonplussed. I could see he was trying to figure out what to say. All he could think of was "You listen to your mother!"

Perfect—a weekend plan gone terribly wrong. We gathered ourselves up and fled out the front door to my car. I took everyone home and drove around until I had enough nerve to go back to my place, where I denied everything, of course.

Since nothing really happened, except for the aborted party at the house, the waves subsided and that was that.

Summer passed and the next thing I knew was that Dad was labor attaché and first secretary of the American Embassy in Manila, and the Kaukonen family was on their way to the Philippines.

I sold my 1950 Studebaker Starlight coupe for a hundred bucks. We packed the house on Northampton Street in boxes and got ready to leave. Of course my Gibson J-45 came with me. I didn't have a hard-shell case for my axe, just a cardboard case with simulated alligator texture on it. Today I would never fly a guitar in an ordinary hard-shell case, much less a cardboard one, but that's all I had so that's how it was.

We flew to Los Angeles. Jaako Kaukonen had passed by this time, but we visited with Grandma Kaukonen, went to Disneyland (which had just opened), and boarded a Pan Am Boeing 377 Stratocruiser. We flew to Honolulu and spent the night. The next day, on board another Stratocruiser, we headed out to Manila. We stopped at Wake Island and Guam. I walked the sandy beach on Wake Island while they refueled. This was little more than a decade after World War II and there were still sunken vessels and downed aircraft in the water. Many hours and naps later, we landed in Manila. In those days you just got off the plane and walked across the tarmac to a couple of Quonset huts.

It would be a while before we got our own house in a little compound on Park Avenue in Pasay City, but that didn't stop Mom from getting me enrolled in the American School immediately. My brother, Peter, and I shared one hotel room and Mom and Dad the one next door. As much as I already loved the guitar and music, it never occurred to me that one might find a career that involved these two things. I just wanted out, but I had no idea what "out" was.

I was sitting on the wall one morning outside the Filipinas Hotel and two guys drove by. One of these guys was a fellow student at the American School named Ng Lun Yun. The other was Bill Hight, whose dad was a contractor in the Philippine Islands. Yun recognized me as the new kid in the school and they pulled over. We found we all were gearheads. We liked motorcycles, cars—mechanical stuff. We became friends then, and we are still friends sixty years later.

One evening some of the other guys from school came by the hotel and picked me up to take me around. One of them had a 1946 Lincoln Continental. He had pulled the V-12 engine and replaced it with a diesel. It was cheaper to run in the Philippines' post–World War II economy. I remember the first thing he said to me was "Welcome to Manila. We do a hell of a lot of drinking around here!" Yeah buddy! I knew I was going to like this place. They didn't have sobriety checkpoints in Manila.

Americans and Filipinos have had a long and interesting love-hate relationship that goes back to the Spanish-American War. In a country with more than eighty distinct languages and perhaps more distinct cultures, we were more than friends. As the kid of an American diplomat, I was able to skate around a lot of the local laws with my pals. For example, you needed to be twenty-one to have a driver's license. I was seventeen at the time, but that was no problem. A carton of Camels and a bottle of Johnnie Walker Black to a "fixer" standing outside the Department of Motor Vehicles, and I was good to go. One of my friends from California had a driver's "license" from Disneyland that he was able to turn into a valid permit in the Philippines. Ah, the glory days in the Far East.

Mom got us a house in Pasay City in a compound that was mostly inhabited by Americans, not all of whom were affiliated with the embassy, but all of whom had something to do with the long-standing American presence in what was then still the Philippine Islands. One day shortly thereafter, Dad drove the family over to the PX on Naval Station Sangley Point and bought me a Lambretta motor scooter. I always wanted a two-wheeled vehicle with a motor, but so far my only real experience with one was that very short and ill-fated trip on the BSA Bantam Major in Pakistan. It boggled my mind that my parents bought me a motor vehicle I had never operated in a country where I still didn't have a legal license. Just because you can afford to buy an airplane doesn't mean you're going to jump in the cockpit and take it for a test flight. Anyway, staying in the metaphor, that's exactly what happened to me. Dad bought me the scooter. As we were getting ready to leave the base I remember he asked, "Can you ride this thing?" "Of course I can," I replied emphatically. I wasn't going to miss this opportunity for anything, and the fact that I had never ridden a scooter before wasn't going to stop me. We wrote "TEMPORARY" on a piece of paper with a ballpoint pen, taped it to the license plate bracket, and I set off for home.

My first scooter ride involved navigating the traffic from Cavite City to Manila. Dodging jeepneys, rickshaws, carabaos, and hordes of people was all in a day's drive, and I felt pretty good about myself when I got home to our pad on Park Avenue. My parents never seemed to give it a second thought.

I began to ride to the American School every day. Time moves so slowly when you're sixteen and seventeen. I realize now that I spent only a year on this sojourn to the Philippines, but it seemed like a lifetime.

It is important to note that one of the important life skills that my friends and I honed was learning to drive with triple vision. I have no idea whether the parents were aware of this or not, but excessive alcohol consumption was de rigueur at the parties that happened at least once every weekend.

By this time I had already been suspended from school for a couple of weeks because of a booze party at a friend's house. It was a *Project X* kind of party and we were sure we wouldn't get caught, but of course we did. I didn't drink every day, or even every week, but when I did my goal was always to get drunk. I was never a "social" drinker, whatever that is. My friend Dave Davis married my neighbor's daughter, Patsy, and at their wedding reception, I got completely smashed, and all I can recall is that Dave lent me his Triumph 500 motorcycle while they left for their honeymoon. On my way home from the party I was passing a line of traffic when I saw a gravel truck coming the other way. There was nowhere for me to go . . . I remember blinking my eyes and feeling a spray of gravel on my face and then there was open road in front of me.

I guess G-d had other plans for little Jerry Kaukonen. There is no other explanation. Some might perceive this as a wake-up call of some sort. I didn't. I just felt I was lucky and drove on. I survived 1957 and moved into 1958. My guitar playing really hadn't advanced much, but I loved performing. In the 1958 Kawayan Yearbook of the American School under Jerry Kaukonen's picture, the only activity is the Musical Cavalcade. I forget what I played for that show—probably some Buddy Holly song.

A perception is shared by those who lived and traveled with parents in the service, either military or government. Those of us who grew up in faraway places, embracing distant cultures whenever possible but always missing the world at home, were a select crew. My experiences as a kid with my folks in Pakistan and the Philippines have given me an appreciation and love for my country that is difficult to adequately express. While we were "in country," our memories of home were put on hold in our hearts. Of course, time doesn't stop just because you're not there, so the world we would come back to was always different in a way that we could never predict. I could only really share my experiences with military or Foreign Service brats. We knew what the deal was, and back stateside, we pretty much just kept that part of our lives to ourselves.

5

A Walk with Friends

I decided that I wanted to finish high school in DC with the folks I had started school with. My son, Zach, has lived in the same town since he was born. He has had some of the same friends since he was in kindergarten. The same is true for my daughter, Izze. My experience was different. I lost a year when we were in Pakistan. My buddies—Bill Haile, Mike Oliveri, Chick Casady—they all graduated before me and were already in college. I guess I wanted to pick up that hometown memory in some way, so I convinced Mom and Dad that I should return home for my senior year.

My grandparents Ben and Vera Levine lived in our house while we were away. In a way, it had become their home. They actually spent more time there than we did. I would be going home, but it would be to my grandparents' house.

Why was it important for me to return to Woodrow Wilson in DC to graduate? My pals from elementary school and junior high were already gone because of the year I lost in Pakistan. I guess I don't really know why this was important, but it was. I think I was seeking that sense of continuity and place in the world that I would never have until I moved to Southeast Ohio in 1991.

I flew back to the District of Columbia with my suitcase and guitar in hand and re-enrolled in Woodrow Wilson High School. Chick Casady was in the army, other friends were in college, but Jack Casady was still there and he was still playing the guitar. Jack had been studying jazz for a number of years. We had yet to become musical friends, but it was coming. Bill Haile was in his second year at what was then Virginia Polytechnic Institute.

Thursday, December 6, 2001

When I go to DC I frequently get to hook up with old friends from my high school years. One of these is my friend Bill who used to live on Northampton St. a couple of blocks down from our place across from Lafayette Elementary School. Anyway, my senior year of high school I had a Lambretta Scooter I brought back from the Philippines with me. In Bill's note, he calls it a Vespa, but it was a Lambretta. The rest of his tale is dead-on accurate and I include it here. Bill sent it to Todd down in Atlanta and it found its way to me.

From Bill Haile, my neighbor and childhood friend:

Mark Ingino has prompted me to send you this brief story about the childhood of Jorma, since he and I were buddies from about 6th thru 12th grades in Washington, DC. Back then he lived two blocks from me on Northampton Street and we spent many hours together. Here is one incident. It was Christmas time in 1957 or '58, and Jorma and I were busy chasing girls. He was driving a motor scooter, a Vespa I think, and took it everywhere. As Christmas approached, my mother asked the two of us to go and get a tree, since she lacked the time. She gave us some cash and off we went, two of us on his scooter. We found a small 6 foot tree at Chevy Chase circle, but how to get it home? We jammed the trunk behind the license plate holder, I sat on the back holding the tree behind my neck with one hand and grasping the seat strap with the other. Jorma drove and we wheeled off in rush hour traffic. Cars behind could only see a tree with a rear wheel, since it completely covered me. Leaning around curves and street corners was specially fun. The "flying Christmas tree" made it home without incident. Mom was happy and Jorma was, as usual, completely unfazed. The motor scooter was used many times thereafter, but never so completely.

This brought back a lot of memories for me. Also humorous in this vein is the image of me on the scooter with my Gibson J-45 on the floorboards in front of me as I drove over to Reno Road to rehearse with Jack. These are sweet thoughts for me today.

By that time I had moved on from old-timey tunes and crossover country to the music that was rocking our teenage world. When you are learning anything it is great to have lofty goals, but it is even more important to have realistic expectations. Buddy Holly was a prime example. His guitar work was much more complex than I was able to realize at the time, but I could sing many of his songs and my rhythm guitar playing was certainly an adequate addition. I felt the same for Ricky Nelson. I was certainly no James Burton—the studio cat who played all the cool guitar leads on Ricky's records—but I didn't have to be. I could strum the guitar and sing "Poor Little Fool," and that was good enough for me.

Looking back, I find I became a guitar player in spite of myself. I just wanted to sing the songs and I couldn't do that without accompaniment, so my guitar evolved accordingly. Jack, on the other hand, had been studying jazz and who knows what else. It is interesting that Jack and myself became partners in crime. He was younger than me in a time when that meant something. Our slight age difference meant nothing to our friendship. Music called to both of us and we answered it. It was immediately obvious that I would sing and Jack would play lead guitar. I never thought of myself as a "front man" back then, but since I could sing, that's what I was. In early outings Warren Smith, my classmate from Woodrow Wilson, played drums, and from time to time when the budget would allow, Mike Hunnicut would "play bass" using the mute pads on his Gretsch Country Gentleman. Ronnie MacDonald replaced Warren on drums at some point in 1959. He had a little more experience and he also had a Les Paul Junior he would lend me. We weren't even a garage band. My grandfather's car was in our garage and Dr. Casady's garage was filled with his cars. We either rehearsed in Jack's rec room or my grandparents' living room.

From my parents' point of view, a formal education was everything. When Ben and Vera came to this country, they went to college. Ben went on to earn a PhD. It was presumed that Beatrice, my mom, would do the same, and she ultimately earned a master's degree. Neither of my dad's folks went to college. They only made it to the eighth grade. They worked with their hands, as did my father's two brothers, Pentti and Tarmo. But my dad went to UCLA and got a degree. He was the first Kaukonen in the new country to get a higher education.

Sometimes people ask me what I would have done had I not become a musician and my answer is always "I would have been an over-the-road truck driver." I have always loved to drive and I like mechanical stuff. Many of my friends went to vocational school and that always looked appealing to me, but it was out of the question as far as my family was concerned. I understood that going to college was the next step.

Ben had recently retired from his long tenure with the Public Health Service, but the concept of retiring was anathema to him . . . as it is to me. Strangely enough at the time, a lot of interesting research into air and water pollution was being done in the former Soviet Union and my grandfather got grants to translate this research into English. He needed someone to help him transcribe these more-than-dry tomes, and that someone was me. My typing was atrociously hunt and peck, so he enrolled me in typing school in downtown DC. I was the only male in the class. Being in what was considered female work didn't bother me. I liked working at the keyboard. Still do. At the end of the class I could type ninety-five correct words per minute, and on a good day over a hundred.

Now I had a job. Back in Ben's office I made clean copies of his translations. It was tedious and I really didn't understand any of the material, but for some reason I liked the work. It was like ironing or cutting the grass. There was neat and immediate gratification. Progress was always visible. There was a bonus too. Ben had this gadget that made photocopies of documents. Now, in this era of sundry digital technologies, most of today's tech-savvy youth would not even know what this machine was. It really was a *photocopier*. It took a picture of the document in question, and then you would sandwich the negative paper with what would be the positive one and run it through the developing chemicals, and the end result would be a positive copy. Before you ran the master through the machine you could make corrections by putting white tape over errors and then typing over the tape. When you made the photocopy, it looked like a clean original.

In 1958 in the District of Columbia, you could drink beer and wine at eighteen, hard liquor at twenty-one. You also needed be at least eighteen to work in bars. Jack and I were starting to get work at various seedy clubs in the DC metro area. Most of them were so shady they never ID'd anyone, but a few did—so we needed IDs. Jack's older brother Chick already had his draft card. I borrowed it and laid strips of white paper over his details. Then I made a photocopy of said card, front and back, and lo—a blank draft card. I typed in the details, one for myself and one for Jack. Then I glued the front and back together and laminated the finished product. All of a sudden, Jack and I were eighteen. Thank G-d there were no photos on IDs back then. When you see pictures of us back then, we look like babies. It was laughable. But there we were, ready to play in any club in DC.

Ah, the side benefits of gainful employment. By day, I was a mild-mannered high school student and clerical assistant to my grandfather; by night, working musician in some very marginal downtown "clubs." "Where are you going?" my grandmother Vera would ask as I headed out the door with my guitar and the keys to my grandfather's 1950 Packard. "I'm playing at the club, Nana," I would tell her. I think she had visions of a country club. Nothing could have been further from the truth.

One of the places we played was the Rendezvous Club. It was a narrow little storefront and the stage was in the front window, our backs to the street. Nobody had much gear back then, so two guitars, a bass, and drums could squeeze into the smallest places. I don't remember what we got paid, or if we got paid. I do remember free beer. Driving home after one of these gigs could be challenging. One time I dropped

Jack off at his house on Reno Road after a particularly boozy evening. Apparently he couldn't navigate the back door, so his mom found him in the yard in the morning when she went out to walk Barney, the family dog. She was plenty pissed, but we denied everything, of course. "It must have been something he ate. I'm lucky I didn't get sick too . . ." I used to lie to the adults in my life as a matter of course. I did it even when I didn't have to, just so I wouldn't get out of the habit.

I didn't booze every day, but I did every time we worked a job that served alcohol. We used to like to go to the drive-ins back then. A big four-door sedan like my grandfather's old Packard wasn't sexy on the outside, but on the inside, it was a love machine. Most dates at the drive-in would require a six-pack of Country Club Malt Liquor made by Pabst. It was a cheap and potent beverage. A special date might mandate something classier, like Miller High Life: "The Champagne of Bottle Beer." Yeah buddy: advertising slogans had already conquered me.

We started to get gigs through Milt Grant. Milt Grant was the DC version of Philadelphia's Dick Clark. He had a local TV and radio show, and the TV show was a dance party just like Dick's was. I'm thinking that our link with Milt was Mike Hunnicut, the guy who played bass on the muted strings of his Gretsch Country Gentleman. Mike was a little older than us and had already developed "connections."

There was a rockabilly artist named Jimmy Clanton who had a hit with "Just a Dream." When Jimmy came to town, Milt hired us to back him up. We did a couple of gigs with him. Jimmy, I apologize for our ineptitude. We got a job backing Jimmy in West Virginia and on the way there we were stopped for speeding in Warrenton, Virginia. In those days, the cops in these small towns took you right to the magistrate's office. In this case, it was in the judge's home.

He put on his robe and sat behind a mahogany table. The fine was around $75. Whatever it was, we didn't have it. We barely had gas money. Fortunately, Hunnicut had two guitars and we left one with the judge in lieu of bond. We drove off to the gig in wild and wonderful West Virginia.

The gig was in a gymnasium or an armory. When we were warming up the crowd to bring Jimmy on, someone threw a bra onstage. "Holy shit!" Women's underwear onstage? I remember thinking, "I'm gonna love this gig!" We did our thing, backed Jimmy up on his hits, got back in the car, and drove home. The judge was still awake so we stopped off, paid the speeding fine with the money we earned, ransomed Mike's guitar, and drove back to DC.

We called ourselves the Triumphs after our favorite motorcycle marque. We stole the cool logo from the motorcycle and were sure we would triumph.

It wasn't exactly stardom for our little band, but we did get gigs. The music scene back then was still elemental; you could see those we considered to be big stars in real first-person situations. Jack and I saw Bo Diddley at a National Guard Armory in southern Maryland. Bo's guitar sound was like nothing I had ever heard. The overdriven amp sound combined with the "shave and a haircut, bay rum" rhythm was complete in its simplicity. At the time there was nothing like it. The doomsayers who believed that music like this was a product of devil-inspired intervention were convinced the End of Days was at hand. It was an exciting time for guitar music. The next guitar innovations wouldn't happen until the sixties, and we would be part of that!

Jack and I and our cohorts occasionally got to open these shows. As far as our musical careers were concerned, the Triumphs and those like us were underpaid throwaways whose mission it was to fill time on the stage before the "stars" appeared. Back in those days, the audience just wanted to hear in person the hits they were experiencing on the radio. With that in mind, the sets for the hit makers tended not to be very long. In my memory, as an opening act, we were not reviled like opening acts sometimes are today. The whole thing became part of a group experience. In a way, any of these evenings might be considered as a gem of performance art au naturel.

When Jack and I started out playing together, he was lead guitar and I was the vocalist who played rhythm guitar. Jack had a Telecaster that he bought with his paper route money and I was still playing the J-45 that Dad got me at Sophocles Papas's Guitar Shop. There was no pickup on this guitar, so to amplify it I took the microphone from Jack's Wollensak tape recorder and hooked it under my belt so the mike faced out. The back of the Gibson was pressed against the microphone. Voilà, an amplified guitar. Our first paying gig had been at a Woodrow Wilson sorority party in Charlotte Harbor's basement. We might have made ten bucks, enough to have a burger at the Hot Shoppes or a shake at the drive-in.

After hearing bands like Bo Diddley live, I realized that my minimalistic approach to amplifying my guitar wasn't going to cut it. Clerking for my grandfather Ben gave me the hundred bucks I needed to buy a Fender Musicmaster, a little single pickup guitar with a three-quarter-size neck. It was all I could afford at the time and it was good enough. I also had enough dough for an amplifier, which I got from Sears and Roebuck. Danelectro made amps for Sears back then, and the one I chose had a single fifteen-inch speaker. It also had a separate channel for PA stuff, so we plugged the microphone into that input.

Today we take for granted many sounds that are made by bending any given amplifier to your will. It is hard to imagine an era where overdriving an amp was avoided. I had no idea how Bo Diddley got those magical sounds back then. It was like he channeled a voice from a parallel universe. I was playing amplified guitar, not electric guitar as we know it today. Kicking in the reverb and tremolo was as electric as it got for Jerry Kaukonen.

When I heard Jody Reynolds's "Endless Sleep," I flipped out.

The night was black, rain fallin' down
Looked for my baby, she's nowhere around

I've always had a penchant for dark lyrics. This song had it all. Gothic teen melodrama, lots of room echo on everything, and a tremolo guitar sound. It was the little things back then. Tremolo was one of the earliest guitar effects. In those days the effects pedals we guitarists all take for granted had yet to be dreamed of. However, many of the amps of the period had reverb generated by a set of enclosed springs and tremolo, which varied the amplitude, or volume, of the signal. There were usually two knobs associated with the tremolo circuit: speed and depth. The speed part is obvious; the depth modified the ratio of affected sound to the original sound. This circuit in the amps of the time was most assuredly responsible for that eerie, rhythmic shimmering sound we all loved so much in "Endless Sleep."

I wasn't looking for guitar licks, but I did like sonic textures. My little Musicmaster through the tremolo/reverb channel was literally as good as it got. The tremolo on that Danelectro always got a good workout. I still practiced songs ad nauseam with my J-45 in the tile bathroom whenever possible.

We need to get back to Buddy Holly and Ricky Nelson again for a moment. When Buddy Holly burst on the scene, it was like—well, we had all found our voice. We could relate to the songs, and the music was accessible to us. "Peggy Sue" with the F chord thrown into the bridge was just about the hippest thing I had ever heard, and Buddy's voice . . . It was different in a really good kind of way.

As for Ricky, "Poor Little Fool" got my vote immediately. Of course it had the mantra of four-chord rock and roll, but it was more than that. The lyrics to this and so many other songs presupposed that adolescent relationships would be baffling at best and disemboweling at worst. All this made sense to me at the time.

There was something else too. Most of the musicians I was beginning to look up to were black artists, and what they were able to do was artistically and technically over my head at the time. Buddy and Ricky gave hope to us young white aspiring musicians.

My home world, either with my parents or my grandparents, was fraught with emotional terrorism. At least that was my perception. I always thought of life at home as being a constant hostage negotiation for quiet time. I think my grandparents loved each other. I know that when Vera died, Ben's life seemed to cease to have meaning. He followed her a year or two later. The same would be true for my mom and dad. Bea would join Big Jorma a year or so after his death.

But in both households the battlefield was omnipresent. Truces might be declared from time to time, but conflict was a way of life in our family.

If you believe that one's emotional makeup is partially predestined by genetics and geography, then folks like me with ancestors coming from northern Europe and western Russia are born with an inherent appreciation of darkness. Though the background noise in my family tended not to be one of joy, I did find a way to navigate those waters. Buddy Holly, Ricky Nelson—their songs resonated with me on a molecular level, and I could sing them too, so they became a large part of my repertoire.

One of the gifts that I got from those early lessons at the Guitar Shop was to pay attention to my right hand. My flatpicking techniques are no longer as facile as they once were, but I am still aware of the basics. Downstrokes, upstrokes: I really focused on all those things in the dawn of my guitar experience. As time went on and I learned more songs as a rhythm accompanist, the nuances of accents were really important. I didn't intellectualize this, but I had a good ear and I extracted what I needed to make the music flow. I heard great players like James Burton or Carl Perkins or Chuck Berry or any of the cool pickers that inhabited my world, and their music set me on fire for sure. For some reason, I never felt compelled to learn their licks. It wasn't an intellectual or artistic decision; it just wasn't where I lived. I was more than happy to work out rhythm parts that fleshed out the songs so I could either play them by myself or with Jack and the guys.

Unlike Jack, I never really found my identity as a band member. The band was a means to an end for me. I just wanted to play and sing the songs. What I did get, though, was a solid right hand and a deep groove. A couple years later while being mentored by the great Ian Buchanan, I focused on my right hand more than my left, an approach that has served me well over the years.

All of that would come in time. However, Jack was without a doubt the prime mover in making me part of the band, and he made me aware of the gestalt creature that a band is and that the whole is always greater than the sum of the parts. I've never told him that because I never really thought about it. Jack always took the initiative when it came to the band and personnel. Maybe it's because he doesn't sing, I don't know. He has always been a man able to focus on what needs to be done, and then finding a way to make it happen. It seemed as if he was always networking and unearthing people to play with. I think he perceived music as a career long before I did. For me to be able to return the favor by bringing him into the Airplane fold was divine providence! I realize now that we were truly colleagues at a young age, way before I would have known what a colleague was.

As 1958 turned into 1959, I had little interest in my grandparents' lives. My approach to life was pretty much "Self will run riot." Aleister Crowley would have loved me. I did what was necessary in school to ensure my graduation, I worked for my grandfather every day, but other than that, it was all about me. After my junior year at the American School in Manila, weekly drinking was pretty much a part of my life. When Jack and I were working clubs, it was all about the buzz. With all this in mind when science fair time rolled around at Wilson, it made perfect sense that I would build a still and make vodka.

Ben had all this scientific gear in the basement of the house on Northampton Street. I found a condenser coil with a cooling jacket around it. There were large Erlenmeyer flasks and beakers galore. I found a five-gallon water jug and started to ferment potato mash in it. It smelled utterly repulsive as this evil mixture began to ferment. Had the Internet been around back then I would have learned how to make booze the "right" way. There were no books in the library on bootlegging so I had to wing it. I forget how long I let that nasty mess brew, but at some point I figured it was time to distill it. I moved my apparatus table near the zinc laundry sink so I could hook hoses to the cooling jacket. The fermented mess went into a giant Erlenmeyer flask with a top feeding tube to the coils and underneath it a denatured alcohol burner.

Bubble, bubble . . . Before long clear liquid started coming out of the business end of the coils and filled another flask. I found some activated charcoal to filter this fine product through and lo, vodka of sorts. I wound up with about a pint of alcoholic fluid that thanks to the charcoal was drinkable if you didn't mind the smell.

End of story: my bootleg rig got no notice whatsoever at the science fair. Given my evolving history with alcohol, perhaps this should have been a tipoff, but it wasn't.

It was just another day in my life.

I got involved in Junior ROTC and found I really liked it. I made it to squad leader before the school year ended. I can still take an M-1 or M-1A apart and put it back together. Good times in an odd era. I registered for Selective Service when I turned eighteen. They weren't drafting for Vietnam yet, and being in high school I still had a student deferment. Many of my pals joined the service when they graduated high school. I had no feelings about the service one way or the other. My folks expected my brother and me to go to college, and to college I would go.

I started filling out college applications. My grandfather Ben was a graduate of Brown University so I applied there, as well as to the Foreign Service School at Georgetown University. Some insightful school counselor recommended Antioch College in Yellow Springs, Ohio. While they didn't have coed dorms, men could hang out in women's dorms and vice versa. Wow! What a concept for a school in the 1950s. In addition, Antioch didn't use a grading scale. All classes were pass or fail.

Ben's PhD from Brown didn't help me a bit. Brown University rejected me immediately. I got accepted to the Georgetown Foreign Service School and Antioch College. I only applied to Georgetown as a sop to Dad, so there was really one choice for me and that was (as my DC friends called it) "that pinko, free love school in the Midwest." There was another aspect in the microcosm of Antioch College that really appealed to me, and that was the co-op job program. Antioch was a five-year undergraduate school because each student would work one or two quarters a year and these were called "co-op" jobs. Having a job and earning a paycheck on some level really appealed to me! I was as good as on my way to Yellow Springs before I even graduated.

The next thing I knew, I was on my way back to the Philippines for summer vacation before heading to college. I took my Fender Musicmaster and my Danelectro amp back to Pasay City with me. In those days, I just checked the guitar and amp as baggage. The airlines took it, and they both arrived in Manila safe and sound. I didn't even take the tubes out of the amp.

When I got back to the PI Dad bought me a BSA 250 cc Starfire motorcycle. Thanks, Dad! Parents worry about a lot of stuff their kids do. Mine never agonized over two-wheeled motorized transportation. Go figure. When I left DC after my graduation, I sold the old Lambretta scooter. It had served me well for a couple of years and countless tough miles. In the Philippines it had been on almost every road on Luzon—most unpaved. From below Manila to Subic Bay I rode fearlessly. Back in the States it took me to high school, to the mountains of West Virginia, and occasionally off road in Rock Creek Park. What a machine! May it rest in peace in some long-forgotten junkyard.

My vision of action and consequence was incredibly shortsighted. I have no idea why that was. The survival techniques that served me in the emotionally hostile Kaukonen household did not serve in the adult world that I was entering. As a kid, I aimed to be noticed as little as possible, to be gone whenever I could, and to tell my parents whatever I thought they wanted to hear. The lens through which I viewed the world was skewed and distorted in a very strange way. For example, I was probably nine or ten and there was a bike rodeo on the playground of the Lafayette school across the street from our house on Northampton Street. I always prided myself on being a good bike rider. I loved every moment on two wheels. Anyway, there was this obstacle course around a bunch of little blocks. They told me the objective was to navigate the path and hit as few blocks as possible. That's what they said. What I heard was "Hit as many blocks as you can." This didn't make much sense, but if that's what they wanted, OK. It was tough, but I hit almost every block and got the worst score of any kid in the competition. I was shattered when I realized my mistake, but just like life itself, there were no do-overs. I could have aced that little competition standing on my head if had allowed myself to understand the instructions.

This kind of self-destructive misperception of reality would continue to haunt me as I grew older.

At the end of that senior summer I flew back to DC with luggage, guitar, and amplifier in tow. My long-suffering grandparents Ben and Vera loaded me and my junk into their 1950 Packard and drove me to Yellow Springs for my freshman year of college. To interact with other people, to make friends, to be a member of society: this clashed with the way I navigated life at home. I spent a lot of time inside my own head, which was not necessarily a good place to be. I loved reading science fiction. My world seemed so pedestrian that any parallel universe had to be better. In any case, I took these dubious life skills with me to Antioch. We crossed the Ohio River at Wheeling, continued on past Columbus and Springfield, turned south on US 68, and rolled into Yellow Springs.

We went to the student union and got my dorm assignment for the second floor of South Hall. The rooms were small and amenities were minimal. I didn't care that I drew the lower bunk. It was all good for sure. My roommate was a really nice African American man from Covington, Kentucky, named Marshall Jones. I knew we were going to get along great. We loved the same kind of music and, hey, we were freshmen in college together!

The first order of business was to check out the local bars. First stop, the Old Trail Tavern on Xenia Avenue, aka US 68. I wasn't working anymore so I depended on remittances from my parents and grandparents for the necessities—some of which were booze, bars, and pizza. I don't remember any of the courses I took that first year, but I remember Carling's Black Label and pizza at the Trail Tavern. First things first, always.

I did what I had to do to stay in school. I really looked forward to my first off campus co-op job, which would be coming up after two quarters.

Marshall turned me onto all sorts of exciting music. He hipped me to recordings of the Reverend C. L. Franklin sermonizing, with his daughter Aretha singing prominently in the choir. He told me tales of seeing the great Ray Charles live. Antioch introduced me to a very real world that was evolving at breakneck speed back then. Things were indeed different in Yellow Springs than in the house on Northampton Street.

Students at Antioch College had much more social awareness than I had at the time. It was rumored that my grandmother hung with Emma Goldman, but this is family legend. In the distant election of 1952 my family was appalled that I found Dwight D. Eisenhower more appealing than Adlai Stevenson. General Eisenhower was the Supreme Allied Commander. For a kid, what's not to like about a war hero? Political leanings had nothing to do with it.

There were always heated political discussions around our house. All of my grandparents' friends had deep political and intellectual convictions. Debates would be loud and entertaining but utterly unintelligible because they were almost always in a foreign language. It might be Russian. It might be Yiddish. It might be French. It might be German. None of this made an impression on me because English was the only language I understood.

My grandmother detested organized religion of any sort. Whether or not she was an atheist I'll never know. My guess would be yes. That said, she was 100 percent Jewish, a life member of Hadassah. She and my grandfather Ben gave me a $100 savings bond every year for my birthday. After the formation of the State of Israel, she switched to Israeli bonds. My first electric guitar with Jefferson Airplane was purchased after cashing in some of those bonds.

So here I was in a school whose student body would be considered radical by most of America at that time. I guess if a vote had been taken, I would have been the resident conservative at South Hall without really knowing what that was. I did notice that Antioch's intellectual atmosphere was about freedom compared to the monochromatic norms of mainstream America. It was so much more than being able to have members of the opposite sex in dorm rooms. It had an undeniable freedom of spirit. I was learning to look at the world and see it as a work in progress, not just as a fait accompli with rules to follow. In a way, Antioch College preceded the freedoms of San Francisco in the sixties by half a decade!

The civil rights movement was gaining momentum in the late 1950s. As in many towns, there existed in Yellow Springs an uneasy truce between students and "townies." The local barbershop was segregated and we were going to picket the establishment. I put on my dad's old World War II field jacket and joined the picket line. It wasn't the freedom marches of the south, but it was something!

As my second quarter was coming to an end I started looking around for my first co-op job. I wasn't ready to really break out on my own, so I took a job my grandfather Ben lined up for me at the Department of Health, Education, and Welfare, Division of Air Pollution. All those Russian translations I had been typing up for Ben during my senior year of high school were for grants from the Division of Air Pollution. I passed the Civil Service Exam as a clerk/typist, and all of a sudden I was an Information Specialist, Junior Grade. I was the only male in the room except for our boss, Richard Head. (Richard Head . . . I kid you not.)

My job was OK and I liked getting paid. I certainly didn't resent going to work in an office, but I never for a moment thought about a career as a bureaucrat. The gig at the Department of Health, Education, and Welfare was just marking time for the experience and a paycheck. All of a sudden though, an epiphany came in the form of Joan Baez's first, self-titled album. What a stunning recording that was! And although Joan's guitar work was not fingerpicking as I would come to know it, I loved her sound. I still had the J-45 and I worked out my own version of "Silver Dagger." The folk music scene was beginning to gather momentum. I certainly found beatnik chicks attractive, and Coffee and Confusion was the joint in DC where they were all hanging out. I'd bring my guitar and play folk music such as I saw it. I wasn't really playing my electric guitar at all; my days with Jack and the Triumphs were long gone.

There was another Antiochian working at the office with me and somehow I got invited to parties with her friends. She had the beat persona I found so attractive, but the cool that surrounded her intimidated me. I did, however, start hanging out with her sister and we partied together. One day she came to me and said that she was pregnant. The immediate solution seemed obvious to me at the time. I said we should get married. This made sense to a twenty-year-old man living with his grandparents while working a temporary job in a government office.

I called my mom to give her the news . . . she was not thrilled. The next thing I knew she had flown to DC from Manila. She pointed out to me that she thought I was an idiot. She disappeared for a day. I don't know who she saw or what was said, but the wedding was off and I never saw that girl again. Did she have an abortion? I don't know. I know I owe her an amends and perhaps someday I'll be able to make it.

Now, one would think that this series of events would be traumatic on some level. I managed to submerge all these memories and transited to another chapter in my life. I wish today I could remember more about that time, but I expunged my memory too efficiently. I was quite simply prepared to push on.

When the fog cleared, I was still single, the young lady in question had been disappeared from my life, and it was New Year's Eve, 1960. Before you could yell "Save me from myself," it was 1961 and I was on a train from Union Station in DC to Springfield, Ohio. Somehow I found a ride to Yellow Springs and I was back at Antioch in an off-campus house called Morgan.

I had foolishly sold my Gibson J-45 to one of the gals in the office at the Division of Air Pollution. I had no acoustic guitar. One of my fellow Antiochians from the neighborhood in DC had a Harmony Sovereign that he lent me. My roommate at the new house was Steve Richmond, who played the five-string banjo. Steve's brother, Fritz, would be the jug and washtub bass player for the still to come Jim Kweskin Jug Band. Also in the house was a guy named Al Heald and his roommate, Ian Buchanan.

Saturday, December 6, 2003, Keene, New Hampshire

Life went on as life does and at the Fur Peace Ranch I met this guy Rich, who knew Marty Brennan, Ian's friend. We started to talk and he talked about his buddy, Marty Brennan back in New York. The next time Rich came to the Ranch I went down to my studio and grabbed a Dobro I had bought eight or nine years ago. I gave it to Rich and told him to give it to Marty . . . that it was a repayment of a long owed debt. He did so, and a torn thread in my past began to be mended.

Last night at the Colonial Theater in Keene, New Hampshire, Rich and Marty came to the show. It had been over thirty-five years since I saw the man but I would have recognized him anywhere. It was such a great pleasure to reconnect. There was more though . . . He brought an old J-200 . . . not just any old J-200, but the big Gibson that Ian had left him when he died. The one I first heard him play. I picked it up and started to pick. I remembered that sound as if it were yesterday. In the case was an old kerchief Ian used to wear to cover his mouth when he rode his motorcycle on cold days . . . so long ago. Brennan entrusted the guitar to me for safekeeping for a while. It sits next to me in my hotel room right now. Time folds in upon itself. I think of those days . . . four decades ago . . . Ian is alive . . . we are all young and strong and full of hope. Linda is beautiful as she sings a Roy Acuff song. The son she was pregnant with would be in his mid forties by now. The music is everywhere. It was all we lived for at the time. New York, San Francisco . . . the transcendental yo yo is everywhere. We were young. What more can you say?

I pull myself back from the well of memory. It has snowed since I went to bed last night . . . about 6 inches. It is cold up here in New England, but my heart is warm with friendship. Thank G-d for friends, new and old! Thank G-d for the chance to plunge into this pool of memory and emerge into the crisp present air dripping with places and people and things long gone.

I am blessed! I think I shall speak to Ian through his guitar. I hope he is resting well . . . and for us here . . . it is another great day!

At a speaker meeting I was at tonight I heard this: "You can count the seeds in an apple, but not the apples in the seeds." So it is with us as sons and daughters. I think if my mom and dad were alive today they would not be unpleased with the way my brother and I have grown. That is a good thought. Another thing I heard that I liked was this: "If G-d had given us justice instead of mercy, none of us would have been here today."

Indeed . . . living . . . growing . . . learning to love and share . . . and finally, going where the road takes us.

Indeed . . .

Our house was filled with string music at all times. My roommate, Steve, might be playing the banjo, Al might be playing guitar or banjo, and Ian—well, Ian was playing fingerstyle music on his beautiful J-200. I had never seen anyone do this live before. I had listened to a lot of blues but I never saw any live fingerpickers before.

I had been playing the guitar for five years. I had made very little technical progress since I stopped my lessons with Sophocles Papas. To be sure I had learned to play and sing at the same time. I had hung with Jack and his DC buddies long enough to start to feel comfortable onstage. I had my Fender Musicmaster and the Sears/Danelectro amp, but I soon learned that my thrashing on the electric guitar was not what was happening at Antioch. With the borrowed Harmony Sovereign in my hand, Ian patiently took me under his wing and started to teach me to fingerpick.

The first tune I attempted was a simple version of Arthur "Blind" Blake's "West Coast Blues." I paid really close attention to Ian's right hand, which has served me well to this day. Back then we didn't have the plethora of picks available to us today. I don't think the thumb picks even had a brand name. Ian wore his pick up near the first joint of his right thumb, so I did too. If the pick was too tight, I would heat it gently with a cigarette lighter until it fit appropriately. The finger picks were steel, made by National. There were no gauged picks yet.

I watched Ian relentlessly and listened to every sound he made. It became apparent to me (even though I didn't realize it at the time) that the key was in the right hand. Being able to play and sustain an independent bass line with the thumb of the right hand was what the deal was all about. It's sort of a counterintuitive set of moves. A pinch between the thumb and fingers is natural: it's how we pick things up. To have a finger stroke in between thumb beats was not natural. Again, I didn't intellectualize this. Ian just showed me patiently how it worked, over and over again, and I practiced it until I thought I had it. With every new tune, when I thought it was mine I would play it for Ian. "What do you think, Ian?" "You suck! I showed you it goes like this," and he would play it again and again for me. I probably did suck, but eventually I did get it.

Since I've now been teaching for a number of decades, I realize that the simplest description is this: in a 4/4 measure, the thumb plays quarter notes and the fingers play the melody, typically eighth notes. Of course, it's not always that cut and dried, but it's a good starting point if you're trying to get your right hand under control. Any time a melody note occurs on a downbeat, have a pinch between the thumb and the noting finger. Anytime the melody is sounded on an upbeat, have a finger stroke by itself.

Hard work paid off indeed, but there was more. I needed to surround myself with the cool stuff the people I looked up to had. Talismans—that's what it was really about when I was younger. I thought that if the right mystical objects were arranged and in the right order, the stars would align and everything would be all right. There was an odd cluster of brand names that commanded my loyalty: Gibson guitars, Mapes strings, Camel cigarettes, Zippo lighters, Case pocketknives, and Triumph motorcycles. Those were the sacred possessions along with steel-toed work boots, jeans, and work shirts such as Pete Seeger might have worn.

The sacred collection was subject to flux, however. It became apparent to me that I needed my own acoustic guitar. In order to acquire this I would have to sell something, and the only thing I had of value was the 1954 Triumph 650 cc bike I bought from Jack's older brother, Chick. I would have to find a buyer and then organize a road trip to DC to pick the thing up and bring it back.

The buyer manifested itself in the person of Al Heald, one of the notables at Morgan House. Al had been lending me his J-50 from time to time to supplement the loan of the Harmony Sovereign. Al also loved motorcycles so he bought the old twin from me.

Another of the housemates, Jos Davidson, volunteered his car and his help. Jos had a 1958 Chevy Impala convertible with three deuces and a pair of glasspacks. I realize that many readers today wouldn't know a deuce or a glasspack from a cloudy day. In this context, that small-block Chevy had three two-barrel carburetors and dual free-flow mufflers that were straight through with a little fiberglass stuffing to make them barely legal in most states. It was the stuff of hot rod dreams! What wasn't to like about this trip? As I recall it was Jos, Joe Zinman (another of my housemates), and me who made the trip to the family manse on Northampton Street. My long-suffering grandparents were not totally pleased to see us show up. We were supposed to be in school, and it was an unannounced trip.

In an effort to placate my always suspicious and terminally acerbic grandmother, Joe said, "Mrs. Levine, Jerry is doing twice as well this quarter as he did last." "Feh," Vera spat. "Twice nothing is still nothing!" This was so in character for our relationship that I just gave her a hug and headed down to the garage where the bike dwelt.

I had rented a trailer and in those days you didn't need a Reese hitch. In fact I didn't even know what one was yet. You got a bumper hitch along with the trailer, and bumpers on American cars were strong enough to take such a gadget. We loaded up the bike, tied it down, and

I bid my grandparents a fond adieu as we headed back to Ohio and Yellow Springs.

One must remember that in 1960 the Interstate System was not yet finished. This meant that the trip to Ohio involved old US Route 40 and the Cumberland Mountains. We were feeling pretty good about ourselves, Jos and Joe and I, driving along happily in that White Impala convertible, dual exhausts rumbling in a comforting way. Uneasy lies the head that wears the crown, as they say. I had insisted on doing the driving, as is my wont. I just felt too comfortable behind the wheel. Coming down the western side of the Cumberland Gap, the brakes went out on the Impala. I knew this because all of a sudden the pedal went to the floor. It seemed counterproductive to mention this to Joe or Jos so I just white-knuckled the ride down the mountain and when I somehow got to the bottom the car coasted to a stop in a real service station.

I remember getting out of the driver's seat, waking Jos up, and returning the keys to him and suggesting that perhaps he would like to drive after getting the brakes fixed. Good times and G-d doing for me what I could not do for myself—saving my ass one more time. Funny about stuff like that. There should have been ongoing fear and trepidation . . . and there probably was at the time. Once it was over, though, it was over. Thinking of it today, I can't recall any fear.

Back at Morgan we unloaded the Triumph. Even though the bike now belonged to Al Heald, Ian took it for a spin, overrevved it, and floated a valve, which hit the top of one of the pistons, bending one of the push rods and damaging the solid lifters. Fortunately, I already had experience with this, having done it myself. Bikes didn't have rev limiters then and some of us didn't have enough self-restraint to prevent that from happening.

It was still chilly in Yellow Springs and we didn't have a garage, so into the kitchen came the old bike and I tore into it. I took off the heads and pulled out the push rods and lifters. The dome of the pistons remained intact so repair involved taking the heads to Dayton for new valves and some cylinder head work, buying new push rods and lifters, and heading back to the house to reassemble that scooter. I put the bike back together, adjusted the valves, and fired it up. That classic Triumph vertical twin sound filled the kitchen to a round of cheers. I took it for a last spin and it passed into Al's hands.

Now I had a little money. Somehow I had acquired an off-brand five-string banjo. I don't remember how this instrument came into my possession but I know how I said goodbye to it. In Dayton there was a little music store called Pop's. I didn't know what I wanted in the way of guitars yet. Martins had cachet at Antioch, but I couldn't afford one. Ian had just introduced me to the Reverend Gary Davis and he and the Reverend played a Gibson J-200—and I couldn't afford that either. Al Heald had been letting me play his Gibson J-50 and I had gotten quite comfortable with it. Right there on the wall in Pop's was a 1958 J-50 just like Al's. I handed off the banjo and one hundred dollars and the guitar was mine, along with a fiber case.

The two records I had were Reverend Gary Davis's *Harlem Street Singer* on Prestige/Bluesville, and Reverend Gary Davis and Pink Anderson's *Gospel, Blues and Street Songs* on Riverside. I also had Brownie McGhee's ten-inch Folkways LP. Today, we have such rich material readily available, but in those days it was limited, and you had to be in the know to find it. I listened to those two Reverend Davis LPs almost exclusively for the next year and a half. My father was into hi-fi when records were still mono. In that world, everything was still modular. A hi-fi needed a pre-amp, power amp, a speaker, and a turntable. I had inherited my dad's old Garrard turntable but I had no amp, so I plugged it into my Danelectro guitar amp. Not exactly hi-fi, but it worked and I could hear what I needed to hear.

I have no recollection whatsoever of the courses I took that last quarter on campus. I remember the hours of practice I spent trying to make my right hand do what my ears told me it should do. There were hootenannies in the early hours of the morning at a bakery in Yellow Springs. The shop was filled with Joan Baez songs, bluegrass, old-timey stuff, and Child Ballads. "Let's play some fingerstyle blues and clear the room," Ian would say. We did, and the room would thin out almost immediately. It's hard to imagine today, but not many people would listen to fingerstyle guitar back then. But those of us who loved it couldn't get enough. There would be other magical times in my life, but this was truly one of the first involving the acoustic guitar. I was beginning to define myself.

Having invoked "fingerstyle guitar," I need to talk a little bit about the right hand. Pianos have hammers, violins have bows to excite the strings, and the guitarist's right hand has a lot of different techniques to do the same thing. As previously mentioned, I started out flatpicking, that is, holding a flat pick between the thumb and the first finger of my right hand and plucking the string either with a downstroke or an upstroke. The right hand fingerpicking style that called to me required a plastic thumb pick on the thumb of my right hand, and metal fingerpicks on the first and second fingers of that hand as well. Flatpicking tended to be naturally louder in this pre-pickup time. When one was playing something fingerstyle, you just had to listen harder, and most audiences back then were not prepared to do that.

My friend and fellow guitar player John Hammond had just finished an Antioch co-op job at the Rusk Institute of Physical Medicine and Rehabilitation in Manhattan. "You gotta take this job, Jerry," he told me. "It's an amazing human experience!" It would be that and more, but it also took me to New York City, where I knew all the music was happening.

Some of the Antiochians had worked in Chicago, where the Old Town School of Folk Music was. Win Stracke had cofounded the OTSOFM with Frank Hamilton back in 1956, and for the folkies in Yellow Springs it was definitely Mecca. But because of Ian and my New York friends, for me the gateway to the new world was not Chicago, but New York. I could hardly wait for the academic quarter to end and for the work quarter to begin.

6

Simpler Than I Thought

If it weren't for what happened to me in 1961 that spring quarter at Antioch and the following summer in New York City, the sixties would have been quite another story for me. My Antioch friends Jos Davidson and Joe Zinman and I decided to room together and we found a joint called the Lincoln Square Hotel, in Manhattan. It was right next door to the Riverside Memorial Chapel on the corner of Seventy-Second and Amsterdam. Jos and Joe shared the bedroom and I slept on the couch in the living room.

Working as an attendant in a hospital as a young man gave me an interesting perspective on life. Our ward had patients recovering from strokes and various forms of spinal cord damage. By today's standards, the way we dealt with spinal cord injuries was something out of the dark ages; back then, it was cutting edge. I made beds on the ward, irrigated catheters, emptied colostomy bags, changed dressings, cleaned decubitus bedsores, and did other tasks the nurses on the floor assigned me. There was an Israeli nurse in my ward who showed me how to make hospital corners. I can still do that to this day. Hospital beds were cast-iron monstrosities but that nurse fresh out of the Israel Defense Forces could lift one with one hand.

That was what was happening during the day. As soon as work was over, I would take the train back to my apartment, grab my guitar, and head out to wherever the music was happening. Ian was still my entrée into this world so I would see if he had some sort of assignment for me. I met two of his friends, Marty Brennan and Linda Fuchs, who were playing a lot of what we now call Americana, but what in those days was just called "country." Linda played Autoharp and sang. Marty played guitar and Dobro—actually a National Tricone square neck. Most of the playing I did with them was flatpicking, but I was still working relentlessly on my fingerstyle and played in hootenannies whenever I could.

I never learned to sing harmony but for some reason the sonic textures of the "high, lonesome sound" that we associate with bluegrass made sense to my ear. My grandmother Vera always made fun of what she called my "hillybilly music." What did she know? Marty and Linda saw to it that there were gigs and they included me in their scene. It was a grand time, scurrying around the Village at night looking for music to listen to or places to play.

As I recall, Gerde's Folk City was down at 11 West Fourth Street, and Mike Porco was hiring a lot of the great folk artists of the time. I got to see the Reverend Gary Davis, John Lee Hooker, and quite a few of the other Great Ones. I hit some of the other joints in the Village, but for whatever reason, Gerde's was the one that resonated.

It seemed like Ian knew every musician in town that mattered. He encouraged me to start playing in the hoots at Gerde's. Brother John Sellers ran the open mikes in those days and I signed up. My fingerpicking repertoire was still limited but I had a couple of songs I could perform. Of course I can't remember what they were today, but I guess I did OK because I got an encore, almost unheard of in the world of open mikes. I had no more songs performance-ready, so I just repeated one I had already played. Yikes!

That summer I played as many hoots as I could down at Gerde's. It was a real incentive to increase my repertoire. Every moment that I was not working at the hospital I was working learning tunes, singing as well as playing. Now, in the background was that fact that this summer in New York and the job at the hospital was supposed to be an integral part of my college "education." The last thing in my mind on any given day was college. The real deal was getting my day job done so I could pick up my guitar and start playing. I never had the talent or the patience to really copy "the Masters," and I caught some flack from some of the Village denizens for that. In this era when original music is encouraged and revered it is hard to imagine why one would be criticized for sounding original. Many folks in the musical generation before me felt that authenticity lay in replication. Back then it was considered important to sound "authentic" and there were those who were very good at it. I guess in retrospect my pals and I were as authentic as anyone whether we copied the licks or not. I just wanted to be able to play the songs, and in the long run that has worked out pretty well for me. In any case, I sound like me, and for better or worse, that's as good as it's going to get.

The summer quarter ended and so did my job at the Rusk Institute. It was time to figure out what to do next. The obvious thing to do was to return to Antioch for the fall quarter—that is, if Antioch would still have me. My academic performance in college had been marginal at best. I wasn't kicked out of Antioch, but I wasn't encouraged to return. I packed up my stuff from our little two-room apartment up on Seventy-Second Street, sold my Fender Musicmaster to Jos, and loaded all the rest into my green '51 Pontiac Chieftain. I bid goodbye to Joe Zinman, Jos Davidson, Ian Buchanan, Marty Brennan, Linda Fuchs, and New York City. As I headed toward the Lincoln Tunnel I was reminded of the New York "driving lesson" Joe gave me when we were driving around looking for an apartment. "Don't be afraid! Assert yourself. If your fender is in front of theirs, you're good to go!" Those were words to live by. Getting your fender in front of the opposition is a good metaphor for life.

Fall, 2004, Yellow Springs, Ohio

Vanessa and I drove to Yellow Springs in Greene County, in this most beautiful time of year. It had been quite a while since I had walked through the Antioch campus. I was there to receive the Rebecca Rice Award, an award for achievement in profession. Antioch did not have an "edifice complex" and the campus looked much the same as it did in 1960. "There's more to this place than architecture," I told Vanessa. I remember in my acceptance speech I told the audience about my dilatory academic performance and we all got a good laugh. "That said," I continued, "I learned what has defined my life here on this campus. Who could ever want any more than that from a school?"

It was decided that I would return to the Philippines and go to college at the Ateneo de Manila for a year. My dad had a year or so to go of his tour. I have no recollection how that decision was made or if I was involved at all. One might think this an odd decision for me to make: to return home again after having been essentially on my own for a while. I wasn't ready to quit school. Getting an undergraduate degree had become a rite of passage for the Kaukonen kids, and perhaps the familial financial teat still had some allure. Mom and Dad weren't going to spring for another college in the States, and truth be told I might not have been able to get into another US school. I *could* get into the Ateneo de Manila in the Philippines. Mom and Dad would pay for it and room and board was free. I was going "home!"

Ben and Vera drove me to Baltimore/Washington International Airport and I flew to Los Angeles to catch my next plane to Manila. When I first flew to Manila in 1956, we left LA in a Pan Am Boeing Stratocruiser. The Stratocruiser was an awesome double decker four-engine prop plane that actually had a bubble on the second deck so you could see the stars. In those days you flew to Hawaii and changed planes. The next flight was to Wake Island for refueling, then Guam for more fuel, and finally Manila. In 1961 the first transpacific 707 jets were coming into service and there were no longer fueling stops in the Pacific. Another era had passed.

I was leaving the many compartments of my life behind. Antioch was gone, New York was gone, and the time in DC was gone. High school was a forgotten universe. I was ready to be reborn again in another world. Of course I had been in the Philippines before, but now I was a college kid. My brother had been sent to Lakeville, Connecticut, to the Hotchkiss School for his junior year of high school, and I inherited his room on the second floor of our house in that little compound on Park Avenue in Pasay City.

One might wonder why I haven't spoken more about my brother. I'm not saying my family dynamic was any more peculiar than anyone's. We all have our oddities. My brother and I were never close. Why was that? I really don't know. The emotional landscape in the Kaukonen household was always volatile; I've said that more than once. My mother and father always seemed to be fighting about something, and neither one of them had any verbal boundaries. I never saw them strike each other, but sometimes objects were known to fly around the room. They were married for sixty years. I remember them still yelling at each other up to the time my father passed in 1997.

My solution to avoiding the minefield was to distance myself from everyone, including my brother. The further away from the battlefield I was, the safer I felt. My brother, Peter, has always been his own person and it is not for me to try to tell his story. I just know that we were not close as kids or as adults, except for rare times when our worlds collided.

In any case, Pete was at the Hotchkiss School, a prep school for Yale and the like. I don't know what I was thinking being back in the Philippines again. Looking back on it, I think I went back because at the time I just had nowhere else to go. If my job at the hospital hadn't been temporary I might have stayed there for years. I guess I'll never know because it was and I didn't.

So here I am, back in Manila. My mother had taken the bull by the horns as she always did and enrolled me at the Ateneo de Manila. It was a Jesuit university founded in 1859. With a Jewish mother and a Lutheran father, neither of whom were observant in any way, it seems odd that they picked a Catholic university for their eldest son to attend . . . but pick it they did. I never gave this choice a second thought. "You're going to the Ateneo," they said, and so I went. In any case, it was the best university in the Philippines.

I had been dabbling in sociology and anthropology back at Antioch, so I figured what better place to study anthropology than the Philippine Islands? I was surrounded by hundreds of islands, languages, and cultures. For the first time I was actually excited by a line of study in school. Father Frank Lynch, S.J., was the head of the department. He was brilliant and exciting. One of his teaching assistants was a younger guy named Dick Stone. We became friends that year.

When we got together for parties, either with embassy folks or friends from the Ateneo, I would bring my guitar and play my small but slowly growing repertoire of songs. Back in the early sixties there probably weren't more than a hundred fingerstyle guitarists in the United States. Today they are everywhere. Back home, I would have been a cultural oddity, but in the Philippines people saw me as some kind of American artifact. Arthur "Blind" Blake's "That Will Happen No More" made its debut in Southeast Asia thanks to me.

The de facto effect of being isolated in an American community in Southeast Asia was that musically speaking I had no outside influences other than the LPs I brought with me. Spending time abroad as a result of my father's job certainly exposed me to a great variety of exotic music, and I loved listening to it all. Whether or not this exposure affected the development of my own art is open to discussion. I never consciously set out to bring world music into the mix that was evolving on my guitar. Listening to my LPs—lifting up and putting down the needle, trying to learn licks and songs—that's how I spent my musical time. I tried to replicate what I heard, and if it did not match the original, that was all right with me. I just wanted to play the songs.

My father was always seeking youthful endeavors, and up until the early 1990s when he had his first stroke he was remarkably fit. He was in his early fifties when I returned home to Pasay City, and although he always played tennis competitively most of his life, one activity was never enough. He had joined the Manila Boat Club, a rowing club on the Pasig River. It looked like fun and for the first time in my life my dad and I seemed to have something in common. I started in the bow of a heavy pair. Dad and I didn't really mesh as a team so I wound up rowing with Vic Niemeyer as stroke. Vic was a World War II vet and at the time he was serving with the United States Information Agency at the American Embassy in Manila. Vic and I made a good team, and with Tony Rittenhouse as cox we won the 1961 Christmas Regatta at the Manila Boat Club. Rowing on that Pasig River was always challenging. The river was unbelievably polluted, filled with large clumps of some sort of moving river vegetation as well as dead animals. Everything from dead dogs to carabaos and pigs were present on that filthy river. That conspired to make one really not want to turn the boat over and fall in the river. What an incentive!

One of the high points that year for me as a son was having a beer in the boathouse with my dad after a river workout. It was an odd rite of passage for me but one fathers and sons have gone through since the beginning of time and the invention of fermented beverages.

In that last year in the Philippine Islands two really interesting events touched my life. Father Lynch got some sort of grant and put together a little expedition to the Sulu Archipelago. His colleague Dick Stone and I and a number of others flew to Mindanao and then to a little village on the island of Jolo in the archipelago. We flew from Manila to Davao in a prop plane, probably a DC-4. We then flew from Davao City to the Jolo Airport not far from Maubo Beach. The plane we flew in from Davao City was a World War II C-47 barely reconditioned for civilian use. Jolo is a volcanic island and the little twin-engine plane came in from the west over the Sulu Sea, skimmed over the nipa rooftops of the village, and landed on a runway that went uphill, scrubbing off speed as the wheels touched down. The old C-47 was a tail dragger, so even this many years later I can say I have never again experienced a landing like that one.

I had my dad's old prewar Rolleiflex 2¼ × 2¼ as well as his prewar 1936 Contax II 35 mm camera. I'm guessing my mission was to document this trip. I brought plenty of film with me. The color film was Kodachrome and I had some Ektachrome as well as Plus-X and Tri-X for the 35 mm. I took pictures of everything. Some things live brilliantly in my memory. One of my fellow travelers for a brief moment was this lovely woman, Dolores Ducommon. Dolores had something to do with the Peace Corps, and since she was an English-speaking American we briefly coexisted on that trip across the Sulu Sea. We were on a small ship going between two islands and we pulled up for a moment midchannel. The water was that glorious blue that seems to only exist in the Sulu Sea and environs. I dove off the stern and swam downward. A strong underwater current caught me and started to sweep me deeper. I quickly realized this wasn't like splashing in the ocean in Wildwood, New Jersey. I managed to swim back to the surface and as I took my first breath of air I realized the ship was almost a mile away. They came and got me and I was told in no uncertain terms how reckless, stupid, and unbelievably lucky I had been. G-d had other things left for me to do or my life could have come to an end not far from north Borneo.

The next thing I knew we were cruising through the archipelago in outrigger canoes powered by a couple of outboard motors. We were in search of Bajau people and villages. The Bajau were water gypsies. The villages were always on stilts, never on land. The people lived most of their lives in their outrigger boats, their upper bodies well developed from the constant paddling and legs nearly atrophied. It was a specific lifestyle with specific physical requirements.

In one of these stilt villages I met a foundry man forging Damascus steel with fire fed by oxygen from hand-driven bellows made out of large bamboo pipes. He was making swordlike weapons. I was able to get him to sell me one that had been in his family for almost a hundred years. It was a kalis. A kalis is similar to a kris, but the blade is only wavy for the first eight inches or so near the hilt. It is a slashing and thrusting weapon. I was told that the wavy part of the blade made cuts of uneven depth that were difficult to heal in the tropics, making what might be a superficial wound more lethal. I was also told that it made the blade easier to extract from a thrust wound.

It is interesting to me that an adventure that was so short in the cosmic scheme of things would be remembered so vividly after all these years. This was more than fifty years ago, and a lot can happen in fifty years. That part of the world down by the Sulu Sea is stunningly beautiful and back then was largely the land that time forgot. There were some anomalies though. The Oblate Fathers who were our connection to the Ateneo de Manila had an amphibious aircraft. It was a Republic Seabee curiously named *Our Lady of the Snows. Our Lady* held four passengers and had a pusher motor mounted behind the wing above the cabin. The good fathers flew Dick Stone and myself around and suffice it to say, it was an amazing trip. We were thinking about flying to Sandakan in northeast Borneo, but for some reason just circled around the Sulu Archipelago.

The last night of our expedition the Oblate Fathers and the people of Jolo had a banquet for us. The food was amazing and after we ate, the folks played music and danced. There was a little—and I mean *little*—microphone and PA, and one of the guys was playing a five-string guitar. They asked me if I wanted to play a song and so I played "Hesitation Blues" on a five-string guitar, in the town of Jolo in the Sulu Archipelago on a generator-powered PA. Reverend Davis would have loved knowing his version of that great tune had such very long legs.

And then it was time to say goodbye to one of the most amazing worlds I have ever had the honor to occupy. It was time for a trip back in the old C-47 to Davao City. You will recall the landing strip at the airport stretched from the edge of town up the side of the volcano. When we first arrived we landed uphill on the strip, shedding speed as we went. To take off, we reversed the process down the side of the mountain, just lifting off in time to clear the nipa huts and head out over the Sulu Sea. As the aircraft gained altitude and began to circle with a heading toward Davao City, I sadly realized that I was saying goodbye to a once-in-a-lifetime experience.

In Davao City I changed to a somewhat larger plane. I had my cameras and sundry souvenirs, including my kalis, in my carry-on. I smile as I think of this. Today it is unlikely that one could board a plane anywhere in the world with a sword as a carry-on.

Back in Manila the school year at the Ateneo was over, and my thoughts turned to finding a summer job. Dear old Dad got me a temp job at the American Embassy. In the early sixties Clark Field, in Angeles north of Manila, might well have been the largest American base in the world. With the navy at Subic Bay and Sangley Point, there was a huge American military presence there in the Philippine Islands. It was more than apparent to us in the American community that a war was brewing in Vietnam. The embassy bristled with all sorts of antennas for receiving encrypted messages, and pouches containing documents ranging from Unclassified to Top Secret came to Manila personally accompanied by couriers. I got security clearance that entitled me to handle top secret documents, and my short career as a Communications Clerk, Pouch began.

I'm sure if I had chosen a career as a Foreign Service staff person, this would have become mind-numbing work after a while. As a temp job it was exciting, and although I didn't know it at the time, the American involvement in Southeast Asia was beginning to unfold under my very eyes. Manila was also a garden of earthly delights for a young man looking to take a short walk on the wild side. There were bars, bar girls, and all that goes along with that. Part of that lifestyle involved me going to the embassy infirmary for penicillin shots. Years later I realized how lucky I was that I never caught anything penicillin couldn't cure. The nurses took care of me, and because I was now considered an "adult," my parents never entered the equation.

If someone had asked me if I was a risk taker, I would have said emphatically no! Alcohol, cars, motorcycles, girls, and all that jazz—yeah, I definitely took risks. I can only say that I was lucky to make it through. One thing was for sure: I wasn't through paying those dues yet. Working in the pouch room, playing guitar, going to the endless parties that seemed to surround the diplomatic/military community: in retrospect it wasn't much of an intellectual endeavor, but that's the way it was.

It's funny to think of it today, but even as a lowly temp communication clerk in the pouch room, I recall feeling what I thought was the majesty of empire. Much has changed in the world since then, and the concept of empire has vanished along with the majesty that probably never was. There was no way I could project how leaving this post in Manila would truly close the doors to a major chapter in my life and set the stage for one of the paths I would follow for the rest of my life.

It was late spring as I recall. Dad's tour of duty in the Philippines was finally over and the Kaukonen family was getting ready to move on. Mom closed up the house in the compound on Park Avenue and packed everything we owned into containers to be shipped stateside. We were planning on sailing back to the States on the *Golden Bear*, one of the flagships of the Pacific Far East Line. Many of the diplomatic families sailed home on the ships of the Pacific Far East Line.

As a Foreign Service dependent brat you get used to the transient nature of your life. You never have the same friends because they are here one moment and gone the next. No matter how dear they might be, there are those you will never see again. If my dad had never been in the Foreign Service, I would have grown up in that little neighborhood in Chevy Chase, gone through elementary, junior, and senior high school with all the same kids; the chances were I might have gone to American University and some of the same people would still have been with me.

Instead, people might rotate out six months after you met them, and if you ever saw them again, it was only much later in life. Friendship certainly had an ephemeral quality. At the time I accepted this transience with certain equanimity. In retrospect, there is a wistfulness, a gentle sadness to this mode of life.

The house on Park Avenue in Pasay City was no longer ours. Up to this point in my life that house had been our home longer than any other in my young life. Everything was packed and heading either to storage in the States or to Stockholm, Sweden, which was to be my dad's next posting. I had a suitcase and my Gibson J-50 guitar. It was back to the Filipinas Hotel, the same hotel we started our Philippine existence in. We spent our first moments in the PI at the Filipinas, and our last moments there too. The night before we were to board the ship, Dad and I walked around the neighborhood together. In Manila at that time a neighborhood could change in half a block. Around the corner from the hotel were a couple of seedy girlie bars. I remember some street hustler coming up to Dad and me and asking if we wanted some poontang. Without skipping a beat Dad said, "Blow it out your ass!"

It was another great father-son moment.

The next day there was a little party on the ship. Some of my friends were there, as well as some of Mom and Dad's friends and colleagues. We promised we would stay in touch—and then they were gone. The gangplank was pulled away, lines cast off, and the *Golden Bear* made its way out into Manila Bay, past Corregidor where I once walked in the Malinta Tunnel; past Bataan, scene of the Death March; and into the South China Sea.

My world had always been compartmentalized into chapters and this was yet another. As I said goodbye to my friends at the dock another chapter closed forever.

The *Golden Bear* put in at Hong Kong, then Taiwan, and then Yokohama. From there it was nonstop deep water to that dock in Oakland. I decided it was time to read *The Rise and Fall of the Third Reich* by William L. Shirer. This was a weighty tome under any circumstances and just the book I needed for a two-week ocean voyage.

I knew that the Pacific Ocean was a much rougher crossing than the Atlantic, but I didn't know how much rougher. The *Golden Bear* was a shorter ship than the SS *United States*. The captain and crew didn't seem to think the crossing was exceptionally rough, but I did. I remember trying to read in my little stateroom, starting to get seasick, going out on the deck, and immediately discovering why it is not a great idea to vomit on the windward side of a ship. Another lesson learned.

Manila, Hong Kong, Taiwan, Japan . . . it all vanished as we sailed under the Golden Gate Bridge and into San Francisco Bay. We docked in Oakland, got our luggage off the ship, cabbed it over to San Francisco where we spent the night and the next day, and then flew to the Baltimore/Washington airport. I was back in my home place again.

Flux was the name of the game for me as always. Neither fish nor fowl it seemed, as if the New York days were nothing but a distant memory. The year back with Mom and Dad in the PI was fading, and here I found myself back in DC under my grandparents' roof on Northampton Street. Mom and Dad were there too. The only thing necessary to complete this maelstrom of family dysfunction was my brother, Peter, and he was about to come back from Hotchkiss. I wandered about the neighborhood and found a job at the local Sunoco station. I got a uniform with "JERRY" on the pocket, a paycheck, and an apartment. I spent that summer picking the guitar, pumping gas, and going to bluegrass festivals, and then as fall approached, it was time to go back to school.

For me, regaled by tales of beatnik revels by Dick Stone back at the Ateneo, I knew I wanted to go to San Francisco. I applied to the University of San Francisco, another Jesuit school. My grades weren't good enough for USF, but I did get into Santa Clara University down the peninsula.

The summer of '62 passed in the blink of an eye, as youthful summers do. At the end I got on a plane at Baltimore/Washington International in the morning and landed at San Francisco International Airport in the late afternoon. I knew I wouldn't be able to catch the bus south that day so I cabbed it into San Francisco and found a hotel for the night on Mission Street. I still had a day to get to Santa Clara to enroll in the university, so I decided to stop off in Belmont and see my dad's younger brother, Pentti, whom I had never met.

Pentti was a master machinist. He had worked for years up in Seattle at Boeing, but after his divorce he moved to the Bay Area and worked at a machine shop on the peninsula near Belmont. I had called him the night before and he was waiting for me at the bus stop. He didn't have a car so we threw my things into a cab and went up to his house.

Uncle Pen was a truly gentle soul. That said, he carried a flame-thrower in World War II as his unit fought its way up through the Pacific to land in the Philippines. For whatever reason, he seemed to have simply let go of life, floating gently like a leaf in the wind waiting for the next landing. His house hadn't been cleaned in months. There were rings from coffee mugs in the dust on the counter that could have been there for years. He lived for working and spending time at the track playing the ponies. In subsequent years I would go to the track with him. It was always an amazing look behind the curtain. He knew all the owners, the jockeys, and the stable hands, even the folks selling beer and racing forms.

After the night at Pentti's I cabbed it down off that hill in Belmont to the Greyhound station on El Camino Real, and within the hour I was in Santa Clara, California, which would be my home for the next couple of years. In 1962, Santa Clara was a sleepy little town. The Santa Clara campus was still small and accessible and the El Camino ran right through the middle of it. The bus station was right on the edge of the campus so it was not much of a schlep to drag my stuff to the administration office and get my dorm and class assignments. My first dorm was in Nobili Hall, and my first roommate was president of the Young Republicans Club. This was an odd match for sure. I was not a very political person, but in my mind at least my lifestyle bordered on bohemian.

In 1961 Santa Clara University became the first Catholic university in California to allow female students. Wow—what a mind bender. The mascot was the Bronco. The male students were Broncos and the female students were Broncettes, or something like that. The male old guard was upset because women were being allowed behind their curtain. I remember thinking, "Have you guys lost your minds?" By this time I had lived in the "real world" (at least on a trial basis) and found I enjoyed the company of women. Being back in a dorm in a very conservative school was an eye opener indeed.

After settling into my little dorm room I took a walk around campus to see if there were any like-minded spirits around. The spirits did not manifest themselves yet, but something else did. There was a flyer stapled to a telephone pole: HOOTENANNY AT THE FOLK THEATRE! Hootenanny? Yeah buddy! It wasn't Greenwich Village. It wasn't Coffee and Confusion in DC. But it would have to do.

My bond with music and lyrics has always occurred on a molecular level. A simple series of chord changes could move me to tears at any given moment. I believe my dad felt the same about music. I remember bringing him a portable CD player and a set of headphones as he lay in his hospital bed after his first stroke. As the music played, tears would run unashamedly down his face. I think I know what he felt.

Anyway, when I played music—be it the Carter Family, the Louvin Brothers, or Reverend Gary Davis—I would be totally involved in the universe of sound. I found myself an alien in Santa Clara, but when I saw that flyer, I believed there was a sanctuary to be found. I grabbed my Gibson J-50 in its fiber case.

The Folk Theatre was just what I expected. It was a single-width storefront with the stage facing the little audience from the front window, strangely reminiscent of the Rendezvous Club where Jack and I played during my senior year of high school. The audience maxed out at forty or fifty. There was the de rigueur espresso machine, which often made musical subtlety challenging. Everything in the room was black, of course. There was a little tuning room in the back. Two of the first people I met were Steve (later Richmond) Talbott and Janis Joplin.

This was a moment of unbelievable synchronicity. My self-image was never that of a college student, and yet I had been one for a long time. I'm not sure what I expected out of life or what sort of dues I would be required to pay. For someone like myself who just wanted to play music, the Santa Clara University was an odd place to be. As things turned out, it was exactly the right place to be.

The first time I met Janis, I realized that I was in the presence of greatness. I knew nothing of her or her past . . . nothing. I just knew that I was as close to brilliant authenticity as I might ever get. She was looking for someone to accompany her. We started fooling around backstage and a set evolved. Along the way I recognized a kindred spirit in Steve Talbott, and we co-opted him (or he co-opted us) to blow some harp. I don't remember who went on first or how the evening evolved, but I played some tunes on my own and then Steve and I played with Janis.

How did all this happen? How did one thing lead to another? Without doubt it was an amazing night of music. These nights are always happening somewhere, but on this night there was a tape recorder present, and these moments are still alive and well and can be found if you look really hard.

Of course I had no idea at the time that any of these tiny shared moments would amount to anything. We were all just doing what our spirits called upon us to do. I had no idea whatsoever what the scene was going to be like when I immigrated to California. Up to that point in my experience Greenwich Village was the epicenter for all things folk-related. That first weekend at the Folk Theatre in San Jose was more than an eye opener to me. That Janis was destined for greatness was undeniable. My relative lack of experience (at that time I had been fingerpicking for less than two years) was more than compensated for by my strong right hand. And Janis in that incarnation—well, I had never heard anyone like her.

No one had!

Janis was already a full-time musician. I was a college student by day, musician by night. If I had gone to UC Berkeley my street cred would have been solid thanks to the radical leanings that school shouted. Going to a conservative parochial university was bad for my image. What serious bluesman would go to a Jesuit university?

I have to smile when I think about some of the fashion persona we affected. Janis was wearing jeans and a work shirt. Most of the time I strove for the Pete Seeger look: steel-toed work boots, jeans, and either a denim work shirt or a flannel shirt. I was hardly a working-class kid, but it made me feel better to look like one. The flamboyant sartorial excesses that came later on in the sixties were light-years away.

There are some wonderful photographs of this first meeting of young musicians, taken by a San Francisco photographer named Marge Scott. Marge and I met at that little coffeehouse and we got to talking; when the evening was over I went up to San Francisco with her in her little Austin-Healey Sprite. San Francisco in the early sixties was still a small town. Earthquake-proof buildings were a thing of the future. Marge and I would become close . . . as close as a self-involved soul such as myself could be to anyone then. She taught me much about photography and darkroom techniques as well as life itself. By some strange miracle, we are still friends today.

Every moment that I wasn't fulfilling school obligations, I spent in San Francisco. However, back in Santa Clara, another momentous event happened. I was walking by the cafeteria in Nobili Hall on campus hugging the wall, as was often my wont, trying to keep as much shade on myself as possible. Santa Clara at the time made the term "clean cut" sound radical, so when I saw a guy with a beard heading toward me, it definitely got my attention. He looked at me and said, "I see you're a wall walker." Wow. What a way to start a conversation. We got to talking. We both liked music. He was into slack key guitar, which was a new concept for me.

"There's this guy you have to meet," he told me. "He was my roommate last year but he dropped out. He's living on the beach in Santa Cruz and he's a folkie too." Yeah, that sounded good. "Let's go," I said. "How about right now?" My hirsute companion's name was Bob Kinzie. Bob loved all things aquatic and had a 1957 Ford two-door sedan with the backseat taken out so he could fit a surfboard in the car. We got in and drove on Highway 17 over the mountain and down into Santa Cruz.

Inside a beach house with surfboards leaning on the walls was Paul Kantner, surrounded by a six-string guitar, a twelve-string, and a long-neck banjo. Paul was not a blues guy but he was dedicated to folk music, and the musical styling I heard in Santa Cruz that day contained the DNA of the Jefferson Airplane, which would be born three years later.

Shortly after meeting Paul in Santa Cruz, I met Jerry Garcia and Bob Weir at the Folk Theatre, as well as Ron McKernan, later known as Pigpen. When I first met Jerry I was immediately taken by what a nice guy he was. I was shy more often than not; usually when I met new people I would let my guitar do my talking for me. If we established common musical ground, the conversation would continue. Jerry was an outgoing guy and we soon realized that we had a lot in common. It also became immediately apparent that he knew a lot more about bluegrass and old-timey music than I did. His sensibilities as a band member and leader were already well developed. At the time, of course, I was uninterested for the most part in ensemble playing. I liked getting together and jamming with my pals but I had no interest whatsoever in forming or being a member of a band. Being a solo artist really fit with my personality at the time. Jerry was also married and had a kid, which made him seem more like an adult. I figured he had to know more than I did. Even in my twenties, when adulthood should have been a goal, it wasn't! At the time, Bob Weir was definitely the silent type on those occasions when we met. As I have come to know him over the years he is a man of wisdom, both in life and music. Pigpen was always a mystery to me. We would share musical space from time to time, but we never really talked.

There were many other musical luminaries back then. Tom Hobson, with whom I would record *Quah* almost a decade later; Mike Wilhelm, who would be in the Charlatans; Janet Smith from Berkeley; Bill Bohn; and a host of others. Who are some of these people and why do I mention them? Some are gone and some you will never have heard of, but in that time they and those like them made the Bay Area sing with a song that was always fresh. It was indeed a time! The whole San Francisco Bay Area scene was more than music-friendly. Artist and writers abounded in an atmosphere that seemed to afford them respect.

I would encounter Joe Novakavich, Page Brownton, Sherry Snow, and others there too. Jerry Garcia, Bob Weir, and Dave Nelson were mainstays of the folk scene in Palo Alto. Dave would be instrumental in creating the New Riders of the Purple Sage with Jerry in later years. For those of us without a car, Palo Alto was a day trip. Berkeley seemed light-years away at times, and in a way it was. San Francisco was a Greyhound ride away. It was easier to get there without a car than it was to go to Berkeley. That said, we all got to know each other and realized that we shared a powerful bond rooted in the music, the culture that surrounded it, and in the bonds of the artistic community that was evolving.

My so-called studies at Santa Clara seem almost incidental looking back from the hillside of time. Something of an intellectual will-o'-the-wisp, my academic studies in sociology seemed to fill the interstitial spaces in my body. The rest of the space was taken up by music. The head of the department back then was Witold Krassowski. He was an amazing man, a Polish resistance fighter and prisoner of the Nazis in World War II. He always exemplified the American Dream to me. I think he saw through my pretensions as a student, and with that in mind assigned me John McNamara as a thesis advisor. He was a jazz pianist in addition to being an academic, so he was perfect for an apostate student such as myself. He understood my passion for the music, but he firmly believed that I needed something to really motivate my life when the bubble broke. I recall that when I had let my homework get behind, he gave me my first Dexedrine, the Adderall of the time. That was my first introduction to speed. The weekend I was supposed to catch up on all this work, my friend Marge and I decided to drive to Tijuana and Ensenada. It was a long drive, but what the heck. Tijuana reminded me of the worst parts of Manila, but sleeping on the beach in Ensenada under the stars was really something.

About halfway back to Santa Clara from Mexico I realized I had a bunch of work to finish up and, yes, it was Sunday. I took the Dexedrine. The rest of the drive went by in the blink of an eye. Marge dropped me off at my dorm and I went up to my room. Instead of completing my assignments, I wrote a short story and submitted it to the *Owl*, the SCU literary magazine. First things first, I always say.

By this time I had a new roommate. Peter Manchester was a theology and philosophy major. It might seem like another odd combination, but in fact we both loved the guitar and music. Peter was perhaps the smartest guy I have ever known. Epistemology, cosmology, ontology, Aristotelian logic, and more . . . he was at home with all these things. He was also a tinkerer and had modified a stereo Akai tape recorder to record fifteen inches per second, which was a pro speed back then. He also had a condenser microphone. Many of the early recordings of Janis, Steve Mann, Tom Hobson, Steve Talbott, and me owe their existence to Peter Manchester.

I came to Santa Clara in 1962 and before I knew it the fall semester was over and 1963 was upon me. It seemed as if the spring quarter also went by in the blink of an eye. Peter and I decided we would room together the next school year and I planned to spend the summer with my parents, who had been posted to the American Embassy in Sweden.

I boxed up the stuff I would be leaving behind and stored it. I had somehow inherited a hard-shell guitar case from David Freiberg, a folkie from LA. David was part of a commercially successful duo called David and Michaela, and in later years he played with both Jefferson Airplane and Jefferson Starship after his tenure with Quicksilver Messenger Service. Just prior to my meeting him, he, Paul Kantner, and David Crosby were sharing an apartment on Venice Beach. The eagles were gathering. Paul had moved to LA during the summer of 1963 that I spent in Sweden.

These were waning years for my father at the State Department. Known and respected as an authority on labor matters in the Far East, he found a posting in Sweden to be another universe. Still, it was a position of respect. He was, again, labor attaché and first secretary at the American Embassy in Stockholm. He still had his Lambretta scooter that he loved dearly and he had it shipped from Manila. As always, within months he and Mom were fluent in Swedish and had made themselves quite at home.

Two of my pals from DC, Bob Lindner and Dave Dawson, decided to join me in Sweden for a month so we could busk our way through the Swedish countryside. The new Kaukonen family house was in the little suburban community of Danderyd. It was a four-story house on a hillside in the woods, and in those days moose would come out of the forest to nibble on the clothes Mom left drying outside in the sun.

My DC pals arrived in Sweden via England, where they picked up a pair of Triumph motorcycles. They arrived in Danderyd with the motorcycles, a banjo, and an Autoharp, and we were ready to hit the road. Mom and Dad were able to tolerate the three of us for a couple of days while we made plans. Dad lent me his Lambretta scooter and I figured out a way to wrap my guitar in a plastic tarp and pack my tent and sleeping bag on the passenger seat. Back in those days every little town, or *commun*, as the Swedes called them, had a folk park. The three of us traveled north through central Sweden playing our music wherever they would let us . . . and they let us a lot.

When we got back to Danderyd, my mom was getting ready for a visit from my grandparents Vera and Ben. Bob and Dave pitched their tent at a nearby campground for their last week in Sweden and before I knew it, my friends were heading back to the States.

Vera and Ben had left Russia around the turn of the nineteenth century, fleeing the murderous persecution of Jews under the czar. They became citizens, went to college, found jobs, and raised a family. For as long as I knew them I never heard a sentimental word about the "old country" or a desire to go back. In 1963 my grandfather was the same age I am now and my grandmother was seventy-three, younger than I am today. That said, they always seemed incredibly old to me; my grandfather Ben was getting old in his fifties. When I saw him that summer in Russia, he seemed ancient. It seems as if the years took their toll on people of that generation at an earlier age. In any case, as age was beginning to wrap itself around them, they decided to make a roots trip back to Russia. In 1963, we were deep in the throes of the Cold War. Americans were not particularly popular or welcome in the Soviet Union but tourists—regardless of nationality and international currency—were always welcome. Ben and Vera planned to get their visas in the States and meet us in Russia. Mom, my brother, Peter, and I got our paperwork through the American Embassy in Stockholm. We booked passage on a tour ship out of Stockholm that docked in Helsinki and then went on to Leningrad.

On the ship was a nineteen-year-old Swedish girl named Lena Margareta Pettersson. In the European tradition she had been working full time as a layout artist for a Swedish girls' magazine since she was fifteen. If one wasn't going to go to university, a full-time job was mandatory. She had long wavy brown hair and green eyes, and she was sporting the bohemian-hipster look I found so attractive. I had my guitar with me, and with the help of Johnnie Walker Black we began talking. She and I and the first mate of the ship became buddies after hours of drinking and playing cards.

After the layover in Helsinki we sailed to Leningrad. We found ourselves with different tour groups but somehow she and I managed to get together a couple of times a day. We were told to bring our own toilet paper so we did. We were warned that the Intourist guides were really NKVD agents so we were advised not to try to sell anything. People offered me unbelievable sums of money for my jeans, but the thought of being shipped off to some gulag kept me honest.

Being in Russia in 1963 was, in its own way, very exotic. It was the height of the Cold War so there was always that tension for us Americans that we were constantly being watched, and maybe we were. What I remember most about Leningrad (St. Petersburg today, as it was before the Russian Revolution) was the Hermitage. Growing up in DC

I learned to love museums at an early age. Now this was no National Air and Space Museum, but they did have a lot of Fabergé eggs and more paintings than one could possibly see in a day or so. My grandmother Vera was from this area, but we were not allowed to wander about on our own so I never got a chance to see where her home place was.

To meet up with my grandparents in Moscow we took the night train from Leningrad. It was like being a player in some black-and-white spy movie. We departed the Leningrad train station, which in those days was as spotless as a Mercedes dealership in Manhattan. In the morning after checking into the Hotel Bucharest in Moscow, we cabbed it to the airport to meet Ben and Vera. In addition to our family, they were met by friends from a lifetime ago as well as science colleagues. Up until the early sixties Ben was busy translating Russian air and water pollution documents for the American government and kept in touch with all his sources. Even this many years later I am touched to recall how these friends, from the old days to the new, greeted each other lovingly. They paid Ben and Vera the highest of compliments with flowers and chocolate.

The day before we were supposed to fly back to Stockholm I was walking near Red Square with Margareta and there, in the shadow of the statue of Karl Marx, I proposed marriage. It just made perfect sense at the time. I had known her for all of a week, maybe ten days.

We decided that when we got back to Sweden, she would come visit me at Mom and Dad's place outside Stockholm. She came to Danderyd while my brother, Peter, was still there. A family dinner at the Kaukonens' might not have been good for digestion, but it was never boring! There was a fiery scene at the dinner table involving Peter's future. There was the matter of ROTC and the draft to consider. I think my father had given up on me being a part of the straight world of the time, but he was still hovering over my brother. Margareta had come to get to know my family; well, she got to know them all right. There was yelling, slamming plates, and kicking over chairs. Welcome to my world!

Since we had planned on a couple of days together I figured they would be better spent away from the folks so I borrowed Dad's scooter again, packed up the tent and sleeping bags, and Margareta and I headed to a campground in Uppsala. Of course it was raining and cold those couple of days. Frankly, the terrible weather, leaky tent, and miserable World War II–style sleeping bags should have been a harbinger of things to come. Both of us should have simply said, "It's been swell. See ya sometime." But we didn't. We got back to the folks' place in Danderyd, had another dinner. Everyone was cold to each other this time instead of angry, and the next day I took Margareta to the airport for her flight back to Malmö. In a couple of days I was on a plane back to California and another year at Santa Clara. We were engaged in a transglobal relationship that would be consummated when she came to California in January 1964.

7

In the Kingdom

That was the last significant length of time I spent with my grandparents. Ben and Vera returned to the old house on Northampton Street, Mom and Dad continued serving at their post in Stockholm, and my brother got ready for his senior year of high school, which he would spend in Sweden. I went back to Santa Clara. I closed the book on another chapter as I headed back to whatever life would provide in California. I did not, however, close the book on Margareta. This would be a much longer chapter.

Back in Santa Clara I settled into my dorm with my roommate Peter Manchester. I was more active than ever in the expanding folk scene in the Bay Area but somehow managed to still keep my grades up enough to maintain my student deferment from the draft.

I was sitting in my room in 329 Dunne Hall on November 22, 1963, playing my guitar when we got the news that John F. Kennedy had been assassinated in Dallas. I had yet to vote in my first election but in some way I viewed JFK as the president of my generation. We have become inured to tragedy on many levels since November 1963, but at the time, the unthinkable had happened. Santa Clara, being a Jesuit school, had many religious classes that I did not have to take since I was Jewish.

But I did attend the Mass in the Mission Chapel on campus after Kennedy's death. It was very moving. No one had his own TV back then, but we all knew that the world was changing faster than our awareness allowed us to fully grasp. The assassination of our president impacted everyone profoundly.

All that profundity in the real world was all well and good. Aside from the emotional impact of that event, I was really untouched by what was happening in the world outside my own. I was into my second year of teaching guitar at the Benner Music Company on Stevens Creek Road in San Jose. The year before, I had been lamenting my lack of gainful employment to Paul Kantner. We were all out playing all the time, but we rarely, if ever, made any money. "You gotta start teaching," Paul said to me. I had never thought about teaching. "What am I going to teach?" I asked him. "How's about what you know?" he replied. It was that simple. I couldn't believe I hadn't thought of it myself. Paul had been teaching for a year or so at the Benner Music Company. Norm Benner, who owned the place, made most of his money renting and repairing band instruments for local high schools, but he had a feeling about folk music and fretted instruments. He and Dana Morgan up in Palo Alto saw the fretted instrument craze coming before any of the big music stores did.

Norm welcomed me on Paul's recommendation, no questions asked. He had two tiny basement rooms that were accessed by climbing down a ladder. I knew nothing about tablature (a notation for guitar) or traditional music writing so I figured out a simple tab system of my own. The lessons were three bucks a half hour. I forget what Norm charged us to rent the "studio," but it wasn't much. He made his money selling Epiphone guitars to the students. It was a good deal for everyone. That little music store on Stevens Creek Road was constantly filled with pickers and songs. It was a glorious time. I continued to teach well into the first year the Airplane was together, and at the time, it was better money.

In any case, I was engaged to be married, I was living in a dorm room in Dunne Hall with Peter Manchester, and I had no idea what-soever how I was going to handle whatever life might dish out to me. Somehow, that all made sense.

The year before I had been turned on to pot for the first time. Rich and Mary, two friends from Antioch, had a lightless pad in a basement on Waller Street in San Francisco. "Come on up to the city," Rich said. "We're getting some pot." I remember seeing a TV ad later, in the eighties or nineties, that showed a drug-addled derelict. The voiceover said something like: "When you were young you never looked forward to being a drug addict when you grew up." If drugs had been available earlier in my life I probably would have fallen prey to them. However, the guitar was my drug of choice at that time. In any case, I remember sitting cross-legged on the floor of that apartment as the pot was cleaned and the joints ceremoniously rolled. I had asthma as a kid, so even when I pretended to smoke cigarettes when I was young, I didn't inhale. It took me a moment to get with the process of inhaling smoke and hold-ing it in that getting high on pot requires.

Nothing happened at first. "Is this it?" I was disappointed . . . for a while. But then the music we were listening to started to take on oth-erworldly characteristics. I began to hear things in a different way and there was that sense of communion amongst all of us who partook. In a very real way, it was the sharing of a sacrament.

In 1963 the demimonde of music and pot connections was an odd counterpart to the relatively staid world of Santa Clara. I was commit-ted to the university there for the duration of my studies, but I spent a lot of time with my friends in San Francisco. My parents were not pleased by my life choices. I convinced them I would stay in school and pay most of my own way outside of school, and they signed on until my graduation. I had to find a place to live that I could afford near the university. Hard to imagine today, but back then the cost of living in the Bay Area was better than affordable. It was cheap.

I found a big house on Fremont Street a couple of blocks from cam-pus. It held four apartments, and mine was a kind of shotgun: a living room into a bedroom into a bathroom into a kitchen into a backyard. It was dingy and nasty. There was no cleaning deposit, because nothing was clean. My roommate, Peter, assembled a bunch of our lady friends from school, and they all came over and helped to clean this dump.

A dump it was, but it was going to be my dump, where I would live as a married man with a wife and classes to go to and, well, it seems insane today, but that's just how it was. I stayed in my dorm room at Dunne Hall until the semester was over. Margareta was coming at the beginning of January and we would get married, and that's about as far ahead as I was able to think.

There is no question that I had always cast my fate to the wind (thanks to Vince Guaraldi for this metaphor), and if one needed proof that there is a higher power somewhere, the way my undirected life worked out should prove it.

That fall semester wound its way into Christmas and New Year's, and then it was 1964. Sometime early in the month of January, Margareta flew into San Francisco International Airport and my friend Lee drove me up to the airport in his MGB roadster to pick her up. Back then you could walk right out to the gate; at some airports you could actually walk out to the plane. I wish I could tell you exactly what crossed my mind as she walked off the plane and out the gate where we looked at each other, hugged, and headed for the baggage claim. The me writing this today looks back and says, "Now what are you going to do, smart guy?"

The next morning I had class and I left Margareta alone in a strange country, strange town, and very strange and seedy apartment. She was one of the smartest people I have ever met, but she was not an academic by nature and she had nothing in common with my schoolmates. I didn't either, but being chameleonic by nature, I played the game better. She wasn't much for games. A couple of weeks went by as we struggled to get to know each other. Right about this time I got an irate letter from my father wondering when I was going to make "an honest woman" of her so we decided it was time to get married. We got a marriage license in Santa Clara County, and with my friend Rocky Free and my brother,

Peter, who was now a student at Stanford, as witnesses, we went down to the courthouse. It turned out my brother was too young to be a legal witness so we collared an off-duty police officer for the job. We were married that afternoon in a six-minute ceremony.

We bought a couple of bottles of cheap wine on the way back to the house and that was our celebration. We got nasty drunk on that cheap shit and got into a fight on our wedding night. "You're a son of a bitch!" she yelled. For some reason the only thing my addled brain could grasp was that she called my mother a female dog. That's what I heard, I swear to you.

She stormed off into the bedroom and I slept on the stained couch in the living room. Morning brought a silence you could cut with a knife, but we ignored it and talked about the paperwork we had to do. We had to take the marriage license to federal court in San Francisco and start the process to get her a green card. While I was still going to class, Margareta was looking for a job. There wasn't a lot of need for layout artists in the South Bay Area, plus you really had to know someone. Anyone who has tried to get a job in an area where you have no connections knows how impossible that can be. There were no magazines being published out of San Jose, and the local press establishment was already filled with a network of old boys and old girls. I have said many stupid things and taken many idiotic positions in my life, but on this day I picked a doozy. "No woman of mine is going to have to work," I remember saying with conviction. "You're an artist. All you have to do is work on your art." For the next twenty years Margareta would occasionally get a paying project, but she never held a regular job.

We didn't stay in the shotgun apartment on Fremont Street for long. The larger unit next door opened up and we moved over into it. Along with the upgrade, I became manager of the building, which lessened our rent. Being manager simply meant collecting rent—sometimes easier said than done—and occasionally waking up in the middle of the night to unclog a toilet.

Living off campus at Santa Clara was a big deal. You had to be married to make this happen. In my circle of college buddies I was the only one with an off-campus dwelling, so for a while it briefly became a hang-out for my pals who were still stuck in dorms. Margareta didn't have much in common with the college kids who surrounded us, and she tolerated their presence with less than benign equanimity. She was very turf-conscious and resented sharing space with other people. There was not much socializing with my friends from school. Back then none in my circle knew much about drugs other than a little pot every now and then. One night my ex-roommate Peter brought over a bottle of Darvon. "Darvon is proof of the existence of G-d," he raved. I had no tolerance for such drugs and I recall getting really high. I decided it wasn't my thing, yet, so that dark desire would lie in wait for me for another decade or so.

It was to the first house on Fremont Street that Paul Foster, who would become one of Ken Kesey's Merry Pranksters, and David Freiberg brought Steve Mann. I wasn't there the first time they called, so Paul left a methedrine-inspired drawing with a sketch of Aladdin's lamp and the words "KEEP YOUR LAMPS TRIMMED AND BURNING FOR THIS OLD WORLD HAS HAD IT." The next time Steve came by, I was home and we spent the better part of a day and a night playing guitar together. We became friends and anytime he was in town we would hang out and pick music. Steve considered any music that involved improvising to be jazz. We played a lot of jazz.

Margareta and I drove down to LA to visit Steve for a couple of days. He had gone back down to do some studio work. We stayed at some cheesy flophouse downtown but the digs didn't matter. We weren't in the room much anyway. Steve was the twelve-string guitar on Sonny and Cher's "I Got You Babe" as well as many other commercial hits of the time and he knew a lot of studio cats. He thought I should meet Ry Cooder, so he called Ry and we dropped by at about eleven thirty at night. It was a small, thin-walled apartment so we couldn't play acoustic guitars; instead we played a couple of unplugged electric guitars for a bit. Ry probably doesn't remember this, but I do.

Back in Santa Clara, eventually a fairly large house across the street from the original 1159 Fremont Street digs came available. We took in two roommates to help with the rent: Joan, who also worked at the Benner Music Company, and Steve Mann, who was back in town. Joan had been working for Norm for some time and we had become friends. None of us had any furniture. This made it tough to find a place to sit, but the cavernous rooms and hardwood floors made for great guitar acoustics.

A couple of amazing events took place at that big house in Santa Clara. One was the making of the "Typewriter Tapes." Janis got a gig to play a benefit up in San Francisco's North Beach. She picked me as her accompanist and she came down to Santa Clara to rehearse. I had just bought a little Sony reel-to-reel tape recorder. I was so excited to have this gadget, mono though it was, that I taped everything. In a very low-tech way it was roughly analogous to what folks do with all their electronic gadgets today. The tape was running, Margareta was typing a letter home to Sweden, Janis was singing, I was picking, and there it was, the typewriter tapes! Anytime I got to play with Janis was momentous. That little rehearsal certainly wound up having very long legs in the cosmic scheme of things. Steve Mann, Janis Joplin, and I were all there that day rehearsing and we taped everything. Over the years the tapes found their way out into the world, and thanks to the Internet they can still be heard today, complete with Margareta's typing in the background.

The other epiphany came through Steve Mann. One night Steve said, "I've got some LSD. This is something you need to experience." LSD was still legal, and even though I had no prior experience with psychedelics I really thought they might be some kind of shortcut to enlightenment. I had been to the Vedantic Center in Hollywood. I read Vedic scriptures and I had done some yoga. It all seemed too much like schoolwork. I needed a shortcut.

Down the hatch! It was a sugar cube. How weird could it be? The answer was "Plenty weird!" It started coming on and it didn't take long to realize this was not just some sort of supercharged version of the crappy pot we smoked. The unfurnished living room of the big house on Fremont Street became a garden of earthly delights. The walls and the air around me were kaleidoscopic and the music was like pillars of sound. Playing the guitar was a little difficult because I watched my hands, but the sounds became visions.

Steve and I played for hours and the effects of the drug showed no signs of waning. Sunrise began to cast its morning rays through windows with no curtains to diffuse the light. This many years down the road I don't know if it was awesome or not, but it sure was different. The time factor to the high was certainly different too. In my experience, you got drunk; you sobered up. You got high on pot; you came down. It was the same with speed. With this first LSD experience, the hits just kept on coming.

Steve, who had been our guide, came up with another great idea. "Let's drive up to the mountains and watch the sunrise." My old '47 Oldsmobile was starting to be temperamental so the four of us opted for Joan's VW bug. I have always loved driving so I'm sure that I insisted I drive. So be it. The mainstream acid high was gone, but the aftershocks were alive and well. Isolating all the functions that make driving a manual shift car possible took a few moments. I did a mental preflight check and off we went.

Some of us remember the VW bug days. There was a certain cachet to that marvelous little machine. My grandmother Vera hated them and called them Hitler Wagons. I always wanted one but never got one. I still learned to work on them though. VW repair was always a neighborhood event. There was a time when I could pull the engine on one and replace it in an afternoon, but that is another story. The bug was small, and even though we were all more sylphlike back then, it was an up close and personal ride. I drove up the Santa Cruz Mountains until I got to Route 35 and that was the moment when I stalled the car. There was a police cruiser with a couple of cops there at the summit and I was sure they could read our minds and knew without a doubt that we were mentally modified. I flooded the engine and that was that. The officers got out of their car and headed toward us. I was sure that our next stop would be prison, but they merely said good morning and helped us push the car until it started. I guess they didn't notice our paisley halos.

As if that weren't exciting enough, what happened next certainly was.

Friday, November 30, 2001, Keene, New Hampshire

It's been almost three weeks since I've visited my Thoughts page with thoughts to write down. Not that I haven't been thinking but I've just really been in the moment and I haven't been thinking that way. My last entry down below was provoked by the passing of Ken Kesey and this one by the passing of guitarist George Harrison last night.

When the Beatles exploded into the American and world music scenes back in the early sixties, I had totally immersed myself in traditional music and had eschewed all things vaguely electric or "popular." When I think about what a stuffed shirt I was then I really have to laugh today. Anyway, my friend Steve Mann came up from L.A. to visit me in Santa Clara and convinced me that one of the sugar cubes he had in his pocket would really open my world as a musician. Steve was such an innovative musician and so far ahead of his time that I accepted his recommendation as gospel and we each ate one. Well, needless to say I was totally unprepared for what followed and at some point a couple of hours later we had to go for a ride with a friend in a borrowed VW. We're driving somewhere on Highway 101 near Sunnyvale, California, and a semi pulls up behind me filling the rear window with its bumper and grill. Now, in retrospect, we were probably only going 20 miles an hour in rush hour but still it really scared the shit out of me. As I was contemplating my impending death and possibly the end of the world, we turned on the radio and as the tubes warmed up (remember tubes in car radios?) the first thing I heard was George's solo in "She's a Woman" and it changed my life! Not only did it get me through that moment of fear on the freeway, but it opened my eyes to more things than I can enumerate here. It prepared me to be, at least moderately, open to Paul Kantner's suggestion that I join some band that he was forming up in San Francisco. In that moment, the electric guitar became a real instrument for me again.

I met George once a long time ago . . . I do not even remember when. I did not know him but of course as a man of my time I was always interested in what he was up to. He was immensely successful, but he and his family suffered all the things that can afflict "normal" mortals. As I grew older, I came to appreciate more and more the huge contribution that he and his friends made to our world. I know that he had been ill for some time. As one who lives in some small way in the public eye, I admired the way he handled his privacy . . . the way he loved his family. I know that he is in a better place. (I always say that when someone dies, but I believe it.) He is all right now and my prayers are with his family.

I thank George for helping to open my heart!

Next thing I knew I was safely off the highway and back in our house on Fremont Street. This chapter in the tale wasn't quite over yet. I was teaching that day at the Benner Music Company, and guess what? I wasn't screaming high anymore, but I was still far from being solidly back on Earth. I got in my old Oldsmobile and drove over to Stevens Creek Road. I've often wondered if my students noticed anything different in my demeanor that day.

I learned a couple of things. There were aspects to an LSD high that held some sort of minor enlightenment, and in that moment I truly saw the world in a different light. It also impaired my ability to play the guitar and I didn't like that. It lasted a very long time, and I didn't like that either. Control issues, I'm sure. Over the next couple of years I would trip again, but it wasn't my thing and I can count the acid trips I've had on a hand and a half.

Communal living has never been my thing, and it still isn't. The four of us coexisted in the house for a bit and then Steve went back to LA and the three of us remaining couldn't afford the rent anymore. Margareta and I moved to a tiny little house at 75½ Wabash Avenue in San Jose, a block or so away from the music store, and I settled into trying to put a little money aside so we could survive after my upcoming graduation from college, when Dad's bountiful largesse of $150 a month would cease.

Right around this time, the mostly faithful 1947 Oldsmobile fastback coupe was beginning to be more maintenance-intense than I was willing to tolerate. I traded it to Steve Schuster, a flautist and horn player who had been one of my brother's classmates at the Hotchkiss academy. I gave Steve the car, and he gave me a soprano saxophone. I'm sure he got more use out of the car than I did out of the sax, but it was cool to have.

My grandmother Vera had relatives in Sacramento named the Josephs. They sold me a 1957 Volvo PV444. It was definitely the coolest automobile I had owned to date. I rebuilt the SU carburetors and the clutch and transmission myself in the driveway next to the little house on Wabash Avenue. Margareta and I put thousands of miles on this little car.

I was about to graduate Santa Clara, and other than my teaching and coffeehouse gigs I had no prospects whatsoever. This didn't really disturb me as much as it should have. I had heard that the great blues pianist, Champion Jack Dupree, was living in Denmark successfully. Rumor had it that American blues and jazz musicians were treated with more respect in Europe than they were in our own country. I began to think about moving to Copenhagen. Margareta's parents still lived in Malmö, just across the sound, and, well, why not?

It all seemed to make sense to me at the time. Short-term vision? Unrealistic? Perhaps . . . but that was me. Rock and roll was rearing its head again in a powerful way. There was the so-called British Invasion, although I wasn't really a big fan at the time. The Byrds were starting to make their mark. "Mr. Tambourine Man" was a big hit, as was "Turn, Turn, Turn." Roger McGuinn and his colleagues had crafted what was undeniably a completely new sound. McGuinn was playing his Rickenbacker twelve-string and he seemed to effortlessly put his axe in and out of alternative tunings. Also amazing was to see my friend David Crosby on the big stage of the San Jose Civic as a big star and not just a talented folkie with esoteric tastes.

Whether I was able to process "modern" rock-and-roll and pop music as valid art or not, it was incredibly seductive and I found myself liking it in spite of myself. My devotion to traditional music had been profound indeed, but in a way, I believe it to have been limiting. In any case, this all troubled my artistic sensibilities but that was not necessarily a bad thing. College was winding down, graduation loomed on the horizon, and real life seemed just around the corner. The Folk Theatre had morphed into the Offstage. I don't know who the original owners were, but it wound up in the hands of Paul Foster, David Freiberg, Paul Kantner, and a couple of others whose names elude me. I'm sure that somewhere there is a great story about Paul Foster, one of the smartest and nicest guys I've ever met. I still have the little rapidograph penned note he left pinned to my door on Fremont Street: "KEEP YOUR LAMPS TRIMMED AND BURNING FOR THIS OLD WORLD HAS HAD IT." That was Paul, and that was the headspace of the time.

The energy that infected the Folk Theatre (and later the Offstage) dissipated as everyone's world began to get larger. Take a guy like Jerry Garcia. I don't think he ever sought stardom, but I think he always sought progress. He was always studying something: songs, techniques. He was constantly experimenting with band formats: bluegrass, jug bands. He played some blues of course. By this time almost everybody did. It was not really his thing although he understood the idiom perfectly. By this time, Jerry Garcia and his friends were getting way beyond bluegrass bands, jug bands, and the like. Rock and roll had reared its head and Jerry and the boys were leading the charge. They were now the Warlocks and, as a bona fide rock-and-roll band, were beginning to play "real gigs" such as bowling alleys and pizza joints. Interestingly enough, even though they "covered" songs, I never considered them a cover band like the rest of the bands on the pizza circuit.

Back in 1963 at the First Monterey Folk Festival, Jerry was already becoming a big dog and had a place on the bill. I drove down with Margareta to see the show and support our homeboy. Bob Dylan, Mance Lipscomb, the New Lost City Ramblers, the Georgia Sea Island Singers, the Weavers, and more were there. It was a hell of a festival. They had an open mike for locals and I signed up. I played an instrumental version of "Follow the Drinking Gourd." It was well received, and it was a real confidence builder for me, getting out of the local coffeehouses and playing on the stage of a nationally recognized festival, small though my part might have been. Jerry was already a seasoned veteran by that time and he nailed his slot . . . of course!

As Jerry was transitioning from folk to rock and roll, I remember he and I were sharing a bill at the Offstage one night. I don't remember how the evening was laid out, but in the break he and Margareta and I decided to get in our car and drive to Alum Rock Park and the Eagle Rock view to smoke a joint. Smoking a joint was a big deal and required clandestine arrangements. Anyway, we got to the park, hiked up to Eagle Rock, and fired up. There was a Hispanic family up in the Rock area as well and the sun was setting. The pot started to take effect and the patriarch of the family watched the sunset and uttered reflectively, "ZZZboofa! ZZZboofa!" That's what I heard. Looking back, I think what he really said was "It's beautiful! It's beautiful!" To this day when I see a beautiful sunset, I may not say it out loud, but what I think is "ZZZboofa!"

We drove back to the Offstage and were late for the set. Audiences then were more forgiving, though, and all ended well.

The Warlocks were making waves. One time, while I was hanging with Jerry at one of his shows, he admonished me to start thinking about rock and roll. With this in mind I got together with a couple of guys and we started an extremely short-lived band. We called ourselves the Head-stones, because we smoked pot and liked the Rolling Stones. I had a 1937 Gibson L-5 and an early fifties Fender Princeton amp that I had bought from a friend a year or so before. The guitar had a DeArmond pickup and that was the axe I played in the Headstones. I can't remember if we played more than one gig. I rather doubt it. I don't think we were very good.

By this time Paul Kantner had put aside his attachments to the Folk Theatre and had moved to San Francisco. He met Marty Balin and they talked about starting a folk-rock band. They got a little group together with Signe Anderson on vocals, Jerry Peloquin on drums, Bob Harvey on bass, and a guitar player whose name I do not remember. Paul came back down to San Jose and stopped by our pad on Wabash Avenue: "We're getting this rock-and-roll band together and we think we might need another guitar player." He was excited, but I wasn't convinced. "We've got this club on Fillmore Street down in Cow Hollow," he said. "It's called the Matrix. Come on up and bring a guitar. Check out the scene." It sounded interesting. I threw my L-5 and the Princeton as well as my J-50 into the trunk of the Volvo, and up to San Francisco we went.

We found a parking place and schlepped my stuff into the club. (More than two trips to the car, and it isn't folk music.) The Matrix was what would be called a yuppie bar in a few years. Ken Kesey was there and for some reason he had brought an Echoplex with him. The Maestro Echoplex EP-2 was a tape-delay unit that used vacuum tubes. The unit used a series of sequential record and playback heads that, because of their distance to the source head, would provide delay. Looping was still in the distant future, but with a very long delay, one could produce looping-like effects. Why would he have been there and why would he have had an Echoplex? Good questions. "Try it," he said. I plugged it into the Princeton and the L-5 into it. It was cool—it was indeed sort of like prehistoric looping. It began to open my mind into the possibilities of electronics merging with the guitar and music. More importantly in retrospect, it was just plain fun!

"Count me in . . . at least for a while." That's what I said. Paul, sensing that he had me on the hook, said, "You're going to need a Rickenbacker twelve-string. Like McGuinn's." I had no experience with a twelve-string guitar at the time, so I didn't realize what an utterly different instrument it is. True, it is tuned just like a guitar (EADGBE), but the octave pairs lend themselves more to chord textures than single line passages. I figured I could adapt myself to this. Since I was giving this gig a shot I decided to buy the Rickenbacker twelve-string. I didn't have the $600 it cost, but I remembered the US and Israeli savings bonds my grandparents had bought me once a year since I was born. I called them in DC and had them send me enough cashable bonds for the axe. I drove up to San Francisco to Sherman Clay at the corner of Kearny and Sutter. The Rickenbacker was mine in the blink of an eye. McGuinn had that crystal-shattering high-end guitar sound, and with a little research I found that he used a Vox Treble Booster, so I bought one of those as well.

I continued to teach at the Benner Music Company and drive almost daily to San Francisco to rehearse. We were getting ready to move to San Francisco and things were slowly falling into place with the band. Marty Balin had brought Matthew Katz into our world as a manager. He had a couple of unreleased Bob Dylan tunes to offer us. Who knows how he got them. He was also filled with promises of record contracts and gigs as well as fifty bucks a week whether we worked or not. It seemed almost too good to be true, and in many ways that would prove to be the case.

Margareta and I decided to spend a couple of days and nights in San Francisco looking for an apartment and rehearsing while I commuted to San Jose for my teaching gig. We found a transient hotel in North Beach. I have no recollection what it was called, but I do know it cost less than twenty bucks a week for the room. Margareta got bored commuting to San Jose with me so one day she decided to stay in the city while I went to teach. I came home around six o'clock and as I was walking from my car to the hotel I saw a paddy wagon and a bunch of cops throwing a handcuffed woman into the back. It was Margareta. Coming from Sweden in an era when even the cops didn't carry weapons, Margareta had no fear of law enforcement. Apparently some North Beach beat cop was used to extracting favors from the working girls on the street. Wandering around the streets in North Beach, a policeman mistook her for one of the street girls and tried to exact his tribute. Margareta was not about to take any shit off this cop and when he got only one handcuff on her the other one became a weapon. It took six cops to subdue her and get her in the wagon.

While my father was stationed in the Philippines he had gotten to know both Edmond "Pat" Brown, the governor of California, and the mayor of San Francisco, John Shelley. I got in touch with Dad immediately and he called his California political pals and they sprang into action.

Up until this time, my thoughts on the government in general and the police in particular were moderately benign. Yeah, smoking pot was a felony back then, but it was a necessary rite of passage so the benefits outweighed the risks. There was a war going on in Southeast Asia, but up until this point I had always had a student deferment. This was a reality that would catch up with me soon enough. At this moment, as my wife was arrested because she would not give some North Beach beat cop the sex he demanded, I began to see the Establishment as the enemy, with little regard for the rights of ordinary people. As a result of father's intercession, the charges were dropped and the cop disciplined. Even as naïve as I was at the time, I could see that if it hadn't been for my dad and his political connections, this incident would have had a far different outcome. I could see for the first time that justice wasn't necessarily equally meted out.

As for the band, we still had no name. Lots of ridiculous names were bandied about. Finally when I couldn't take it anymore I said, "You want a stupid name? Howzabout this . . . Jefferson Airplane?" It was one of those rare moments when everyone in the band agreed, and that was that. I think it was the only band meeting that ever allowed me to come away smiling.

Here's where the name came from. I had a couple of blues-playing pals. We always used to joke about when we would qualify for an authentic nom de blues. Tom Hobson from San Francisco settled for Blind Outrage, Steve Mann from LA picked Li'l Son Goldfarb, and when I couldn't think of anything for myself, Richmond Talbott from Berkeley told me that I was Blind Thomas Jefferson Airplane and that was that. The newly named band had bumper stickers and buttons made up that read "JEFFERSON AIRPLANE LOVES YOU." A couple of gals from one of the local high schools took it upon themselves to start a local fan club, and as Paul Harvey would say, "Now you know the rest of the story."

We opened at the Matrix on August 13, 1965. San Francisco then was a weird place on a lot of fronts. It had some bizarre city ordinances that made no sense whatsoever. One that affected all of us was that you could not have a dance without a permit, and in clubs that did not have such a permit, dancing was against the law. The Matrix did not have such a permit and so ostensibly it was a sit-down joint. Hippies did not really exist yet. We were all still imbued with the tailings of the Beat Generation. I wore dark jeans, a black turtleneck, and a sport coat. Beatle boots when I could finally afford them. My hair is naturally wavy so it required careful drying and an occasional touch of hairspray so that I could actually effect bangs. I guess we needed to look like contemporary rock and rollers. It seems whatever one does there is a uniform that accompanies us, a look that affirms that you are real in your endeavors. That said, we all looked pretty conservative compared to what would become the norm in a couple of years.

I had never been in a real band before nor had I been a "professional" musician on this level. This was a new landscape that needed a different sort of navigation. Marty Balin had been a professional musician for a number of years. By the time we met, he had already been in and out of record deals and already paid a lot of dues. He had a pretty good vision of what he wanted and how to go about getting it. Marty is an intense and very private individual. He always kept a lot of shade on himself and I always found him to be a tough read. I didn't know much about the music he made in the past. I did know, however, that he possessed one of the great male voices of my time. He was also always looking ahead. He could see a place for us in the galaxy of stars that already graced the scene. It was just a matter of time.

The creativity that Marty brought to the table was different from anything I had encountered. First of all, his songs rested on his voice, not his guitar. He gave me an important lesson that I try to teach my students today. It is always about the song! You can geek out and get under the skin of instrumentation and arrangements, and to be sure they are important. But without a song, they are nothing! Marty brought songs to the table every day.

When I listen to our first album, *Takes Off*, I hear a folk-rock album, and yet it is more than that. Take a tune like "Blues from an Airplane," written by Marty and Paul. It's really a blues in name only. It's too electric to be folky, and the groove and hook lines are, well . . . different. It's Marty finding his way with some assistance from Paul, and the rest of us blending in.

We rehearsed relentlessly; it's really all we did. Skip Spence had replaced Jerry Peloquin on drums by the time we opened on Friday the 13th, August 1965. I had met Skip when I was teaching at the Benner Music Company. He was a salesman at a local Levitz furniture shop, was already married, and had kids. In addition to all these responsibilities, he managed to hang out in the South Bay music scene and play guitar. He was a real nice guy, but I don't recall paying much attention to his music. I was still agonizing over what "authenticity" was, so he was off my radar. Marty thought Skip looked the part of a rock-and-roll star, so he invited him to join the band. I think what Marty saw was raw musical talent, and he was right about that. Skip learned to play the drums more than well enough for what we needed at the time. Had his powers of concentration equaled his talent, Skip could have done anything.

Moving into September 1965, we of the Airplane were both cursed and blessed by our association with Matthew Katz. It is true that he was giving us something like fifty bucks a week to rehearse and advance ourselves. It is true that he got us gigs and it is true that he was beginning to pitch record companies to see if he could get us a contract. There was a darker side to this, however, and I'll get into that in a bit.

The band was beginning to be more electric and Bob Harvey, who was a fine bluegrass upright bass player, was pressured into getting a Rickenbacker bass and framing his music in a more electric setting. At another one of our interminable band meetings I told the crew about my old friend Jack Casady, who was playing bass back in DC. The funny thing is that I had never heard Jack play the bass. Back in our old band in high school, he was the lead guitar player, and I played rhythm and sang. But with Jack's obsessive attention to details as well as having one of the deepest grooves I've ever heard, I was confident that he would be great for us. "Give him a call," I was told. "See if you can get him to come out."

He was a little surprised to hear from me, and he was more than a little surprised when I told him what was going on. "You're in a rock band? You . . . the traditionalist?" He couldn't stop laughing.

"Yeah, I know it's hard to believe," I told him. "You can laugh all you want but we're getting fifty bucks a week whether we work or not." That got his attention for sure. We said it then, and we say it now, only half joking: "A gig's a gig!" He dropped out of school and we sent him a plane ticket to San Francisco.

Margareta and I drove to San Francisco International Airport to pick him up. Remember, I had never heard him play bass before, so my first words to him were "You better be able to play that thing!"

By this time Margareta and I had found a third-floor walk-up at 1145 Divisadero Street between Turk and Eddy. We took Jack back to our pad and he set up his world in the front room. There were only three rooms. There was a bedroom with a bathroom, a kitchen where the entrance was, and a living room that became Jack's world. Jack, brilliant though he is, takes up a lot of psychic space, and like the rest of us, he likes things the way he likes them. Our being roommates would be short-lived. Margareta also didn't share space well and Jack wound up at a hippie commune run by some gal who called herself the Queen Bee.

I recall a funny story as we welcomed Jack to the three-ring circus that was San Francisco in the sixties. We all felt so special that we had the secret handshake of pot and LSD. Booze and other hard drugs were sometimes looked at a little askance. Jack had never done any drugs and we were intent on ushering him in with a Technicolor splash. My friend

Paul Zeigler came up to San Francisco with his wife Catherine. Margareta and I snagged Jack, some pot, and some acid and met the Zeiglers down on the street and got into their car. As always, I made myself the designated driver and off we went. Paul, Catherine, and Jack were in the backseat and Margareta was in the passenger seat. We dropped the acid as we headed north over the Golden Gate Bridge. I'm sure we fired up a joint or two as well. This particular day was golden in San Francisco, golden across the bridge and golden into Marin County. On the Sausalito side of the bridge we got on Route 1 north toward Fort Ross. As we passed behind the backside of Mount Tamalpais, wisps of fog were beginning to cross that narrow road. By the time we drove a couple of miles on Route 1 the fog was everywhere and the Pacific Ocean had vanished. As we headed toward Jenner the acid was truly beginning to make its presence known. Fog is mysterious enough by itself. This was ridiculous! The fog-shrouded highway seemed like a portal to another dimension. Route 1 is twisty, and with sheer cliffs on the right going up and sheer cliffs on the left plunging into the ocean, we were definitely heading into another dimension. We were all flashing and I used all my powers of concentration to be a "responsible" driver. Catherine had taken her shoes off. Jack started to get carsick and before I could pull of the road he threw up into Catherine's shoes. Now, pulling off the road on that part of Route 1 is always a challenge and it took a bit to find enough space where I could get two wheels off the road. I finally got the car stopped and everybody tumbled out. Jack continued his barfing duties by the side of the road, Catherine emptied her shoes into the culvert, and Paul looked bemused. As I stared north, out of the fog rode about twenty Hells Angels out for a run. You can't make this stuff up. Skulls riding out of the fog, kaleidoscopic panoramic vision, and a tolerance for vomit all make for a memorable drive.

We weren't done yet though. Back in the car, we continued north, past the old Russian settlement at Fort Ross. By this time, the sun had burned off the morning fog. Mountains on the right and a sparkling Pacific Ocean on the left surrounded us. We came to some beach town;

I forget what it was called, but it was a public beach with a little café
and a parking lot with easy beach access. We were all still surrounded
by paisley visions but a barefoot walk in the sand seemed like a great
idea. Our feet felt strangely uncomfortable. What could the matter be?
A kid was running toward me from the beach. My expanded consciousness thought he looked a little like the Pillsbury Doughboy. He
was making what seemed like unintelligible sounds. As he got close to
us, the sounds began to take shape. "The sand hurts my feet! The sand
hurts my feet!" I got it. The sand was very hot and hurt his feet. Wow.
That's why it was hurting our feet too. I absorbed this wisdom and put
my shoes back on sans socks. My feet no longer hurt. Another lesson
learned.

But wait, there's more. I went to the restroom in the café and as I
was coming out people were yelling and running around. Apparently
someone had drowned in the surf. I analyzed the landscape and determined it was time for us to drive on. Somewhere north of Sea Ranch
we headed inland and got back to Highway 101 around Cloverdale. I
was still driving, but now we needed gas and I had to go to the bathroom again.

I must point out that this was Halloween weekend. Pumpkins, corn-
stalks, goblins, witches, and the like were on sale everywhere then as
they are today. I pulled into a gas station in Cloverdale and stopped by
the pumps. A kid was walking across the station tarmac with a pumpkin on his shoulder. The pumpkin was bigger than his head. Shades of
Ichabod Crane! By this time we were all on the back slope of the acid
high, but things were still plenty weird. I tried not to look at Ichabod
as I went into the station to pay for the gas and use the facilities.

Hells Angels, sand burning my feet, the Headless Horseman . . .
how weird was it going to get? Back on 101 we drove south through
Santa Rosa, past Sausalito, over the Golden Gate, and into San Francisco in time to go to Longshoremen's Hall to see the Lovin' Spoonful
play. All enjoyed a fitting end to a fine day! I can't help but wonder what
really went through Jack's mind on that amazing fall trip. He just

seemed to accept it as the new normal, as if he had shifted gears seamlessly from the more than conservative atmosphere in the nation's capital to the psychedelic adventure land that San Francisco was fast becoming. And thus it was that Jack Casady was welcomed into the New World of life in San Francisco in the sixties. As that most interesting Saturday receded, it was back to business as usual and nose to the grindstone.

We started rehearsing like crazy with Jack, but since he was used to doing a lot of pickup gigs, he was a quick study. On October 30, 1965, he played his first gig with Jefferson Airplane at the Harmon Gymnasium in Berkeley, California. All things considered, Bob Harvey took his being replaced with an amazing amount of equanimity. He even lent Jack his almost-new Rickenbacker for the gig.

I realized that my beautiful old L-5 was inadequate for rock and roll, so I sold it for $250 and bought a Guild T-Bird. I remember thinking that I had made a killing selling the old L-5; I bought it and the Princeton amp for sixty bucks, so selling the guitar alone for $250 seemed like a killing. I remember briefly thinking I should have opened a music store. Such an instrument today would bring about $25,000. Remember, this was before some genius thought up the "vintage" concept. Back then secondhand meant cheap!

We had seen the Lovin' Spoonful at some bar in North Beach earlier, and Zal Yanovsky was playing a Guild Thunderbird. He was a great player so of course I checked out his gear. The T-Bird was one of the most different-looking guitars I had ever seen. It was a solid-body guitar with a shape like Mr. Tooth Decay. I had to have one . . . and I got one. This was the six-string guitar I used on *Takes Off*, as well as the Rickenbacker twelve-string. I made another trip to Sherman Clay. I think they were the first establishment to extend me credit. I also bought a Standel Super Imperial because Zal was playing through one. It was a completely solid-state amp with two fifteen-inch speakers, and no guitarist today would probably voluntarily choose one. That said, it's the gear that I used for the solos on "Somebody to Love" as well as "White

Rabbit." It worked out OK for me. Years later at a gig in New Jersey at the Tabernacle I found myself sharing the stage with John Sebastian. We got to talking and I told him how I got the Guild and the Standel because the Lovin' Spoonful guys had that gear. "We hated those amps," he told me. "We had to use them because we were endorsers." I couldn't stop laughing. Again, it worked out for me.

As we were becoming a band we used to rehearse at Marty Balin's apartment on Belvedere Street. We did this either acoustically or with the small amps we owned. Marty Balin and Paul Kantner were supplying all the material at the time, both originals and covers. They along with Signe Anderson were the tip of the singing spear so it made sense. I did bring in the Memphis Minnie classic "Chauffer Blues" for Signe to sing. We rehearsed for hours on a daily basis. I had not yet written any songs so I was not part of the song-writing process, but I was always there when it came time to learn the material. This was all uncharted territory for me and I worked hard to fit into what I perceived as a different approach to songs. The good news for me was that it allowed me to adapt what I knew into a genre that was new to me. In a way, that made it easy to come up with new stuff since it was all new. We wanted to be successful in the music business. We wanted to have hit songs. We wanted to be heard and seen. We took it all very seriously!

Ralph J. Gleason, the noted San Francisco jazz critic, took notice of us. Ralph wasn't even fifty years old yet, but to us, in our mid-twenties, he seemed venerable. I am not really knowledgeable about jazz, but Ralph's column in the *San Francisco Chronicle* was fun to read. He truly loved the music and his passion was infectious. He came to the Matrix and heard us play and he took our music seriously. He gave us respect in print, and made us real in the eyes of the reading world. The trickle-down effect helped Matthew Katz open doors to record companies in LA, which was where the action was on the West Coast. The so-called counterculture had yet to define itself, and at the time Jefferson Airplane wanted to find our place in the industry. The battle with the music business establishment would come with the recording of our first album. We all needed to spend time in Los Angeles auditioning for contracts, but there was no money yet for hotels. It was a time of up-scale couch surfing. Matthew had access to a two-room apartment in West LA belonging to the actor Pernell Roberts. Signe and her hus-band Jerry shared these digs with Margareta and me. Everyone else in the band would hang out there all day long and practice when we weren't auditioning. These are lifestyle decisions that only young artists would make. Under normal circumstances, no adult couple would sub-ject themselves to living conditions like these. It certainly didn't help to advance Margareta and me toward a more enlightened relationship.

We did a bunch of auditions, but the one that sticks out in my mind was the one we did for Phil Spector at his house in LA. We were in this cavernous great room with a bunch of equipment set up and Phil expected us to play for him. He was behaving erratically and waving around what looked like a .22 caliber pistol. This wasn't what I signed on for so Jack and I walked out. That was that for Phil Spector.

There were other auditions, but the one for RCA sealed the deal. We got what was at the time an unheard of advance—$25,000. Mat-thew absorbed most of this but we were now on the board and pieces were in play. Tommy Oliver produced our first album. Matthew Katz is also listed a producer, but this was just his way of keeping his fingers in the pie. He also bagged the publishing with a company called After You. He would say with a predatory smile, "I named it After You." We learned from this, and in the future we owned our publishing ourselves. Dave Hassinger, who had worked with the Rolling Stones, would en-gineer. Tommy Oliver's wife, Suzie, fed the band lunch every day.

At that time, getting signed was the only way to become successful in a commercial way. Today anyone with a decent computer, a good sound room, and some mikes can record a decent project. Back then studio time was limited and very expensive; you had to have a deal to get into the studio. We had a deal and so we got into the RCA studio at Sunset and Ivar. *Takes Off* was recorded in the small room, studio B. The tape machine was a three-track. You had two tracks to record to, and the third was for bouncing and collapsing tracks. An open track was always left to combine, or collapse, the other two onto. This left two more open tracks for recording. This was before Dolby noise reduction became the standard, so there were a very finite number of times you could do this before the sound degraded. You actually had to be able to nail your take in two passes at the most. It's funny to think about today. Today my daughter could record a project on her iPhone with an endless number of tracks and no sound degradation.

In the studio you try to capture the life and the excitement that infect a live performance while dealing with a recording technology that by today's standards had inherent limitations. We hung in there though, and got the project done. I listened to *Takes Off* recently after all these years, and it's an interesting piece of work. The creative and skill set differences of the members of the Airplane with no studio experience whatsoever, mixing with the old guard producers and engineers in LA, made for a stressful but effective freshman project.

And so it came to pass that we had made our first professional recording. Success was starting to seem less ephemeral. Right around this time our drummer, Skip Spence, took off for Mexico with some babe. That's what I heard anyway. Regardless, he was gone and Matthew found Spencer Dryden for us. Rumor had it Spencer had been playing in a burlesque house somewhere in LA. Now he was playing with us. We found out later his half uncle was Charlie Chaplin. Spencer was without a doubt the most creative drummer we had in all our incarnations of the Airplane. He had chops, he had music, he had taste, and he could listen. With Spencer, Jack, and Paul in the rhythm section, it was becoming a Garden of Eden for me as a lead guitarist. Musical life was getting better and I was feeling more comfortable in my new role.

8

Seasons in the Field

In 1966 Jefferson Airplane and the Paul Butterfield Blues Band were invited to play the Monterey Jazz Festival. The winds of change were beginning to stir even in the confines of the jazz world, although the old guard so-called purists were not pleased by our presence. We were well received by the crowd, but the jazz critic Leonard Feather did not agree with Ralph J. Gleason. He detested us: "All the delicacy and finesse of a mule team knocking down a picket fence!" We loved that quote, and used it in our print ads for *Takes Off*.

While all this stuff was going on in my professional life, my personal life with Margareta was at a standstill. The band had not yet begun to go on the road. The cornucopia of earthly delights that would soon be available had not yet arrived. Margareta and I were miserable without knowing why. Neither of us was mature enough for a real relationship, much less marriage. We couldn't talk to each other, and fear of the unknown ruled our every move. Smoking a lot of pot and taking speed didn't help us much. We coped by letting problems go unspoken.

The Butterfield Blues Band had come to town, and Mike Bloomfield came to our house on Divisadero Street with his wife. Mike's wife had on a vinyl skirt. I remember it seeming quintessentially modern. Mike took me under his wing and started to show me electric guitar tricks. Up to this point, I still thought of myself as playing an "amplified" guitar, as opposed to an "electric" guitar and all the magic that goes along with that beast. He showed me how to bend strings in a pitch-specific way and many other techniques. Butterfield had just released *East-West,* which, in my opinion, is one of the seminal albums of that time. Somehow Paul and his band managed to play perfect Chicago blues in the style of the time while also forging ahead with some very adventuresome sounds! That year they were in a class by themselves.

The Airplane had a gig with Mike and Butter and the boys down at Stanford University. During their set, Mike bumped the peg head of his Les Paul Goldtop and snapped it off right at the nut. I lent him my Thunderbird. He hated the axe but he still sounded just like himself. It's the man, not the machine. This is a lesson I constantly remind myself of. Never mind the gear, pay attention to the music! Even though we rarely hung after that, he helped start me on the road to being an electric guitar player.

We started to work a lot more in this time. Matthew got us some gigs up in Vancouver, BC. We did a show with Muddy Waters at the Queen Elizabeth Theater, as well as others at some local oddities such as Simon Fraser University. I couldn't believe Muddy was opening *for us*. It just didn't seem right, but there it was. I remember him as the most gracious of human beings. The order of the bill didn't seem to bother him at all. There was only enough money for a hotel room for Signe, and Matthew of course, so the rest of us couch surfed. It was trying. The hippie scene was just getting a head start up in Vancouver that year, so there were lots of drugs going around. I thought, Whatever happens in Vancouver stays in Vancouver. It was a libertine atmosphere where anything went. Being away from my wife for the first time found me in a moral free-fall zone and I did not resist any of the temptations.

Back in San Francisco, I got off the plane and got a ride back to the apartment on Divisadero Street and walked up the three flights of stairs with my guitars. Margareta wasn't there and she had left no note. I locked the dead bolt and started unpacking my stuff. I heard someone try to open the door, but I had locked it. The knocking continued. I answered and found a woman I didn't recognize. She was slender, even anorexic, and had flaming short red hair. As I stared at her I realized it was Margareta. When I had left a week or so before, she had dark hair and dressed in a way that I described as "wild gypsy." Now she looked like something out of an Andy Warhol movie.

If our relationship was uncomfortable before, it had atrophied now. Amphetamine-based diet pills still came via prescriptions back then and apparently she had gotten a scrip for them and had been speeding her brains out the last ten days or so. She had lost a good twenty-five pounds, maybe more. I was not pleased. For me at the time it was a "do as I say, not as I do" moment. I would take prescription amphetamines too, for performances. I considered them a "working" drug, maybe not even a drug at all. I know, double standards. The cold hard facts are that we were two tweakers living under the same roof.

I've heard it said that if a marriage can survive a home renovation it can survive anything. I would say if a band can survive band meetings, it can survive anything. First there has to be the creative magic that brings the members together. Then business rears its head and over-night there are too many chiefs. In our case this led to unfettered chaos. Some liked Matthew Katz, some hated Matthew; either way, Matthew tended to be the focus of our band meetings. Signe said about him, "He doesn't have dime one. He's a crook!" She turned out to be right, but it took more time for us to figure this out. Everything was accomplished with smoke and mirrors. He did finance us in a small way in the beginning, which was true. He did architect a record deal with RCA for us. He did get us gigs. There was also no transparency in his machinations and he was a compulsive liar.

The white noise surrounding the band reminded me of life in the Kaukonen household. I would have done anything to make it stop. A band is a business and to be successful you need to make rational business decisions. My emotional immaturity prevented me from being able to make decisions without being influenced by the chaotic environment. The constant sniping reminded me of my parents and I recoiled from participating in it. It became apparent that Katz's days were numbered. Toward the end of August 1966 Signe left the band to raise her family while the Jefferson Airplane pondered the next female voice. Paul Kantner, as the architect of the Airplane's vocal sound, absolutely required a female voice.

We considered Sherry Snow, a fine singer out of the South Bay scene, but she had a group with Jeff Blackburn. We had all seen the Great Society play, and regardless of how they perceived themselves, the focus in that group was on Grace Slick. Her phrasing and delivery were one of a kind. She had perfect pitch, and a passionate voice that came out of a beautiful, almost deadpan face. She also played piano and composed mostly from the keyboard. Her later compositions for the Airplane are nothing short of brilliant. Give a listen to "Eskimo Blue Day" and you'll hear what I mean.

From Jack Casady, Nov. 5, 2017

GRACE SLICK JOINING JEFFERSON AIRPLANE

It seems to me that toward the end of the summer, August into September 1966, Jefferson Airplane realized Signe Anderson, our female singer, wanted to start a family, and not withstanding continual friction throughout with her husband Jerry, we knew the time had come to make a change. Looking locally for a female singer was not too difficult, as the Great Society featured Grace Slick. All the bands of San Francisco at that time would regularly check each other out at shows—after all, none of us were working on a continuous basis in those early days. We were all young bands, and spent most of our time writing and rehearsing our material. We had plenty of time on our hands to be in the audience as well as onstage. Writing our original material was encouraged and separated us from "cover" bands. After rehearsal one afternoon we agreed to see if Grace might be interested. I had had some light conversation with Grace a few times before, and offered to talk to her after a Great Society show at a Chet Helms–promoted Avalon Ballroom event the coming weekend.

Grace was a stand-up-in-your-face singer, and unlike many of the female folk singers of the time, she possessed a distinct aggressive personality with a unique vocal approach and a killer vibrato! The fact that she had had a classical background on the piano would later on show itself in the more evolved pieces she wrote, along with her personal wit and lyrics.

The Avalon Ballroom dance/concert scene at the time was really something quite amazing to be a part of. The audiences came dressed in their own unique clothing and paraphernalia . . . all shapes and sizes each trying to make something original in look, while making up their own dance movements and generally putting on a show of their own! It was a great and different scene that was taking shape in these early days in San Francisco.

After the Great Society show, I approached Grace and asked for a quick chat. I explained that Jefferson Airplane was seeking a new female singer, and would she be interested in coming to one of our next rehearsals to check things out. She said right away "yes," much to my delight! A period of time followed where she would do vocal rehearsals at a flat Marty Balin and I shared at Fell and Cole streets across from the San Francisco Panhandle. Paul, Marty, and Grace would work on the vocals while Jorma and I would work on the music. We would then work the practices into full band rehearsals at the Fillmore.

I am sure it wasn't easy for her, as she had to consider how to fit her vocal style and range into and between Paul and Marty harmonies. I knew she was a perfectionist and wanted lots of rehearsal to figure things out. So much for the grand plan! A couple weeks later it seems, the night of a Bill Graham Fillmore Jefferson Airplane show, Signe was a no show. Grace was at the show to listen and digest our material, and without hesitation Bill asked her to step in and start singing! From then on, we never looked back.

Signe was gone, we still had gigs, and Grace fell right into the obsessive rehearsal schedule that we always set for ourselves. We were a band . . . we were *the* band! Over the years of Jefferson Airplane, many talented people came and went. To me, the classic lineup was the band that made *Surrealistic Pillow*: Grace Slick on vocals; Marty Balin, guitar and vocals; Paul Kantner, guitar and vocals; Spencer Dryden, drums and percussion; Jack Casady on bass and guitar; and myself on guitar. That's when the magic really happened!

What does it take to make one a success in the music business? If any of us really knew the answer to this question, we'd bottle it and sell it. Obviously talent plays a part but it's not enough. There are lots of talented people in this world. One must have passion and dedication. You've got to fritter away a lot of time to get good at whatever it is that you do. We frittered away a lot of time and we got good at it. We were also more than lucky. Synchronicity just can't be overvalued. We were in the right place at the right time and we made the most of our good fortune.

So there I was, twenty-five years old. Many of my friends who weren't in the music business already had families if they weren't in the service. My career chose me, and at twenty-five that's all I thought about. It didn't make me a good husband and it would have made me a lousy father. I always believed it was a good thing I didn't have children back then. I wouldn't have been good for the kids. It did set me on the path to being a good musician and a guitarist with a style all my own. It was one foot in front of the other, running it all up the flagpole to see who would salute. Perhaps my bandmates had a master plan, but for me it really was all about the music, and the life, one day at a time. Margareta and I continued our nonrelationship. We circled each other like bodies in orbit, but we never touched. Did we have some good times? I guess so . . . depending on your definition of a "good time." I realize today that we lived two separate lives in the same house.

While my personal life marked time, my professional life was picking up speed. Another album was on the horizon. Grace brought "Somebody to Love" and "White Rabbit" into our fold from the Great Society. Marty and Paul were writing, and we brought in one song, "My

Best Friend," from our ex-bandmate Skip Spence. In the blink of an eye we were ready to start recording again. Rick Jarrard produced that album. All these years later I can hear Rick's brilliant work pulling all the elements together. *Takes Off* had been a folk-rock album. *Surrealistic Pillow* was a rock-and-roll project and a harbinger of things to come. I find it interesting that the two songs that really broke us out of the woodwork were not really Airplane songs at all, but rather Great Society songs. Still, a great song is a great song. We made those ours and as a result we would be inducted, years later, into the Rock & Roll Hall of Fame.

One must remember that when *Pillow* was recorded, we used two four-track machines so we would have backup. There was still no noise reduction yet, so we were still limited in the part overdubs we could do. We actually had to nail the parts. We had more creative freedom than we did on *Takes Off*, but we still had a limited budget, so there was no time for fooling around. Our pal Jerry Garcia would weigh in to give us some creative oversight. Over the years there has been some discussion over Jerry's part in the project. I used to think about him as a co-producer, but now that I really know what a producer is, the producer of that record was Rick Jarrard. Jerry was a combination arranger, musician, and sage counsel. Everyone who was a part of that project was equally important.

We cut *Surrealistic Pillow* in about two weeks. This economic efficiency would be left in the dust with ensuing recording projects. I was in a transitional phase with my gear. To recap my gear choice, I had seen the Lovin' Spoonful at a club in North Beach. Zal Yanovsky was playing through a Standel Super Imperial. Back then I knew nothing about gear so when I heard him, I had to have what he was playing. As if the Super Imperial weren't brittle enough, I added an upholstered box from Kustom with two high-frequency horns. Around the time of *Pillow* I was transitioning from the Guild Thunderbird guitar and the Standel amp to the Gibson ES-345 and two Fender Twin Reverbs, but I was still waffling between the two setups. The solos on "White

Rabbit" and "Somebody to Love" were done with the Thunderbird and the Standel (minus the horns). Saturating the sound with the spring reverb was the deal. The other tracks were done with the Twins and the ES-345 Stereo.

As the session was beginning to wind down, I was sitting out in the reception talking to one of the guards and picking my old Gibson J-50. I chanced to play "Embryonic Journey" just as Rick Jarrard was passing through the foyer. "Embryonic Journey" was the first song I ever wrote, and in a way, it wrote itself . . . with a little help from me. I was giving a guitar workshop at Santa Clara University sometime in 1963. A friend had lent me a Martin D-18 twelve-string. I had never really spent any time with a twelve-string before and I had also just learned that dropped D tuning. My right hand, my picking hand was always good . . . always. I was messing around with an alternating thumb pattern in dropped D that afternoon and my roommate Peter Manchester happened to record the session. We got back to our room. "You gotta listen to this. It sounds like a song," he said. I listened and had to allow that he was right. I took a little time to work on it and the result was "Embryonic Journey." I had a good picking hand, and that combined with the inherent beauty of the dropped D tuning blessed me with the song. Talk about synchronicity!

Rick was fired up. "We are going to record that and put it on the record," he said. I thought that he had lost his mind. A folky, fingerstyle piece on a rock-and-roll record? I thought there was no place for it. I went into that great sounding room in Studio A, sat down, and played the piece. Rick did a brilliant job with the final mix. The guitar sound is drenched with room echo—*real* room echo. It sounded as good to me as when I would practice those old Carter Family songs by myself in the tile bathroom at my parents' old house on Northampton Street in DC.

And then, the record was done. There was no way we could have known at that time what an important part of the sixties soundtrack this project would become. We all returned to our apartments in San

Francisco and waited for the release of the album. We found ourselves sharing an agency and a publicity firm with the Doors, who were just starting to hit with their first, self-titled album. Paul Williams, the editor of *Crawdaddy* magazine, told me on the way to the Monterey Pop Festival that he thought I would find the Doors to be the most innovative of rock bands to date. I have to admit, even though I was consumed by the blues, Paul was right.

In June 1967 we drove down to Monterey for that iconic festival. Lou Adler and John Phillips, with a lot of help from their friends, put that first pop festival together. It was such a thrill to be part of it. There were so many memorable performances, and so much has been written about these elsewhere. One of the great moments for me was Otis Redding. Of course there were many others—Janis, Jimi, the Who—but Otis stands out for me. This was also the first time I did cocaine. Owsley Stanley, the legendary audio engineer for the Grateful Dead, gave me a couple of lines and intimated that you got higher if you snorted it through a hundred-dollar bill. Just another day in the life! Monterey Pop did, however, give us visible respect as members of an artistic musical community, and none of us ever looked back.

We found ourselves doing a number of gigs with the Doors. I'm not sure the music business establishment knew what to do with either one of us. We were both making money for them so they had to put up with our collective shenanigans. I would have paid to see any of these shows. We played the O'Keefe Center in Toronto with the guys, and later we did a European tour together. One of the shows was in Amsterdam. We were opening the show that night and as we were finishing up our set, Jim staggered onstage and began mouthing unintelligible noises as Marty was singing. He collapsed and was taken to the hospital. When the Doors went on, Ray Manzarek sang the songs, and you know, he sounded damn good! There have been many dull moments on the road, but not on that trip.

It seemed as if all my life I had been looking for some sort of acceptance, some place to belong. When the guitar found me, that home began to manifest itself. I began to briefly feel comfortable in my own skin. As the counterculture society of the sixties gathered steam, new outside pressures evolved. When the band got rolling I really had no baggage outside of the clothes on my back. It was easy to think that you were turning your back on the accepted modes of fashion. Even though it was unspoken, we were expected to look a certain way. When I started to have a little money, I bought some clothes at a men's shop on Polk Street called the Town Squire. Threads from this joint had sort of a faux Carnaby Street vibe. Soon, however, California hip fashions began to evolve at an alarming rate. Nonestablishment, handmade clothes were everywhere. In LA we met a young seamstress who was known internationally: Jeannie Franklyn, aka Genie the Tailor. I remember when she first met us she told me we looked like farmers and freaks. I took it as a compliment, but ordered a handmade white brocade suit with rhinestone buttons anyway. I wore it once when we played the Hollywood Bowl, and that was that.

Back in those early days we used to stay on Santa Monica Boulevard at Sandy Koufax's Tropicana Motel. Just west of the Tropicana on Santa Monica was a hip clothing store that was just short of what we would come to know as a head shop. It was called Sidereal Time and we bought all kinds of stuff there. I actually did buy some clothes that I truly liked. I got an elk-skin fringed pullover that I wore for years. If it still fit me, I would still have it. It doesn't, so it's at the Rock & Roll Hall of Fame in Cleveland. I remember they used to have essential oils at the counter. I discovered I liked Vetiver. Shopping became de rigueur. We had no idea what we needed, so we bought stuff whether we needed it or not.

On one trip to LA, Margareta and I shared a two-bedroom apartment with Paul Kantner on the second floor of the Tropicana overlooking Santa Monica Boulevard. We had been working at the Whisky a Go Go up on the Strip with a band called the Peanut Butter Conspiracy. They were staying at the Tropicana too. Hell, everyone did. Drugs and paraphernalia were absolutely a membership card to musicians in those days. Even though pot was a serious bust, everyone smoked and surrounded themselves with accoutrements that were impossible to hide if you ran afoul of the law.

In our room, we had a hookah that was about four feet tall. There was pot and pot cleaning gear and rolling gear as well as a tackle box with pills in the little compartments. If someone came knocking on the door, there was no way to hide any of this stuff. There was a rumor that Jack had messed with one of the other resident band's girlfriends, and as a result we got rat finked. Paul and I were out somewhere when the police came to our room and arrested Margareta, who was surrounded with "evidence." I found a place to crash for the night and didn't come back to the room until the next afternoon. Margareta was charged with possession, and a lengthy legal process began that involved frequent trips to LA to go to court. Brian Rohan, the erratic but often brilliant San Francisco attorney, would defend her. We met Brian when he was defending Ken Kesey; he ultimately got Margareta off on some technicality. As the page turned, we would never stay at the Tropicana again. We ultimately found our way to the Landmark Motor Hotel on Franklin.

For me this was a period of musical and professional development, but my personal and spiritual life languished. Don't get me wrong. I don't think I had any idea about these lacks in my life at the time. We were in the beginning stages of affluence. Margareta and I moved from 1145 Divisadero Street to 3228 Washington Street in Pacific Heights. It was definitely a step up in real estate. From the Western Addition to Pacific Heights, from the hood to the carriage trade we went. Bill Graham lived next door, and as Grace and our drummer Spencer Dryden became an item, they would move downstairs. We were making money, and I was starting to spend it.

The second-story flat at 3228 Washington Street was sort of a shotgun flat, but it was a big one. There was a large front room with a fireplace. Down the hall there was a kitchen on the right, two small bedrooms on the left, and at the end of the hall a larger bedroom that

Margareta and I claimed for our own. My old 1957 Volvo 444 died before we moved from Divisadero Street and was replaced by a Sunbeam convertible. I remember washing that car on the street in front of the apartment as Jerry Garcia chanced to walk by. We were talking life and music and generally enjoying the warm day together when some down-on-his-luck guy walked by and offered me a ring for a buck. I couldn't pass the deal up. It turned out to be German silver with a large carnelian stone, and I wore it for years. That ring now lives in our Psylodelic Gallery on the Fur Peace Ranch compound.

Anyway, the Sunbeam made a couple of trips to LA, but ultimately it wasn't long for this world. As I was driving by British Motors on Van Ness Avenue, I saw a beautiful Morgan SS in British Racing Green on the showroom floor. It was a right-hand drive and had a crash box tranny. You had to double-clutch it to shift gears. Mom had taught me how to double-clutch years before so I was good at it. I had a new flat, I was making money, and all of a sudden I had credit. The Morgan was mine. Street parking spots were at a premium in San Francisco even then and we had no garage. Most of the time I just parked the car on the sidewalk in front of the steps.

I was filling empty places in my heart with stuff, and the Morgan didn't satisfy for long. I traded it in for a Lotus Europa. This was a slinky little mid-engine vehicle. It had absolutely no frills. The windows didn't roll down, it had no air-conditioning—it was strictly business. The luggage space under the bonnet could barely accommodate a lady's handbag. One of our pals, Charlie Cockey, had become a de facto roommate in the Pacific Heights digs, and he suggested we visit his mom in Sun Valley for Christmas. It seemed like a good idea so the three of us squeezed into the little Europa. There was only one passenger seat so Charlie and Margareta were compressed to say the least. From San Francisco to Sun Valley and back in the winter for three people in a two-seat car was quite a feat. By the time we got home I was no longer quite so infatuated with the Europa, so I traded it in for a Lotus Elan. Credit is a wonderful thing when you pay your bills.

Wheeled transportation always meant freedom to me. Whether eight wheels on roller skates or two wheels on a bicycle, any of these modes made it possible for me to "ride free to the ends of the earth," in biker parlance. When wheeled conveyances with motors became an option, it was the frosting on the cake. I could get on my scooter or into a car and drive and drive and drive, until I just had to stop for some reason. Free, the captain of my own ship . . . all these things and more became possible. I still feel the same way. People who ride in one of my vehicles can expect me to drive until I just have to rest and turn the wheel over to a trusted companion. The sound of the car door closing, the wheel in my hand . . . it is always where I need to be. Motorcycles are even more liberating, although sometimes not as practical. I became a "car guy" at an early age. In the summer of 1950, all of a sudden I knew the make and model of every car on the road. Mom started me at the wheel of our 1950 Packard Eight when I was twelve. I had my first car a month or so before I got my license. You get the picture. Driving meant a lot to me.

With this in mind, when we started to have a little money in the sixties, it was important to buy a car. The Morgan SS was "pre-loved," as they say, but the Europa and the Elan were new. These were impulse purchases. I have bought many things on impulse, and lived to regret some of them. The Morgan and the Europa were a little ill-thought-out, but the Elan wasn't. It was a tiny little two-seat roadster. It had a soft top but electrical windows. Colin Chapman's nod to American-style luxury, I guess. This little car was just plain fun to drive, and I drove it a lot when I wasn't on the road. It had a 140 horsepower motor, which was a lot for a little car back then. It only weighed fifteen hundred pounds, so in its day it had a lot of bang for the buck in terms of power to weight.

I may have had a conflicted view of my place in the universe in everyday life, but behind the wheel all was right with the world. What's not to like about a good machine, a full tank of gas, and a place to go? These were the salad days, that's for sure. At the time, it seemed as if they would last forever. As I'm looking back, they were there for the blink of an eye! Perhaps that blink of the eye is what it's all about.

Our sophomore project was out and it was starting to define us. All of a sudden, psychedelic was no longer either a door to perception or an excuse to party . . . it was becoming a genre! As for us, we had entered the "mainstream" music business in spite of ourselves. We wanted to be successful, but we wanted to define success in our own terms. There was a price, and one of those prices was that RCA wanted new recordings on a regular basis. The pressure wasn't really on me as a writer. I had yet to really start writing. Paul, Marty, and Grace seemed full of songs. It was a rich creative time.

The great producer Al Schmitt would help architect this magnum opus. The Beatles had rented a mansion in the Hollywood Hills while in LA working on some project. Paul convinced us that if it was good enough for the Beatles, it was probably almost good enough for us too. *Surrealistic Pillow* turned out to be a big commercial success, but when we recorded it we had no budget; we had to work quickly and efficiently. We had more bargaining chips now. With the big production budget we were able to do a lot of experimentation. This was our first foray into the realm of true communal living. The entire band, significant others, and everyone who worked for us as well as their families moved into the mansion in the hills. Needless to say, there was a lot of partying going on. It's hard to recall where my head was at. It was sensory overload.

This place was palatial. Countless bedrooms, a large compound, lots of vehicles, and a swimming pool next to an underground shooting range with windows that looked out underwater into said pool. One weekend we had a gig up at the Earl Warren Showgrounds in Santa Barbara. We packed our gear into our truck, hopped in our cars, and drove to Santa Barbara. When we got back from the gig later that night, we found the house filled with people we didn't know having a massive party. It looked like the street gang from the Sunset Strip had made themselves at home in our house. The pool was filled with naked folks. I had a pellet gun and Bill Laudner, our tour manager, had a .22 pistol. A couple of rounds into the pool and the house emptied. The invaders did leave the Airplane Family some gifts though. There were crabs in every bed in the house. It took us a day or two to realize this. No one ever said life at the top of the food chain would be easy!

We still had an album to make. It didn't seem to me that I had much voice in making band decisions. I felt the big house was a waste of money and that we were wasting a lot of time in the studio. Truth be told, I really had yet to find my creative voice in this dynamic. I might have not liked many of the decisions "we" made, but I wasn't able to offer any better ones.

All that being said, I did write a song, and it did make its appearance on the album: "The Last Wall of the Castle," from *After Bathing at Baxter's*:

> *Gone swirling tears came,*
> *She went today*
> *Down falling years go by*
> *No grace in learning how to cry*
> *I went astray*
> *Understanding is a virtue, hard to come by*
> *You can teach me how to love, if you'll only try*
> *So please, don't give up so soon*

I had never really written lyrics before. Writing is best done about what you know, what you live, and the only thing I could think about was the unfolding disaffection in my marriage. On some levels my songs were confessionals; on others, songs of contrition.

Musically, this tune is an amphetamine-fueled barn burner. I can't even think that fast anymore. The band is in top form and it's a hell of a performance. In one of the guitar solos, the opening notes are Gary

Blackman making a monumental sound blowing his nose. Gary was an extremely eccentric friend of our manager, Bill Thompson. He was like a walking personality cult. Creative minds hard at work!

This was our third album, and although we were certainly comfortable working in a studio environment by this time, none of us were "studio musicians," so we were not constrained by having to fit in with anyone else's vision of us. We had no real expectations to fulfill; we just wanted to create music in our own way, and we did that for sure. Band members and friends came up with wacky ideas, and we knew no fear when it came to trying them out. We were more than fortunate to have Al Schmitt as a producer. Al somehow rendered order from the chaos that was our modus operandi.

Ron Cobb, the LA satirist, did the cover for us. The flying Victorian mansion has taken on a life of its own after all this time. It really was a sign of the San Franciscan times. We were all connected in those days by politics and current events. The Vietnam War could not be ignored. I have to wonder how much Vietnam War antipathy was genuine and how much was simply following the lead of our peers. I chose not to go with the help of a psychiatrist, but my choice was really predicated on the premise that playing in a band and having a career in the music business looked like more fun. Civil rights issues were center stage as well. This was a dark time for Americans on many levels, but as the drama played out every act shaped much of the art, literature, and music of the time. The so-called counterculture was defining itself, and its voices began to inhabit a universe parallel to mainstream America. We were becoming a "We!" This became patently obvious at Woodstock in 1969, but even in 1968 it was hard to ignore. Having the courage of your convictions is a great thing—but first you have to have convictions. Working for racial equality was a no brainer. I certainly don't like everyone I meet, but my likes and dislikes are not predicated on race, gender, or religious specificities. As I am fond of saying, "To not stand against injustice is to stand for it. Don't confuse my personality and my attitude. My personality is who I am, my attitude depends on who you are." (Thank Frank Ocean for that one!) That said, at that point in my life I did not really have a cogent political rationale. It would be a while before I truly realized how important well-thought-out opinions are.

My bandmates always encouraged me to write. I didn't write a lot, but whenever I did, there was always a place on the album for at least one of my songs. I tended to write from the acoustic guitar and I always had my old Gibson J-50 with me. Even though I was now totally immersed in our brand of rock and roll, I never let my acoustic playing get away from me. I was spending a lot of time on the road with the Airplane and there was always a cornucopia of pleasures waiting for us on the road. Margareta rarely came along on tour unless it was to some exotic or otherwise fun place, so there was a lot of partying and cheating. I remember one incident, which at this point is darkly humorous. I had come home from somewhere and realized that I had crabs. A day late and a dollar short, I was in the process of confessing my obvious sin when she interrupted me. "I have to tell you," she said. "I slept with someone while you were gone and I think I have crabs." This confession allowed me to be magnanimously forgiving while bypassing my own confession. Another missed opportunity to be honest, but so it goes.

Spencer and Grace were still living underneath us at 3228 Washington Street. We were all on the road somewhere and they let a couple of eccentrics stay in their pad. I don't know how it happened, but they set the apartment on fire and we wound up with smoke and fire damage on the second floor. We had been thinking about moving anyway, but this certainly made the decision for us. Just prior to the fire, the band actually got together and made a rare decision with a minimum of stress. We bought the mansion at 2400 Fulton Street at the corner of Fulton and North Willard, just across from Golden Gate Park. There was some logic to this at the time, but I'm not sure what it was. The good news was that we now owned real property and Margareta and I had a place to live after the fire. For a brief moment in time, we were all communal in a San Francisco kind of way. Marty was already staying there. Paul had a room on the top floor and Spencer and Grace bunked there for a bit as well. Margareta and I had this room with a bathroom on the second floor. It was a large bedroom with rosy-cheeked cherubs on the ceiling. You can't make this stuff up. We had a rehearsal space in the basement with a little four-track studio and a place to store our gear. There was a beautiful Tiffany stained-glass window on the landing and a couple of large rooms on the first floor. One of the rooms had a full-size pool table, and next to that there was a large kitchen with a Viking commercial stove.

I remember one time sitting in our room and listening to Jimi Hendrix's "All Along the Watchtower," which had just come out. I had my Koss headphones on and I was blasting it. All of a sudden I smelled this utterly noxious odor. I took off the headphones and ran downstairs, following the smell. In the kitchen covering four burners was a huge metal kettle filled with what looked like the leftovers from a slaughterhouse. Augustus Owsley Stanley III was standing in front of this mess trying to agitate it with a giant spoon. Now some of us know Owsley from his time architecting the Wall of Sound for the Grateful Dead, as well as his PA innovations. "What are you doing?" I was nonplussed and irritated by the stink. "Rendering down the fat," he said. "You have a bigger stove than I do." Now, Owsley was way ahead of the Atkins Diet. He had been eating only meat for years. "Vegetables are what food eats," he was known to say. He was hard to stay mad at, plus he had a rationale of sorts. "Well, wind it up. You're stinking up the whole house." I couldn't think of anything else to say, and that was that. I remember Janis Joplin stopping by to shoot some pool and humiliating me in a game of nine-ball.

Now I realize that it is not up to any of us to make another person happy, but we can certainly make the landscape more hospitable. My marriage was stagnant on so many levels. I don't blame Margareta for that; it takes two to tango. Margareta was miserable and could be heard crying in our room when she was alone. I paid attention to what was required of me to function as a band member, and that was about it. I didn't share space well either. The communal life was never for me, and the time spent living at 2400 Fulton Street was an interlude while we waited to find another house. We never really considered leaving each other, but most of the time we were so distant that we might as well have been oceans apart. Business with the band was great, but personal life for me was not so fulfilling.

Right around this time our tour manager, Bill Laudner, was moving out of a house he had rented on Kensington Way in the West Portal neighborhood of San Francisco. It was a nice little place on the side of a hill, with a little apartment underneath it and a garage farther down the hill. By this time we would have taken anything, but this little place was a godsend.

We rented the house on Kensington Way and moved in. All our stuff came out of storage and soon the little bungalow was filled to overflowing with oddities. There was not much time to think of domestic tranquility. It was back to LA to make what would come to be called *Crown of Creation*. At this point in my life, almost all my creative instincts were channeled into Jefferson Airplane projects. I never put my old Gibson J-50 aside and it never stopped being my guide, but there was always pressure to be a visible part of the creative mélange that was the band! It's easy to second-guess oneself decades after the fact.

I'm not sure what I wanted. I couldn't even begin to think about kids. Margareta and I were so childlike ourselves that kids were out of the question—and that certainly was a blessing for the children we didn't have. I followed the path of least resistance, which was to remain a member of Jefferson Airplane. The upcoming recording was still to be done at RCA's venerable Studio A in that grand building at the corner of Sunset and Ivar. Al Schmitt was still our producer and as always, he managed to get the best out of us. I wrote two songs that got included on *Crown of Creation*. The first, "Ice Cream Phoenix," I co-wrote with Charlie Cockey.

You don't know just
When to stop and when to go
City streets in the dead of winter
Stop your mind with dirty snow

I remember how I wrote this song with Charlie. One day sitting around the room I put my first finger of my left hand on the seventh fret of the fourth string and my third finger on the ninth fret of the same string. Using the open fifth string as a drone with a flat pick, I picked strings five and four and bent the fourth string two frets, or a whole tone. I let the bend come back to the ninth fret and then picked five and four with the fourth string at the seventh fret. Then I did the same thing using only strings five and six. The first move is in A and the second resolves in E. That was my point of departure and it became the opening lines of the chorus. My approach to songwriting is usually, but not always, inspired by the guitar itself: the guitar tends to tell me what to do. Words tend to follow, one after the other.

Grace, Paul, and Marty were such strong and prolific songwriters that it is to their credit that they always allowed room for at least one of my tunes. In the case of *Crown of Creation* there were two, the second being "Star Track."

If your head spins round try to see the ground if you can
My busy eyes missed her path through the air as she ran
My sensory mind is too old to cry
Not ready to live and too strange to die
So stop your doubt push the world on by
With your hand

All my writing at the time reflected disconnection and alienation. Come to think of it, over the years that has always been a recurring theme for me. I was certainly aware of the problems that plagued Margareta and myself, but we never discussed them. But they are all over the lyrics of my songs from that time.

Time was moving at an accelerated pace for all of us. Everything was about the band for me. It was all that made sense. There was lots of stuff going on 24/7 but some things stick out in my memory. I recall that Bobby Kennedy flew us all to DC in a Learjet to play at a fund-raiser. We played and went to a reception at his house. He and Ethel were very gracious to us, and although we were surrounded by Democratic Party elite I was able to consume enough alcohol to stay sufficiently insulated. We also got a nice picture of Brumus, Robert Kennedy's dog, which we included in the vinyl release of *Crown of Creation*. In this time I found myself surrounded by all sorts of people I had nothing in common with, but as always I made myself appear comfortable. In any case, after the Kennedy benefit in DC it was back to LA to record *Crown of Creation*. We were at the Landmark hotel on Franklin when I heard the news that Robert Kennedy had been shot at the Ambassador Hotel, which was not that far away. It was unthinkable . . . more than surrealistic. How could this be? The Kennedys were young enough to almost seem like our generation. In the wake of this tragedy, Richard Nixon was elected—another tragedy. JFK, Martin Luther King, Bobby Kennedy, freedom marchers in the South, our soldiers in Vietnam, and countless others made the Reaper always feel close at hand.

We finished recording *Crown of Creation* in June 1968 and it was released in September. Looking back from the lofty perch of time, one can see that there was a lot of creativity happening for the band. This was our fourth album in three years, and we certainly made a lot of artistic progress from 1965 to 1968. As always, we didn't take direction well, so even from a production point of view the Airplane marched to our own drummer. As always, Al Schmitt deserves so much credit for his patient ability to get the best out of us. He always came up with great artistic ideas, and then somehow made it seem as if we thought of them ourselves. The rhythm of our lives became wed to professional necessity. Write, rehearse, record, tour: that was pretty much the deal. All of these things required a lot of attention, so it was pretty easy for me to put development of my personal life on hold and just pay attention to the gig.

With the aid of prescription amphetamines, Margareta drew and painted relentlessly. She drew with a rapidograph drafting pen and filled endless sketchbooks with incredibly complex drawings. She had found herself interested in Art Nouveau pieces, and that led into the works of the great illustrators of that time like Harry Clarke and Maxfield Parrish, Aubrey Beardsley and Gustav Doré. *Madman's Drum* and other wordless novels by Lynd Ward were on the bookshelf next to Edgar Allan Poe's *Tales of Mystery and Imagination* and the like. The illustrations by Harry Clarke were showstoppers. She also developed a technique for painting on a long discontinued paper stock called Eaton's Corrasable Bond. This was a brand of typewriter paper that was coated with an invisible wax finish that allowed one to make corrections with a pencil eraser. Her oil and acrylic paintings on this stock had distinct qualities of their own.

Margareta and I both had prescriptions for 20 milligrams of Obetrol, an amphetamine concoction that allowed you to stay awake for a really long time as well as consume large quantities of alcohol. Today we know this delight as Adderall. We had scrips for this stuff and used it regularly until legal amphetamine production was curtailed in the 1970s. I am convinced that many of the blazing and crystalline solos on those Airplane recordings were directly related to that little orange pill. It's funny to think that my life could have been so completely ruled by mood-altering substances, but at the time it would never have occurred to me that there might be another way to live. The bipolar mood swings that accompany this lifestyle served to make my "home" life with Margareta a ticking time bomb. It could be good . . . it could be bad . . . we learned to drive on.

9

Turn My Life Down

Nineteen sixty-eight came and went, and in 1969 we started to work on our sixth album, *Volunteers*.

By this time Wally Heider had finished his studio, with great sounding rooms and state-of-the-art (for the time) gear down on Hyde Street between Turk and Eddy, and it was no longer necessary to go to LA to record. It was a dream come true for Bay Area musicians. *Volunteers* might have been the first album to be recorded at Heider's. We gigged, we recorded . . . I marked time. It is amazing given my inherent lack of direction that I was able to grow as an artist at all. The reason then, as it is now, is the guitar.

The guitar has always told me what to do, and my love for the instrument has always allowed me to listen. When I pick up my guitar I can almost guarantee that I will learn something and that there is a possibility that something will become a song. The little instrumental "Embryonic Journey" is a case in point. I was exploring the landscape in dropped D tuning and fortunately a tape machine was running. Voilà! A song is born. On a more transcendental level I might be practicing or just fooling around and something will smack me in the face. If I have been granted at least one lyrical line and I choose to follow that lead, I will have a song. Earlier in 1969, I was walking through the East

Village in New York and Smokey Robinson's "Tracks of My Tears" was everywhere. The record had been released in 1965 but for some reason it surrounded me as I walked those Village streets at night. I'm sure no one but me can hear this, but it inspired me to write "Turn My Life Down." I wrote this tune for Marty to sing. There was no way my vocal range could handle this tune.

I see the shadows softly coming
Taking me into a place
Where they turn my life down
Leaving mourning with myself
And nothing to say

As always, my bandmates took my little song and dressed it up in artistic finery. The whole was certainly greater than the sum of its parts!

The other tune I got to record on *Volunteers* was one I called "Good Shepherd." Back in 1963 or so I met a great pair of folk singers, Roger Perkins and Larry Hanks, who stopped to play the Offstage on their way through the San Jose area. In the tuning room of the Offstage, Roger slipped into dropped D. I had never heard anything so cool and in a most profound way, this moment of musical synchronicity would change my musical life! I was enthralled with this tune on so many levels. It was in the key of D with an E minor and an F-sharp minor chord thrown in the mix. In the world of pentatonic blues, this tune is an eye opener.

If you want to get to heaven, over on the other shore
Stay out of the way of the blood-stained bandits
Oh good shepherd feed my sheep

I remember my old friend Tom Hobson telling me that he thought the song was called "Blood-Strained Banders," but I wasn't buying it. I had no idea who wrote the song and/or who originally recorded it, I just wanted to play it and that's what I did. Sometime within the last ten or fifteen years I learned from Eric Shoenberg that "Good Shepherd" was indeed called "Blood-Strained Banders" and that the author was one James Strother, who was reportedly sent to prison for murdering his wife with an axe. Since he was reported to be blind, this conjures up a number of scenarios.

When I was a student at Santa Clara I had a classmate named Jim Steinke whose dad was a professor there. Jim has turned out to be a respected guitarist and quite the authority on all things involving wooden music. When I ran into Jim in Berkeley a couple of years ago he was able to peel back a few more layers of the onion. Apparently there was no axe in this story, but rather a pistol and an unfaithful and abusive wife. The woman had beaten James several times before: "One time with an iron poker and the other time a radio stool. I still have a hole in my head from one of these blows" (from James Strother, Prisoner #33927 to the governor of Virginia, James H. Price, in 1935). The governor pardoned him and apparently he went to live with relatives in Baltimore. The great folklorist Alan Lomax went to the state farm in Goochland County and recorded James Strother and Joe Lee.

By the time we were looking for songs for *Volunteers* I offered up "Good Shepherd." With Grace leading the charge with her vocal, it made a hell of a good rock song. The high-singing electric guitar lines are my Gibson ES-345 Stereo with the neck pickup through an Ampeg Scrambler into two Fender Twins. The bridge pickup was run through an original Thomas Organ Cry Baby Wah, also through two Twins. The neck pickup also had all the treble rolled off. The Scrambler liked that setting a lot.

I should back up just a little here. I almost glossed over our live album, *Bless Its Pointed Little Head*. Recorded in late 1968 at the Fillmore West and the Fillmore East, this album shows the Airplane in absolutely top form. What we had been learning over the last couple of years was blossoming in live performance. The natural boundaries of studio recording were shattered and we could go anywhere the music decided to take us. I still considered Obetrol to be a "working" drug, and as such, it didn't really feel like a drug at all. After one of the nights recording at the Fillmore East, I was in the elevator at the Chelsea Hotel on Twenty-Third Street with a couple who had been at the show. "You're a fabulous entertainer," the woman told me. "You never stopped dancing!" That night I was so wired I just couldn't keep still onstage. That was so atypical for me because usually I was planted like a rock and just played the guitar with no expression on my face whatsoever.

Whatever the collective reasons, on these nights, we could do no wrong. There were no mistakes, there was just adventure. The really good news is that it was all caught on tape! Even these many years later I still think it is not only a great recording but one of our best musical outings! With all this relative success going on, you would think there would be plenty of time for rejoicing, smelling the roses, and who knows, perhaps even planning a family. That wasn't the way it was for me. I really lived day to day and even though I got easily sidetracked, the guitar and the music that went along with it always got me through the day. I never let my acoustic guitar lie fallow. Any time I wasn't gigging and playing electric guitar, the old 1958 Gibson J-50 was getting the call. For years I listened to Reverend Gary Davis's *Harlem Street Singer* and the album he split with Pink Anderson, the Brownie McGhee ten-inch Folkways albums, and the first Robert Johnson album. Then, in the late sixties, Nick Perls started the Yazoo label. I would go to Tower Records a couple of times a week to see what Nick was releasing and I bought them all. I still have them. There was so much great stuff that I could never decide what to learn next. It was overwhelming. At that point, my serious study of "The Masters" was over. They were always on my play list, but I was no longer frequently sourcing material from them.

"Civilian" life when I wasn't on the road seemed to leave me without an identity. I think I was always marking time when I wasn't working. This didn't make for a good partner in a marriage. Thinking back, I can't fathom why we actually stayed married, but the sad truth is that we just didn't know any better. Our parents seemed to stay married long after whatever magic they had was long gone. I guess I learned from their misadventure and decided to stick it out. Given this state of mind, I missed out on a lot of joy. Living life on life's terms was an unknown concept. Being a recognized artist helped make up for some of this though, and I accepted this odd mode of existence as natural.

Thanks to Robin Richman, art editor at *Life* magazine at the time, on June 28, 1968, the good old Jefferson Airplane made the cover of that classic magazine in a lengthy piece about rock and roll. *Life* magazine . . . who would have thought it? It was at this moment that my dad, Jorma Sr., finally realized that I had a career of sorts. Where Margaret Bourke-White once reigned, Jefferson Airplane briefly held sway. The great photographer Art Kane took the pictures in a gravel lot on the East River in New York. Getting us to pose for photos was never easy. We did not take direction well. Art hung in there, however, and for a brief moment we were professional models. This was heady stuff. One of the really amusing side effects of the *Life* magazine cover was that it made my career choice credible in my father's eyes. All of a sudden he could see that we had real jobs. We got to hang with the great musicians of our time: Jimi Hendrix; the Doors; Crosby, Stills and Nash; the Grateful Dead; Janis and Big Brother; Quicksilver Messenger Service—these were our colleagues. Things were about to start moving even faster.

In the first week of August, the Airplane played the Atlantic City Pop Festival. With the Woodstock Festival coming up two weeks later, we had a little time off and drove up to check out the site. It looked like it would be idyllic. Today we might be appalled by the lack of amenities, but at the time it all looked pretty state of the art. The stage was certainly one of the largest and highest I had ever seen. It had a rotating platform on it, which would have been great had it worked, but it failed almost immediately on the first day of the concert. In any case we got to the hotel in Liberty Saturday afternoon, the day before our set. The Holiday Inn was filled with artists and relentless partying.

Many of the artists were getting flown to the site in helicopters, but on the day of our show we drove our Ford LTD wagons in ourselves. We drove in on back roads, which were still traffic-free. No one really had any idea yet what was going to happen although the writing was on the wall. By the time we got our station wagons backstage and settled in, it was well apparent that this was no ordinary festival. The logistics turned out to be a nightmare of misadventure. We had recently played festivals that seemed big, but this was indeed something different.

Now in that time, we found ourselves big stars among big stars. We were at the forefront of our game and hanging out in the stratosphere with the other performers just seemed to be part of our droit du seigneur . . . it's just the way it was. Today in memory everything is dimly seen across a smoke-filled room, the faces unrecognizable. This doesn't make for a good story, but it's true. One of the other things that led to a chaotic weekend for me was that Margareta originally had not planned on joining me, and with that in mind I invited another woman to come along. At the last minute Margareta did come and this led to me wanting to stay in the shadows as much as possible. (As Sir Walter Scott would say, "Oh what a tangled web we weave, when first we practice to deceive.") Hard to do in the environment that Woodstock became. On one hand this memory is uncomfortable, but on the other . . . it's hilarious!

I am often asked how the festival affected me and the truth is that for all the people, for all the stones in the pathway, for all the entropy and descent into chaos and for the intensity of the performance itself, it was really just another gig—but on this weekend there was special magic in the air! I wish in retrospect that I had been stone cold sober so I could truly get a read on the event, but then it wouldn't have been Woodstock. There were people as far as the eye could see. The energy emanating from this mass of humanity is hard to truly describe. The high point for me at Woodstock was seeing Carlos Santana's set. Prior to that, the greatest live band I had seen was Cream. Now there was Santana! That set a new bar for me.

One delay led to another and we wound up going on Sunday morning instead of Saturday night. It was only twelve hours or so late. All things considered, in spite of being utterly exhausted we acquitted ourselves pretty well. We finished out the set and got back in the station wagons to head to Manhattan to be on *The Dick Cavett Show*. By the time I started driving, the little dirt road I drove in on was clogged with cars. My deepest apologies to anyone whose parked car on that back road lost trim that morning. In Manhattan, Dick Cavett was a lucid and intellectual interviewer whose take on life would be lost on the late-night shows of today. "What was that show like?" he asked Grace and Paul. I was not a target for interviews back then but had he asked me, I would have said, "Chaotic and eye-opening." On this day it was Paul, Grace, and Crosby and his pals who got the call to speak, and they always had plenty to say. It was a heady time for sure, but in some respects I found myself to be a bystander and that was really okay. Left to my own devices without a guitar in my hand, I was something of a wallflower.

All this being said, Woodstock is one of those amazing occurrences that could not be planned and could never be re-created. In a way, in those three days we were all accidental tourists in a parallel universe whose portal opened unbidden and closed just as mysteriously, leaving a vivid, almost racial memory. There were other festivals in that time, some bigger than Woodstock . . . but there is only one Woodstock and that's that. The Catskills have always seemed mysterious. I remember when I lived in Mount Tremper in the eighties I sometimes felt surrounded by forces from another time—and I am not normally prone to such perceptions. In any case, did Rip Van Winkle and his pals conspire to elevate that festival to another plane? Was it an intersection of ley lines? Who knows? It was more than special: it was a one-of-a-kind moment for all of us who were there. It was one of the events where there were no real barriers between the artistic events on the stage and the equally important artistic events created by the audience itself. Indeed, this was a happening of cosmic proportions. I can still remember thinking when I got back to San Francisco it was all like a dream. I found myself wondering what just happened back in New York.

You just never know when some seemingly small thing will occur that in some way will affect your life. Sometime in the late sixties I met two guys, Rocky Williams and Big John Clark, who would change my life in unexpected yet very profound ways. I met Rocky Williams in San Francisco, undoubtedly at some music-related gig. We found we had a lot in common, especially motorcycles. Rocky had all sorts of really fast toys and I wanted to be part of that world too. My little Lotus Elan was a cool little car, but I had to up my game. All motorcycles are cool, just as all guitars are cool, but the 500 cc Triumph Scrambler I bought during the *Crown of Creation* recording session had to go. I had Sandy Kosman of Kosman Specialties start a hot bike project for me. We started with a 900 cc Harley-Davidson Sportster iron-head engine and built it until we were getting a hundred horsepower out of it. It was mounted on a Trackmaster frame with Ceriani forks and a Fontana front wheel with dual leading shoe brakes and a rear wheel with a disk. This was still a new concept at the time. It was a hell of a little motorcycle.

Rocky and I became pals. His freewheeling bachelor lifestyle sure looked appealing. Rocky was a bona fide outlaw. It was like that eighties TV show *Miami Vice*, but it was real! In my world one of the binding agents was getting high. To be sure, there was the social activism of the time, but it seemed as if every discussion happened over a drink or a drug. Back then being a pot smoker was a clandestine club. Any bit of visible paraphernalia was a tip-off that we were brothers against the Establishment: "Yeah man . . . we get high. We're important, knowledgeable, and cool." As a youngster, my milieu prevented such side trips, which is why alcohol and then drugs became an important life medicine. It turned off my moral compass and quashed the fear that seemed to always be with me on some level.

Rocky was from Florida but he had a place in Mill Valley. Rocky's friend Big John Clark came out to visit and stayed for a while too. Decades later John Clark would sell Vanessa and me the property in

Meigs County, Ohio, that would become the Fur Peace Ranch. There are no coincidences. For a while there it certainly seemed as if the ladies loved outlaws because there was always a surfeit of beauties and expensive toys around. Both Margareta and I had lived lives based on lies in the past, but things were really starting to accelerate. Almost every day became a clandestine party.

From the very beginning Airplane proved that in the world of bands, there is undeniable strength in teamwork. All that being said, it is easy to take the flow of creativity for granted. It's almost as if you deserve it. But as time passed, it seemed to me we had to dig deeper than we did in the beginning. Early on we in the band might not have always agreed, but we always worked together. There was joy to be found in our differences. It was easy to come up with new ideas because it *was* all new. After a while, for me, the process started to become formulaic; personal agendas, mine included, began to obscure our collective vision. The magic that Jefferson Airplane brought into my life was beginning to dissipate, along with the place in the world that it gave me. We might have acted like it, but none of us were kids when we started the band, and I was pushing thirty in 1969. Hanging out with my outlaw buddies was certainly a parallel universe. I began to ride my motorcycle more, but even that had some bizarre side effects. Hanging out and riding with the boys did not include "the old lady." Margareta really didn't enjoy riding much anyway and this was just one more thing that distanced me from her world. I've heard the term "loveless marriage" bandied about, and I don't know whether that is what Margareta and I had or not. What I do know is that we had a marriage without understanding or communication. Back then I don't think I ever considered for a moment that I might have a problem with substance abuse or that there might be some "isms" in my life that might bear looking into. Alcohol and drugs were just like eating, sleeping, or breathing. I found myself leading a parallel life on the road and, as time went on, more and more at home as well.

Musically I had been toying with some ideas for another band with

Jack. The financial success of the Airplane allowed Jack and me the wiggle room to nurse our young band through its infancy without financial constraints. I had maintained a strong connection with my San Jose pals after I moved to San Francisco. My old buddy Paul Zeigler and his wife, Catherine, were close friends, and for a while he ran a little venue in San Jose called the Shelter where I played sometimes. He and Billy Dean Andrus had a rock band called Weird Herald and we would all get together and play occasionally. It was fun and a real relief to be able to just get together with friends and play music without it being a "career move"!

From the very beginning Jack and I would play together in our hotel rooms, me on the old J-50 and he on his modified Guild bass with a little amplifier built into a Halliburton flight case that Owsley had made for him. In these times of plugged-in "acoustic" guitars, playing with an electric bass is not uncommon, but back then it was really unheard of. An amplified acoustic guitar was a major oxymoron. Back then if you played an acoustic guitar on stage, you did so in front of a microphone. Now all of us who perform with acoustic guitars are plugged into a myriad of gadgets that make us sound like we would in the living room, only louder.

Hot Tuna was born before we even thought of Hot Tuna. One night at the Fillmore East, Paul Kantner said, "Why don't you guys play an acoustic tune?" I walked up to the mike with my Gibson J-50 and started picking. Much to my surprise, that tough New York audience dug it. Many celestial bodies were in motion, that's for sure. We could hardly wait to do it again!

After Woodstock in August, we continued to gig and it was beginning to seem like endless stops on the way to nowhere. The Palm Beach International Music and Art Festival was held November 28 to 30. At that festival the Airplane played on the last day—the same day the Rolling Stones played. I remember two things about that gig. The first was that Spencer Dryden for some reason walked off a pier into the water. Spencer was dressed in a western motif, as he almost always was. Fancy slacks (pinstripes as I recall), dress shirt, dark western sport coat, sunglasses, and a cowboy hat. He was carrying one of those metal Halliburton briefcases . . . you know, like drug dealers in eighties TV shows. Spencer stepped off the pier and disappeared from sight, almost without a ripple. Seconds later his Halliburton surfaced followed by his cowboy hat . . . and then him. We pulled him out, dried him off, and headed to the stage. The second thing I remember was that we were really good that night . . . really good! Well, that's how I remember it anyway.

After that gig we flew back to San Francisco. There was a storm brewing over that now-infamous free festival the Rolling Stones were trying to put on. They had been denied permits for Golden Gate Park and Sears Point Raceway and settled on Dick Carter's Altamont Speedway. Now other people more competent than I have written treatises on what happened at Altamont. I can only write what happened to me. If you're driving west on I-580 from I-5 you will find yourself surrounded by wind farms as you cross the pass not far from the scene of the festival. There is majesty in its bleakness that is only relieved by the hundreds of giant wind turbines. There was no majesty on that day in December 1969 as the members of Jefferson Airplane boarded a helicopter and choppered up to the pass. I remember being tired after the flight back from Florida, but I was always tired flying home. Margareta and I and sundry band members got off the bird in Altamont and it became immediately apparent that this was indeed like nothing we had been involved in before. The chopper took off and showered us with dust. Since we had no personal vehicle, we were there for the duration. There were zero amenities—perhaps a porta-potty or two. Rocky had driven up from the Bay Area in a converted school bus with the blister from the top turret of a B-17 on the roof. We spent most of our time getting high in Rocky's bus waiting for our time to go on. As the day moved on it became apparent that things were devolving and no one seemed to be driving this train.

Life always presents you with a gaggle of intersections, and out of these crossings you might find yourself on a path you never would have imagined. It was through one of these little intersections that I met a couple members of "The Club." Through Rocky I met Frank Berry, aka Pathfinder. Pathfinder was a fine leather, silver, and turquoise craftsman who was proficient in the Native American idiom. He made some amazing leather clothes for Margareta and myself and also did some interesting work on my little Sportster. Through him I met Badger, a member of the Richmond Hells Angels MC, and then a couple of other Club members. It's always good to have friends. As the sun rose in the sky and things got hotter, dryer, and more chaotic, one of the riders from San Jose was assigned to keep an eye on Margareta, who seemed to always have a penchant for getting herself into trouble.

With the added clarity of hindsight, I have to wonder what any of us really expected at Altamont. It was certainly ill omened from its inception, but I think we just expected everything to work out. It always seemed to in the past. Woodstock could have been a disaster of unbelievable proportion and it all worked out . . . in a way. Why should this be any different? Of course wishing and hoping for the best is not the best way to plan for anything. On this day anything could, and did, happen.

What happened to us there was documented in the film *Gimme Shelter.* In my imperfect replay, we started our set and at some point Marty got into it with one of the Angels and was punched in the face. Paul and Grace had things to say to the crowd, and Jack and Spencer and I just played on until the conflict finally got to us and we got pushed onto the drum set, and in that moment our Altamont set was truly over. As I was leaving the stage I realized that things were only going to get worse. There was no one to even talk to about getting back to San Francisco. I don't remember what happened to Paul, Grace, or Marty. Spencer and Margareta and I started looking around for a way out. Rocky was staying for the duration and we really didn't know anyone else. The three of us walked out of the backstage area into the dusty parking lot and looked around. We found some guy passed out on the rear deck of a Mustang and woke him up. I told him, "If you let me drive you and your car to San Francisco, I'll buy you a Mexican dinner." Spencer and Margareta got into the backseat of the Mustang, I got in the driver's seat, the owner closed the passenger door, and off we went. Before we knew it we were in San Francisco at the Little Fiesta on Geary Boulevard eating dinner, and then we were home.

There is a lot written about Altamont as the apocalyptic end of an era. Perhaps this is true; perhaps not. One must ask oneself what that era was really all about. What did people really expect? I know Paul Kantner's mantra was always free love, free music, free dope, et cetera, and it's an interesting utopian dream, but as John Brent and Del Close would say on their great tongue-in-cheek language tutorial, *How to Speak Hip*, "Someone's got to run the subways!" On some level there are always bills to be paid. In my opinion what happened at Altamont was a perfect storm of incompetence, fate, and unrealistic expectations.

What about Jefferson Airplane? Were we a casualty of the so-called Death of the Hippie? What is a hippie anyway? In the tell, Jefferson Airplane is usually considered a hippie band. I guess on some level we were, at least visibly. I guess I really don't know. We could probably talk about this for a while. If you have to live in a commune to be a hippie, my colleagues and I were not hippies; we were also affluent and most of our problems were upper-class, first-world ones. I'm going to go out on a limb and say that Jefferson Airplane was not a hippie band. The so-called straight people might have considered that we lived an eccentric lifestyle, but consider this: we were successful in a mainstream way, contracted to an old guard establishment corporation (RCA), and we all had money. I never lived in the Haight-Ashbury, and except for a year or two on Divisadero Street in the Western Addition I always lived in solid middle- or upper-class neighborhoods. It's hard for me to really grasp the expectations that people who find themselves at a free concert might have. There is plenty of responsibility to go around for Altamont. Some of it may fall on my bandmates and me, but we certainly weren't the only ones culpable. The whole thing looked dodgy all along. There were plenty of negative signs, but we chose to go anyway. Was it the end of an era? I don't know. The postmortem discussions about Altamont were endless, and when the subject comes up, they still are! The audience helped create the environment on that day, and the mob gestalt that evolved must take some of the blame as well. The grandiosity of putting on a free show coupled with the entitled demands of a crowd who felt they deserved a free show made for a nasty witches' brew. In any case, it came, it went, and it was over. Our page was turned for us, and back in San Francisco we started to get ready for another recording project.

Joey Covington replaced Spencer Dryden as the band's drummer, and Paul Kantner replaced Spencer as Grace's significant other. A nascent Hot Tuna was swimming in the shallows and a revolving cast of characters began to make appearances. Even before the band had a name it was always Jack Casady and me. There's no Tuna without Casady and Kaukonen. One of the early incarnations had my brother, Peter, in it as well as Marty Balin. My brother and I were never close. That's just the way it was. Over the years I tried to involve him in projects with me, but for whatever reason, they never jelled. We were always distant but cordial. After our mother died in 1998, we just became distant. In any case, Paul Zeigler was part of it for a while. Joey Covington played drums in the very early days before Tuna really emerged. I didn't have a vision for this project yet; it was a jam band in the true sense of the nomenclature. I bought a Stratocaster and covered it with American flag stickers just to chase a different persona and a different sound. I've never really been a Strat guy, but I definitely wanted to play something other than my de rigueur ES-345. The band that would ultimately be the first incarnation of Hot Tuna had been playing late at night in hotel rooms for years. In the beginning Jack and I frequently shared rooms, and in those days, and as hard as it is to believe, there were rarely TVs. We spent a lot of time picking, me on the old Gibson and Jack on an electric bass guitar through a tiny amp. We were so comfortable with this that it became our show for the first recorded Hot Tuna project.

Woodstock and Altamont came and went, 1969 slid into 1970, and as the Airplane marked time getting ready to start recording the next album, Jack and I finalized a record deal for ourselves. We decided to record a live duo record somewhere. This was before there were pickups on acoustic guitars (what an oxymoron). It would be a live recording at the New Orleans House in Berkeley, and Jack and I were going to play standing up. This would make my staying consistently on the mike with my J-50 problematic, so the folks at Alembic made a set of clamps with a gooseneck mike holder on it that affixed to the lower bout of the J-50. This allowed the mike to sit firmly by the sweet spot above the sound hole, be out of the way of my right hand, and allow me to move about the stage. The microphone we picked for this application was a nifty little Sennheiser condenser, which was plugged into a little pre-amp direct box and sent directly into the PA. This gave me the controlled proximity a mike would have in the studio, but in a live, onstage situation.

It was a perfect moment for us to record. We had spent years playing these songs in hotel rooms and they were as ready as they would ever be. This is a rare luxury, to have road-tested songs ready to record. It made for great performances! There are two Kaukonen original tunes on that album. "Mann's Fate" had been written years before in San Jose. It was originally called "75½ Wabash Ave.," which was where we lived when I wrote it. The signature tag lick was inspired by some of the playing of my friend Steve Mann. I used to call them "Steve Mannerisms." It was an inspiration, not an adaptation; no one played like Steve. As a pretentious college student I had read *Man's Fate* by André Malraux. The song's title is just a play on words and has nothing to do with the Communist insurrection in Shanghai in 1927. Years later while thinking about titles I would do the same with Robert Graves's *Watch the North Wind Rise.*

Steve had unwittingly mentored me as a younger musician, and even though I play nothing like him at all, I learned much from his music. By the time Jack and I were getting ready to record the first Hot Tuna album, Steve had been in and out of institutions, and he found it increasingly difficult to live in the world the rest of us inhabit. He passed in 2009 in Berkeley where he lived the last years of his life being cared for by Janet Smith, one of the great Berkeley personalities and musicians. Anyway, Steve came by the house on Kensington Way and brought the young Berkeley harmonica player Will Scarlett with him. I had just finished writing "New Song (For the Morning)" and I played it for the guys. It was a little fingerpicking ballad and Will's harp fit right in. Al Schmitt produced this project, and we had the usual RCA cast of characters on board. Owsley Stanley himself was also in attendance for the recording project. One must not forget Betty Cantor-Jackson, whose incredible ear for recording acoustic music was profoundly felt not only on the New Orleans House recording but also on my solo *Quah* project. It was an incredible crew.

All the other tunes were either songs that Ian had taught me back at Antioch or other Reverend Davis tunes I learned myself. It occurred to me years later that this record should have been dedicated to Ian, for without him, none of this would have happened. I was able to correct this oversight years later on one of the reissues. Apologies to you, Ian: you always were the man.

Margareta and I drove over to Berkeley and met Jack and the gang there. I had planned on having Will play on "New Song," which he did. He never left the stage after sound check and became a de facto participant and consistent figure on our stage for the next couple of years. As a nod to the sometimes strange behavior of fans, someone noticed a glass breaking during "Uncle Sam Blues," and for many years thereafter some idiot would always break a glass during that song. There certainly is no accounting for the way people perceive things.

Jack and I are still very proud of this project after all these years. The performance is right where it should be.

We used one of Margareta's paintings on one side of the cover. With the artwork done and the record mixed, mastered, and pressed, Hot Tuna had an identity in the real world. In those days reality was measured by having a corporate product. Jefferson Airplane had measured up, and now it was Hot Tuna's turn.

10

Trial by Fire

At the same time that Hot Tuna began to circulate in the cosmos, another Jefferson Airplane project was coming due for RCA. The organic creative process that had driven us in the early years was mutating. To me, our art was becoming formulaic. There were fewer forays into the unknown, fewer all-day rehearsals. This was the first album we did with the first major personnel changes since the band was formed. Marty Balin was gone. Spencer Dryden was gone, replaced by Joey Covington, and Papa John Creach was now on board.

As always, the view is clear looking back. For some reason I had expected the creative energy that had nurtured and driven the band for five or six years to always be with us. I just didn't expect that the constant of change that touches all of us would be so profound. I was still looking for the excitement that newness brings and we weren't new anymore. (All these unsettling feelings would really come home to roost in their full maturity in the making of the album *Jefferson Airplane* in 1989.) One of the real creative bright spots that happened in this time was meeting Papa John Creach.

Papa John was an amazing man and it was an honor to have shared space with him. We were playing Winterland one night, and Marty and Joey brought Papa John along and asked if he could sit in. He became a de facto member of the Airplane that night, and later, a member of Hot Tuna as well. That was also the night that Janis Joplin was found dead in the Landmark hotel on Franklin in LA. It was becoming apparent that our generation was not immortal. Janis was gone, preceded by Jimi Hendrix less than a month before. At the time it seemed unimaginable that this could happen to any one of us. I guess we thought we were special. The Reaper knows no boundaries.

With Marty gone from the band, the writing really fell on Grace and Paul's shoulders. This made it possible for Joey Covington and myself to get in the act, and as a result we got some songs on the LP. The Airplane wasn't doing much gigging in those years, but Hot Tuna was. Jack and Will and I were playing a gig in San Jose at an outdoor venue somewhere as an electric trio without drums. We met Sammy Piazza, who was playing with Dry Creek Road at the time, and had him sit in with us. All of a sudden we had a fine drummer in the band. Papa John Creach was family so when Tuna worked, he did too. RCA wanted another Hot Tuna album, so we got the remote truck together and headed down Route 17 up into the Santa Cruz Mountains to the Chateau Liberté.

The chateau was back off the highway via tiny dirt roads. I don't know its original purpose, but to us it was a dark universe where things happened that should never see the light of day. The gigs happened in a moderately sized log cabin with a little stage and a very low ceiling. It was certainly the most unlikely of places to record a project. There are only a few songs on this album because every last one of them is so long. In my defense, it was the seventies.

Before these sides were cut, Jack and I had brought Paul Zeigler, Marty Balin, and Joey Covington to Jamaica to record an ill-conceived project. Big John and Rocky had extensive business dealings in Jamaica, and Rocky suggested that we record our next project there. The boys rented a mansion in Runaway Bay for us and we headed down to the islands with all our gear, including RCA's remote recording stuff and their tech crew. With the moderate success of our first New Orleans

House record, we had some bargaining clout, but I had no self-confidence as a bandleader and had not written any new material suitable for recording. I was leaning on those around me: Marty, Joey, and Paul. There was nonstop drinking and drugging and the whole trip lives in my memory only as a dim, boozy haze. Jeff Tamarkin has some interesting perspectives from his book *Got a Revolution!: The Turbulent Flight of Jefferson Airplane*. I'm not prepared to argue these ancient opinions with anyone. They are probably all true to some extent. The feeling that I cannot escape is that I squandered another opportunity. It never occurred to me at the time how fear dominated my life, and as long as I was unable to confront this ephemeral darkness it would always be my master. However, like it says in the song "Fool's Blues" by J. T. "Funny Paper" Smith, "G-d takes care of old folks and fools." At the time I certainly met the expectations of the second category. *First Pull Up, Then Pull Down*, Hot Tuna's second album, filled the vacuum left by what didn't happen in Jamaica.

Back in Airplane land, we were finishing the *Bark* album. In retrospect, my complaints at that time were utterly absurd. Musicians complain about two things—having a gig, and not having a gig. For a while it seemed like Jefferson Airplane was working all the time, although by the standards of the work schedule that I keep today, we hardly worked at all. In any case, we found ourselves working the New York Tri-State area and staying in the Chelsea Hotel on Twenty-Third Street for three weeks. If I found myself at the same hotel for three weeks now, I'd have business cards printed up. The winds that would scatter the Airplane were already in play. The love and commitment that launched us in the first place were no longer present. With these thoughts occupying my head, I went to sleep one night after a gig. I always had my J-50 in my room, and it was always out of its case. I also had a little Sony cassette recorder that lived on the nightstand. Apparently the song came to me in its entirety in a dream, and in that dream state I picked up my guitar and recorded it. When I woke up in the morning I hit the PLAY button on the recorder; the song that would be named "Third Week in the Chelsea" was there, intact and in the form it would be when it was recorded on *Bark*!

Sometimes I feel like I am leaving life behind
My hands are moving faster than the moving of my mind
Thoughts and generations of my dreams are yet unborn
I hope that I may find them 'fore my moving gets too worn
If only I can live to see the dawning of the dawn .

The music was certainly a product of what I was up to in the finger-style world. The words came straight from the heart. Some were true, and some were wishful thinking.

Lines were drawn around a pair of eyes that opened wide
And when I looked into them I saw nothing left inside.

I was doing a lot of speed and drinking back then. Oftentimes when I would stop in front of a mirror, I was changing in a way that I was not pleased to see.

Margareta suspected that that line was written about someone I was cheating with, some New York late-night vampire. It was not . . . it was about me. As for the "carrying another's load" line in the tune, that's a little self-indulgent but hey, it's a song, not a confession. That's what I felt at the time, though. Objectively speaking, it turned out to be a good song. Will Scarlett's harmonica part is stunning, and Grace's harmony part, which I just listened to a few moments ago, brings tears to my eyes. What a great singer she was! She is a one-of-a-kind artist! There will never be another quite like her. There would be one more Airplane studio album and then Tuna would swim on its own.

Lots of things were coming due. The Hot Tuna album we would call *Burgers* was on my front burner. It was our first studio recording with

Papa John and Sammy Piazza. I had songs from my repertoire: "99 Year Blues" by Julius Daniels, "Truckin' My Blues Away" by Blind Boy Fuller, and "Let Us Get Together Right Down Here" by Reverend Gary Davis. I also had "True Religion," though at the time I didn't know who wrote it. It has similar lyrics but different music than a song by the Reverend Robert Wilkins. I learned this tune early on from the great Ian Buchanan and I suspect that my arrangement is based on his. I was starting to write more by this time, and for this project I came up with "Sea Child," "Highway Song," and "Ode to Billy Dean," as well as two instrumentals: "Water Song" and "Sunny Day Strut." I had started writing "Sea Child" a couple of years earlier while living on Washington Street in Pacific Heights. At the time, the musical process on the guitar in the drop D tuning was a revelation.

> *Daily games run off like water*
> *Falling down like summer rain*
> *We see each other in confusion*
> *And wonder why we came today*

Like so many of my songs then, this is a young man's song, not about unrequited love but unrequited dreams. Could that dream girl on the beach be the gateway to what I was looking for? My dreams were so shrouded in late-breaking adolescence that the lyrics could have been about just plain wishful thinking. The song has lived for a long time now and regardless of my intentions at the time of the writing, it's a good song. The dropped D guitar part pulled the tune together and turned it into a piece. Even after all these years, I can see that my truncated emotional state did not damage the song beyond repair.

With the logic of a thirteen-year-old, I often thought that the answer to my problems would be to get in a vehicle and start driving. Whenever that nameless destination would be reached, all problems would be solved. With this questionable logic in mind, I wrote "Highway Song."

Rolling down the highway
Living in the spring
It's raining somewhere down the road
That don't mean a thing
If I knew where I was coming from or going to
I might make you happy little girl
Living here with you

Sitting here at the computer, I find myself listening to this tune for the first time in years. Basically it's a little fingerpicking ditty with Papa John playing fills and Jack Casady and Sammy Piazza laying down a truly badass rhythm track. My vocal rides the crest of that wave with David Crosby gently lending a hand. Bo Diddley would sing, "Tombstone hand and a graveyard mind / just twenty-two and I don't mind dying!" Far more dramatic to be sure, but I was in the same headspace. Ah, the indestructability of youth! Talent alone could not have surmounted the shortcomings in my maturity. The fact that I worked very hard at my craft did.

Back in the real world of the music business—inspired, I guess, by the Beatles' own record label Apple—the Airplane decided that it would be a good idea to have our own record label too. We called it Grunt Records. Even at the time this made no sense to me. I could barely deal with my own productions, much less someone else's. Even after all these years I can't believe that we were able to make the deal with RCA to fund this. None of us were competent as artists & repertoire (aka A&R) people and we certainly weren't talent scouts. Except for Papa John, all of our other "big discoveries" have long since been relegated to the dustbins of history. My old friend from San Jose, Richmond "Steve" Talbott, had played and sang with me on Julius Daniels's "99 Year Blues." He was such an awesome and genuine talent I thought he should be given a chance to record. Sad to say, the project never really amounted to anything and was scrapped before it was released. There is a sample of his work on the Arhoolie album *Out West,* featuring Berkeley-area musicians. In any case, the vanity label turned out to be a headache and a money pit for me. I did not know it yet, but my time in Jefferson Airplane was drawing to a close.

My time at the little rented house on Kensington Way was ending as well. I had decided to buy a house. Margareta was less enthusiastic. It was indicative of the way things were in our relationship. She never wanted kids. Perhaps buying a house was also too much of an anchoring commitment that smacked of adulthood. Conscious long-term commitment was always a problem for us. I found a small but nifty little house on Yerba Buena Avenue in Saint Francis Wood, San Francisco's oldest residential community. At the time it was very conservative; we were certainly the youngest and most eccentric people to buy there. My Lotus Elan and 1940 Buick were certainly eye catchers when we moved in. The "yard" was tiny, hardly enough room for a weed whacker. It would be ours though! The homeowners' association looked at us with a jaundiced eye, and in retrospect they had some good reason to be horrified.

On the first floor there was a little maid's room and a bathroom next to the garage. I immediately tore out the wall between the room and the garage and built a wood shop. I had a radial arm saw, an eight-foot-tall drill press, a milling machine, and all sorts of other tools. I sold the 1940 Buick and bought the 1934 Buick Victoria, which is on the cover of the *Burgers* album. I also sold the Lotus, but before I did, in the spring of 1971, Grace and I left Wally Heider Studios at around four in the morning, she in her Mercedes and me in the Lotus. I don't know what we had planned and I'm sure she didn't either, but she careened into a wall on Doyle Drive on the approach to the Golden Gate Bridge and spun across the road. I was behind her in the Lotus and she was leaving me in the dust! All of a sudden her car was spinning out right in front of me, crashing into the wall and swirling to a stop. I was able to get her out of the car and waited until the cops and the ambulance came. All things considered, she was lucky and so was I. When I got home around five thirty in the morning, Margareta's comment was "What were you doing following Grace at that hour of the morning?" Good question indeed. That fact that it made sense at the time was not a good answer.

I sold the Lotus and I bought a Maserati Ghibli with a speedometer that went to 180 miles per hour. There was always something wrong with that car. On one drive to Half Moon Bay something went awry and when I pulled into a garage, the mechanics just started laughing. I immediately traded it in for a 1972 Corvette LT-1 as a companion piece for the 1971 Camaro I had as a daily driver. We were certainly doing our best to help out the economy. Obviously pieces were missing from my life and I tried to compensate with toys.

A number of things were beginning to transpire as the Airplane got ready to record *Long John Silver*. My alcoholism was accelerating. I drank every night. My world should have been golden but nothing seemed to give me a vision of a future in which I would find fulfillment.

This was the mind-set that followed me into the studio as we made *Long John Silver*. I had written a song in dropped D on the acoustic guitar that was inspired by my daily relationship with Margareta. That song was "Trial by Fire."

Gonna move on down the highway, make this moment last
Till it closes with the future, leaving out the past
Rolling 'long and doing fine now, what do you think I see?
That bony hand come a beckonin', buddy come and go with me
'Cause that engine just ain't strong enough to get you round the turn
Lie on your back in the middle of a field and watch your body burn

Chorus:
Don't try to tell me just who I am when you don't know yourself
Spend all your time running out on the street with your mind home
*   on the shelf*

Looking at me with your eyes full of fire like you'd rather be seeing
me dead
Lyin' on the floor with a hole in my face and a ten-gauge shotgun
at my head

As always I drew my images from life. The first verse harkened back to an incident years before in San Jose. A guy I knew was driving an old Volkswagen while sucking on the hose of a tank of nitrous oxide in the passenger seat. He flipped the car while turning into an off-ramp, never dropping the hose. He woke up on his back in a field, reasonably safe, with a burned VW about fifty feet away. As for the ten-gauge shotgun, someone gave me one for Christmas and it was a very impressive single-barrel item. I used to think that some day Margareta would just wind up shooting me. I had already been to the emergency room twice to get stitches on my face and head where she had struck me with various household items. At least I got more than one song out of my experiences with my wife.

Hanging out at the Chelsea Hotel in New York, we had gotten to know the actor Rip Torn; Rip is the pirate on the packaging for *Long John Silver*. There is not a lot of cohesiveness with this project. "Eat Starch Mom" is a jam thing that I came up with and Grace put words to. The music that Jack came up with for *Long John Silver* evolved the same way. With the completion of this album, it was almost over for me.

11

Genesis

The Winter Olympics of 1972 pulled me back from the brink. Margareta and I were glued to the TV watching the limited coverage of the speed skating events. Both of us had skated as kids. In fact, I had briefly taken figure skating lessons from the great American skater Dick Button. I had gone to see the Ice Capades with my mom and the drama of the whole show completely infected me. I was a pretty good roller skater on the blacktop across the street from our house on Northampton. One afternoon after school I grabbed Mom's old pair of white figure skates and took the bus to the ice rink across the street from the Hot Shoppes on Connecticut Avenue. They were too big for me and my ankles kept flopping over but I was determined to get it. They had a race and it made sense for me to enter. It was a hockey rink and I don't remember how many laps the race was, but I finished. My feet were covered with blisters from Mom's skates and I walked home because I spent all my money at the rink, but I was hooked for a while. I didn't know about speed skating back then and the ballet didn't interest me, so I quit my lessons with Dick in the middle of my fourth- or fifth-grade school year. I didn't skate again until our winter trip to Charlie Cockey's mom's place in Idaho in the mid- to late sixties. In any case, here we were watching the speed skating events and it just looked so cool.

"Do what thou wilt shall be the whole of the law" might have worked for the Thelemites, according to Aleister Crowley, but it didn't work for me. I pretty much did what I wanted to do on the road, and hoped that it would never follow me home. However, it did. I don't think I ever really considered it "cheating" until I got caught. Right around this time my activities were finally too obvious to hide or ignore, and in one of the rare honest conversations that Margareta and I would ever have, we took a cursory look at our lives and decided to really start over. Needless to say this was an extremely emotional time, and it fed into my solo album *Quah*. The flagship of the tunes I wrote for the album was "Genesis."

> *The time has come for us to pause*
> *And think of living as it was*
> *Into the future we must cross (must cross)*
> *I'd like to go with you*

I was hoping it was not too late to find a state of grace. This proved to be a false hope, but in retrospect at least it was a start. There were some other cries from the heart on that album, like "Song for the North Star."

> *They gave me money to find the sky*
> *And I took it with no questions, didn't even ask them why*
> *But days are open and skies are free*
> *And the time it took to learn that didn't leave its change on me*

In this moment there were a lot of songs in me clamoring to get out; another was called "Flying Clouds."

> *Say there's gonna be some sailing on the morning tide*
> *The breakers clear your ears, the ocean's here to take you on a ride*

Building houses made of paper, living for the day
That one way ride, on gravel slides, begins to fade away

Right or wrong, for many years I felt that I had abdicated personal responsibility by following the star of the Airplane. My growing process took a long time and I was utterly unaware of its progress. But because of these feelings, writing for myself was more inspiring than trying to come up with a suitable tune for Jefferson Airplane.

The Airplane played our last show together at Winterland in the fall of 1972. Margareta and I, still fired up by the Winter Olympics, went to West Allis, Wisconsin, to go skating and soon realized there was more to this than desire and a pair of skates. The relentless wind in the backstretch and the abrasive qualities of the concrete dust from the nearby factory wore us down. Christmas came and we had our holiday dinner in a Chinese restaurant there in West Allis and returned home.

The Airplane wasn't touring at the time. After the final gig in the fall of 1972 I just never told them I wasn't coming back. If I had it to do over again, I still would have left, but I would have done it in a more adult way. Back home, hanging out at the rink in Belmont, we met a bunch of speed skaters. The big dog in this pack was a Dutch guy named Jack Lutt. He was a friend of Kees Verkerk, one of the Dutch skating heroes of that time. Jack began to harangue all of us about spring and summer training so that the winter's skating could be fruitful. We were sold. My life became an uneasy dichotomy between serious skating training and the usual excesses of my music business life.

So here's the deal. I walked out of my life as a member of Jefferson Airplane as if it never had been. That said, if it truly never had been, I would never have gotten Hot Tuna started with Jack Casady or had the chance for what became a solo career. It's hard to stop a train, and even by the early 1970s the Airplane was a very long train indeed. In the beginning it didn't matter if Hot Tuna was self-supporting. Being under the aegis of the Airplane machine at 2400 Fulton Street really took care of that.

This next version of Hot Tuna was certainly inspired by Cream. They were one of the most powerful performing bands I had ever seen. When they came to the Fillmore the first time, we had all dropped acid. At moments like that watching a toilet flush could be inspirational, but watching Eric Clapton, Jack Bruce, and Ginger Baker play for the first time was celestial.

Aside from their great original material, I can't think of another band that adapted traditional acoustic blues numbers into a power trio format better than they did. I remember going back to our apartment on Washington Street after seeing Cream play and grabbing my Rickenbacker 360 twelve-string and hurling it through a Sheetrock wall like a spear. That was it for my career as a folk-rock twelve-string player. The good news was that the guitar was undamaged (unlike the wall) and I was able to sell it.

In any case, I was ready to explore power rock and roll. This would be Sammy Piazza's last recorded work with Hot Tuna, and as always, he did a hell of a job! The album would be called *The Phosphorescent Rat*. Where did that name come from? Never satisfied with the present day, Margareta and I were checking out all sorts of art and writing from the early twentieth-century Dada movement out of Zurich. What is Dada? I was taught that Dada is nada, and that fit into the absurdist vision of life that I had at that time.

While kicking a soccer ball around on the polo field in San Francisco's Golden Gate Park, we met a Polish expat artist named Marek A. Majewski, who did the artwork for the cover. Who today remembers the beer can pull tabs that grace the front cover? Another staple of the past lost in antiquity. They seemed modern at the time and now no one knows what they are.

The training for speed skating gave purpose to my relationship with Margareta. This was a creative time for me as a writer. I wrote all the songs on *The Phosphorescent Rat* except for "Sally Where'd You Get Your Liquor From?" I wrote "I See the Light" on a Martin D-18 twelve-string I had acquired. I never played it on a twelve-string again, but the instrument inspired the tune.

In this world I'm living in, I see the light
Sins are gone and now I know what is wrong and right
Morning came on slowly, pushing back the night
Good times now that I can see the light

I was fired up and kept on writing. I had a cluster of chords from an outtake on *Quah* that I turned into "Letter to the North Star." When I was a teenager I was a huge Ricky Nelson fan, and listening to this song now, it reminds me a little of him. The lyrics were obviously inspired by what wasn't happening in my relationship with Margareta. Again, writing about what I wished would happen, and letting it go with that.

Winter's been a long, long time
Summer's here again
I've been trying to make you mine
Since I don't know when

There were many things I wanted to do back then, and one of them was to be a motorcycle gypsy. My hot little Sportster was not passenger-friendly and Margareta didn't like me riding by myself. Keeping the peace at home was difficult at best. I did write a song about it though, and that song was "Easy Now."

I got the ridin' pneumonia today
Well the weather's too fine to stay
Now I wanna go down to Mexico
Got a feelin' we'll be heading that way

Nice little rocker, even if I never got the ride. Finally, in 2003 my buddy Jerry Bayha and I rode from Ohio to California and back on Route 66. In 2010 we also rode "The Dragon," the Cherohala Skyway, and Natchez Trace. By the grace of G-d, I'm still riding and will continue as long as I can hold the bike up.

In 2011, as Hot Tuna got back in the studio for the first time in almost twenty years, I wrote an update to "Easy Now" called "Easy Now Revisited."

I got the riding pneumonia today
And the weather's too fine to stay
Well I want to go, down to Mexico
Got a feeling I'll be heading that way

Follow the horizon, decades down the road
Living life, the way it comes, ain't such a heavy load
There's still time, to ride the line, I'll find a song to sing
The echo of my engine, its sound makes freedom ring

Better late than never, I say. Back then, I was on a writing binge and I just kept going. Back in *The Phosphorescent Rat* land, I wrote this next tune, "Living Just for You."

I've waited all my lifetime for a moment like today
Our love is really real and really here to stay
And now I know what's happening, this starting all anew
I've been living lately just because of you

Mallory Earl got Andrew Narell to play steel drums when we recorded this tune. This was definitely a stroke of genius on Mallory's part. I was attempting to solve my problems in songs and not in real life, but from an artistic point of view, it worked. In any case, I was rising to the occasion, which required me to write enough songs for the album projects that Grunt and RCA were expecting. *Rat* was in the can and Hot Tuna began to tour to support it. At home our lives revolved around training and skating, and sometimes the touring schedule suffered for it. I realize today that at the very least, the time I spent in athletic endeavors probably saved my life in the long run. As for Hot Tuna, Papa John was gone and Sammy left while Jack and I spent some time touring acoustically. As we got to thinking about our electric incarnation, I set out to find a new drummer. Michael Casady's girlfriend knew a gal whose boyfriend was a drummer named Bob Steeler. I got in touch with Bob and he drove over to the Yerba Buena house in a VW bug with all his drums in the car. When I saw him walking up the sidewalk with almost his entire kit in hand, I knew he was going to work out before I even heard him play! Bob fit right in with where Tuna was starting to go. In October 1974 we started to work on *America's Choice* in Wally Heider's studio in San Francisco. Mallory Earl produced it with us. I wrote all the songs except one, a take on Robert Johnson's "Walking Blues."

The first song on side one was written in Strömsund, Sweden, the year before while skating up there. Strömsund is in Jämtland in northern Sweden, where it is very dark in the winter. There were many occasions when Margareta could not sleep, and when that happened, violent reactions were never far away. One time she tried to stab me in the back with a broken bottle while I was putting up the Christmas tree. I would play the guitar and write songs softly so as not to wake the neighbors. One of them became "Sleep Song."

> *Shoreline's smaller, every day wonder why we feel this way*
> *You don't know then I got nothing left to say*
> *I been blown across the water, like a ship ain't got no sail*
> *That ain't no way to be*

For the most part I have always been a blind optimist, even when faced with obviously disastrous conclusions. In the spirit of hope springing eternal, I wrote "Soliloquy for 2" for the project.

Fog rolled in from the ocean yesterday
The beach had disappeared within the gray
And tomorrow almost drowned at sea
Without a trace of living that's to be

Another tune on the album wound up being called "Funky #7." Jack came up with the opening riff. I wrote the lyrics and the rest of the music.

Walking talking breathing trying to smile yourself to death
With your finger on the pulse of time there ain't no time to rest

Now I realize that song lyrics do not necessarily make good poetry, but if you're lucky they do. In the context of the music of the time, these lyrics worked. "Invitation" wound up being an epic rock-and-roll number for us. On the record it was almost seven minutes long. In person the jam could—and often did—last much, much longer!

Come along with me my lady, gonna ride this road together
You can see my love for you ain't dependent on the weather
Living with you by my side such an easy road to follow
With the future as our guide as we ride into tomorrow

This was hard rock for real. We shed our folk-rock skin and emerged clad in rock-and-roll armor. We were not a hit-making machine but with the takeoff assist from Jefferson Airplane's reputation, we were making ripples if not waves. A song that started as a jam on the TV show *Don Kirshner's Rock Concert* evolved into "Hit Single #1."

Every time I touch your face I get a feeling in my shoes
Marking time ain't the way to race you got to make some headline news
Jump back now don't let your feet go slow, you got to let your body
  sway
Won't you tell me what I want to know, there's time enough to play

The music came first, as it usually does for me, and then I would chase words until a song evolved. Picking riffs on that old Martin D-18 twelve-string inspired the next song, "Serpent of Dreams." I was fond of mythology involving dragons and the like. To be sure, I had read and reread *The Lord of the Rings* trilogy in the sixties, and this was my dragon song.

Flowers today, blooming by the pathway
Lining the edge of tomorrow's grave
Bright shining way, living in the shadows
Trying to be the master of tomorrow's slave

For the guitar geeks out there, that's my ES-345 through, among other things, an Oberheim Voltage Control Filter. I was still evolving my electric guitar sound, and by this time I had moved away from Fender Twins and the occasional Marshall to a double stack of Orange Amps. More pedals were beginning to emerge by this time, and in addition to the Ampeg Scrambler and the Cry Baby there was now the MXR Blue Box octave splitter and the MXR Distortion Plus as well as a Roland Chorus Echo. Good times as always.

There was another original on this project: "I Don't Want to Go."

Up this morning saw Death coming 'cross a field far away
"I've been looking all night long, I'm coming for you today"
I looked up, all around . . . hiding I don't know
Lots of things I got to do so I don't wanna go

I think that on some primal level, I was always aware that Death begins to stalk us the moment we are born. The stupid risks I took most of my life were gentle tugs on his beard. Of course at some point, if you are lucky, you realize that the Black Marauder will come for all of us and that it is our duty not to rush him. For me, these are thoughts that come to an old man. As a young man I would have pretended they did not exist.

So, I'm listening to this last song on the album, trying to ferret out the words. The song is "Great Divide, Revisited" and if I had to do this one over, there would surely be some rewrites. Too many mixed metaphors and let's face it, some of this stuff is unintelligible. People always wonder if I have trouble picking songs to be on albums; the truth is that I'm not very prolific, then or now. When I get enough material, I'm done. This last song has potential, but I should have followed the rabbit further down the hole.

On some level *America's Choice* began to define Hot Tuna. We had become self-supporting, with our own crew and truck, and were gigging more than ever. Again, my professional life was shining and my personal life was bogged down in an emotional quagmire. But this was nothing new.

The next album was *Yellow Fever*, recorded in June and August 1975 at Wally Heider's and produced by the great Mallory Earl. My pal Paul Zeigler and I came up with the music for "Free Rein." This little number is truly a dark landscape of sound. Looking at the lyrics after all these years, I like some of it and some of it I don't. To me both the writing and playing reflect an amphetamine-and-liquor-drenched state that somehow wasn't able to kill the spirit I had left. When I read the lyrics to "Free Rein" without the music, it's like they came from different realities, but together . . . well, that was Hot Tuna back then.

Tell me why you look so free
Looking back, you don't see me
I don't know if I can stay
Living in the world this way
One fine day gonna jump and shout
Ain't nobody turn me out
While that freeway drives me down
That old highway round

I was certainly rising to the pressure of putting out one album after another, but I think my writing was becoming stressed. I just didn't have that much to say, but I found some different ways to say it. "Sunrise Dance with the Devil" is a dandy though. I had a great time wrapping myself in the language when I wrote it, and I still have a great time listening to it today.

Time will come you're gonna see things my way
    And maybe you won't mind
When a heavenly spire eludes your seeking
    And grabs you from behind

"Song for the Fire Maiden" is really just an excuse for a jam, but the next tune, "Bar Room Crystal Ball," was a dark premonition of things to come.

Early this morning someone hot on the line
Says me and my friends are downtown, drinking wine
Trying to help me but they ain't got time
To see which way I've fallen
Well this sawdust's feelin' fine, and my body sure don't mind
This solitary flying,
Past summer's stare again,
I don't remember when

When I wrote that tune, we had some friends visiting from Sweden. We were doing a lot of partying, and in a rare moment of solitude I picked up the old Gibson J-50 in a G tuning and started to play. The words just flowed. In that moment I knew I was an alcoholic and that most of the people I hung out with were as well. Why bother with someone who didn't party the way I did?

I could see that I was confined and defined by the disease, but I absolutely could not see that there was another way to live. I was so used to darkness that a world with light in it was out of the question. Of course this moment of epiphany came, reflected itself in the song, and was relegated back into the recesses of my mind, only to surface much, much later. In any case, it was just life at the time, and since I knew no better I just accepted it for what it was.

We continued to tour. Margareta and I continued to train for skating, and I believed I had filled my life with purpose. We moved our field of operations to Inzell in Bavaria, about ninety clicks from Munich. The four-hundred-meter track in Inzell is now enclosed, as modern times dictate, but in those days it was open in the shadow of the Falkenstein. It was truly beautiful and we should have been enjoying every moment.

12

Watch the North Wind Rise

Carving out that month of December to go to Europe to skate was an expensive endeavor. Money was flowing out for the trip and none was coming in because I wasn't working. At the end of one of these vacations I would be more than broke and would always have to scurry with Jack to get the band back on the road. I was generally hamstrung by the codependent relationship I was perfecting with Margareta. I realize now that I had no idea whatsoever what she wanted from life or expected from me in particular. It never occurred to me that by their mid-thirties most people had families. That was not my path.

My real moments of communication happen when I play music. The music that Jack and I made back then and still make today has always been honest and reasonably unpretentious. With us, what you see is what you get. This does not mean that we never have bad nights. You bet we do, but our fans always allow us to be us. We are allowed to experiment and make frequent changes. In any case, Grunt/RCA needed another project. We recorded *Hoppkorv* in July 1976 and released it in October.

The title for the album came from the winter of 1975–76, which turned out to be the last time we would visit Strömsund to skate. Margareta and I skated the Prinsloppet, an outdoor race on the Ströms

Vattudal. There were two distances, 100 kilometers and 50 kilometers. We did the 50. Then Esbjörn Jacobsen played drums, a homeboy named Tommy played bass, and with me on guitar we re-created Hot Tuna for the Strömsund Pop Gala. I also wrote "Watch the North Wind Rise."

Well up in the morning watch the north wind rise
Bringing fire down from the skies
Hey we got a long way to go
So keep on lovin' and make it slow
We're going home, won't be long
Hear in my song,
That lovin' you ain't never done no wrong

One of my local pals was a skater named Håkan Sannemo. His girlfriend had just given him a beautiful white cable-knit sweater, and after his race he had changed into civvies and we all wandered over to Ante's Korv Bar across the street from the track. A *korv* is a Swedish hot dog and, boy, are they tasty garnished with local mustard. As Håkan raised the dog to his mouth the sausage itself launched from the bun and ricocheted off the white sweater and onto the ground, leaving a trail of yellow mustard. "Jävla hoppkorv!" Håkan said. *Jävla* is a tough word to translate into English. I think a close approximation for Håkan's exclamation would be "Friggin' jumping hot dog!" It's more emphatic in Swedish. Anyway, I loved the sound of it. *Hoppkorv* it would be.

Back in the States, the motif of the 1976 Tuna tour was the American Bicentennial. Our equipment truck had patriotic murals painted on the box. We worked enough to pull me out of the financial hole that the skating "vacations" always left me in. We put in some months of hard touring and got back into the studio at Wally Heider's in July 1976 to record *Hoppkorv* surrounded by bicentennial madness. We had great hopes for a San Francisco fireworks gala, but the relentless fog always made such aerial displays troublesome. I never could really put my finger on the musical vision I was looking for. I don't think I was artistically mature enough at the time to work in creative proximity with someone other than Jack. I felt I didn't have enough to give at that time so I co-opted others into our world. John Sherman, a guy I met through Paul Zeigler, played guitar with us on "Bowlegged Woman, Knock Kneed Man," and Nick Buck played keyboards and synth on a number of tunes as well as toured with us. I wasn't the easiest person to work with and I'm sure that fear was part of this equation. In retrospect I wonder about fear and overdubs and guest musicians. When is enough? When does an artist look in the mirror and say, "I have given enough and it will have to do"? I guess we're always fishing around for answers to these questions.

The great producer Harry Maslin got the call for this project. Sad to say I remember nothing of the making of this album. I'd like to blame this on age, but I think the real reason had to do with self-medication. I wrote a couple of other tunes for *Hoppkorv* in addition to "Watch the North Wind Rise," but for me today the only other noteworthy lyrics I wrote are found in "Song from the Stainless Cymbal."

Get down child; you've got to find another way
Stop running in the alley now, that ain't no way to start the day
I hear people talking 'bout the time that you spent living in the clouds
You know I ain't no fortune teller still I hear your future singing loud

There are only two lyrical verses here but there are lots of parts to the song. I just wish I'd written more verses. I was tiring as a writer, and even though I work well with words I just wasn't able to see truly what I wanted to say, so I did it with metaphors and guitar solos. Jeff Tamarkin, the author of *Got a Revolution! The Turbulent Flight of Jefferson Airplane*, commented that some of the songs from that time were drug songs— not about drugs, just written by them. I can't argue with this. In my opinion my spiritual, personal, and artistic development had been stifled by my lack of clarity. I was lucky to have achieved what I did.

Harry Maslin, hit maker though he was, certainly had a tough time finding hits for Hot Tuna. As a kid I was a huge Buddy Holly fan, and Jack and I had played many of his songs with our little band in high school. We wound up doing a Tuna version of "It's So Easy" for this project. I think we had a vision of a hit here. However, Linda Ronstadt put "It's So Easy" out at the same time. She had a well-deserved hit with it and that was that. When I look at Harry Maslin's online information he doesn't even mention his part in *Hoppkorv*. We were probably not easy to work with. Sorry, Harry.

This was the final Tuna studio album for Grunt/RCA. We would record one more live project, produced by Felix Pappalardi in 1977. How that came about is interesting indeed. Margareta and I wound up in Malmö in southern Sweden after another skating "vacation" in Inzell. We were there to visit her parents, Svea and Uno, in her hometown before we returned to San Francisco. For Margareta, going home was always filled with dark ghosts. We heard that there was a rock concert in Copenhagen at the Falconer Hall with the hugely popular Danish band Gasolin'. The Øresund Bridge from Malmö to Copenhagen did not yet exist so the ferry was the way to go. Traveling on the ferry meant tax-free liquor, so much of this trip is shrouded in a fog of booze. What I do remember is that we got to the theater, watched the show, and somehow made our way backstage, where we met the band as well as Felix Pappalardi, who was producing their latest record.

Felix, in addition to his own work, had produced *Disraeli Gears* for Cream and I loved that project. In the early sixties Steve Mann had spoken to me at length about Felix's prowess as a producer. Steve told me that Felix would build all his arrangements from the bass line up. This was certainly a powerful concept from the groove point of view. Felix and I got to talking and I thought he would be right for the next Hot Tuna project. I'm lucky I remembered any of this after the fact, but when I got to back to the States I gave him a call and he said he would work with us on our next project, which ultimately was called *Double Dose.*

I don't know if my life was starting to implode or whether I just didn't have what it took to continue . . . or both. The beginning of the next chapter certainly began with the recording of the album *Double Dose* at the Theater 1839, which was a door or so west of the old Fillmore West auditorium in San Francisco. Between the 1839 and the Fillmore was the Peoples Temple in the old Scottish Rites location. This was shortly before the infamous Kool-Aid tragedy in Guyana. The Peoples Temple on Geary had a powerful ham radio system that was constantly in communication with the colony in Jonestown, Guyana. It was improperly shielded and bled onto our tapes, so when we began recording we had to block out time with them so they could put their communications on hold.

Side A was just me on an amplified Ovation guitar . . . an omen of things to come. Sides B, C, and D were the band: Jack Casady, Bob Steeler, Nick Buck, and myself. We got enough material for the project and said goodbye to the Theater 1839 and moved down to Wally Heider's, where all the vocals were replaced with studio takes. The album was recorded on August 5 and 6, 1977, and released on March 13, 1978.

In the summer of 1977 Margareta and I got to know the amazing tattoo artist Ed Hardy. He did a back piece first for Margareta and then for me. I got my first tattoo from the legendary Lyle Tuttle in his studio two floors above the Greyhound station in San Francisco. That started the tattoo ball rolling and I also got some traditional roses from Pat Martyniuk. Ed Hardy and I had become friends. Elvis died while I was on the table. How can you forget a landmark moment like that? One of the other great artists working with Ed was Bob Roberts; I got a piece from him as well. Bob played sax and we co-opted him into part of our fall tour where he made an appearance on such great numbers as "The Party Song." There were some good laughs on that tour!

Margareta and I set out to skate at Inzell again in the fall of 1977, but when we got over there, her behavior became more erratic than ever. She always had a problem sleeping, but now she wasn't sleeping at all and she was losing weight at an alarming rate. We went to a local clinic.

They ran some tests and it was determined that she had a hyperactive thyroid and needed immediate medical attention. We left for California and that was it for the skating that year. At home, the doctors were all about this operation or that one, this medication or that one. Real life had smacked us right in the face, and neither one of us could really figure out how to deal with it in the real world. Acupuncture did not yet have the respect that it has today, but our doctor reluctantly told us that it might help. George Long had a White Crane martial arts studio on Post Street as well as an acupuncture clinic. George began treating Margareta and we also enrolled in a tai chi class there.

At first nothing seemed to change. The hyperactive thyroid exacerbated Margareta's proclivities to act out and one day she put her fist through our bedroom window, severing several tendons. We were lucky she missed her arteries. I wrapped her wrist in a towel and rushed her to the Mount Zion Hospital. They admitted her immediately into the emergency room and began to repair the damage. Of course in the report we both swore it was a terrible accident. The operation took many hours and I left the hospital to run some errands. When I came back to pick her up, I was told that she had escaped when she came out of the anesthetic. I was losing my mind. I drove the streets looking for her but she was gone. I went to make some phone calls and moments later our sometime Hot Tuna tour manager, Jamie Howell, drove up with her. He had run across her wandering the streets and convinced her to let him bring her home.

This was only the beginning.

13

Roads and Roads &

You would think that being faced with a life-threatening illness, you would talk to people, find a support group, research possible treatments . . . talk, share, or otherwise communicate. We did none of these things. We never really talked about anything. We talked *at* each other or yelled or just scorched the earth with our silence. One of the many casualties of this was that I walked away from Hot Tuna. Hot Tuna did not break up in 1977. Hot Tuna did not "hiatus." I handled this problem the same way I handled leaving the Airplane. I told no one what was going on and just walked away. It is a testimonial to my deep friendship with Jack Casady that he was able to forgive me without really knowing why I did what I did.

The acupuncture treatments seemed to be working and Margareta's thyroid improved. She was not a good patient. She broke her cast off several times and it was a miracle she did not undo the amazing reconstructive work the surgeons did on her tendons. Her response when she finally got her last cast off was to have a dragon tattooed on her wrist to cover the scar. We had a young friend from Marin County named Warren, and through all these trying times, he was the only one I allowed myself to talk to. Warren would come over every day and hang out with us for a couple of hours. He was able to talk to Margareta better than I could, and his presence was very important to us at the time.

Margareta was getting better but money was a problem. Since I walked away from Hot Tuna I started to tour solo. I began playing my Ovations amplified through a half stack of Hiwatt amps. Acoustic music at its finest I say today, with a wry grin. My performances in this time were uneven at best. Amphetamines and alcohol were the remedies for my pain, and back then we still convinced ourselves that cocaine was only a recreational drug. I had no long-term goals whatsoever. It was one day at a time in the most negative sense. We went back to Inzell again but this just put me deeper in debt. The skating trips were beautiful and uplifting and a Technicolor change from the bleak corner of my universe at home. For whatever reason I began to find my voice through songwriting again. Somehow I was able to grandfather Hot Tuna's recording obligations into my own projects, and I got ready to record the *Jorma* album.

The very talented producer and musician David Kahne agreed to work with me on this project and we got started. I have no recollection how David got assigned to this project. David was the director of A&R for 415 Records, which was America's first punk and new wave label. As always, the music scene was evolving. That which was new in 1965 for the Airplane and in the seventies for Hot Tuna was fast becoming if not dated, at least old school. David had produced hits for a local SF band called Pearl Harbor and the Explosions. My guess is that RCA figured that somehow David would make my music relevant to the evolving SF scene at the very least—and nationally in the best-case scenario.

I'm sure David would have preferred to work at the Automatt, which was owned and run by his friend David Rubinson and where he had an office. At the time, RCA had lots of irons in the fire at Wally Heider's, so that's where David and I started work on what would be the *Jorma* album. Over the years David pursued amazing projects and gathered all manner of awards, including a Grammy for his work with Tony Bennett in 1995.

Bob Steeler and I had continued to jam together off and on after I took that time off from Hot Tuna. He and I had been working on a number of tunes, one of which became "Straight Ahead" on side one. It's a nice little rock song, but the album's lyrics start to get a little more meaningful to me with "Roads and Roads &."

Walkin' down that lonesome road
Set my soul on fire
Thinkin' back before I left
The passions I desire
Can't you help me anymore
To live my life more freely
Instead of twisting like a rope that's falling at your feet

I'm dancing with images with a lot of the writing on this album. I played all the guitar parts with some very creative direction from David Kahne. I truly missed having Jack in my corner in the studio but I had completely isolated myself from all my colleagues. When the time came to record the *Jorma* album, it truly was just Jorma! Sometimes art comes from necessity, and this was what the corner I had painted myself into gave me. Like other important decisions I had made in my life, there was no logical thought about consequence. The music business machine that was Jefferson Airplane allowed Jack and me to morph into Hot Tuna, and the momentum that Tuna gained carried me into my world as a solo artist.

As always, my writing was inextricably intertwined with my personal life. The emotional dysfunction with Margareta was now compounded by her hyperactive thyroid and I was certainly complicit as a codependent enabler. Still, I was able to write some songs. I recall a conversation I had with Jim Lauderdale about songwriting. Jim is certainly one of the finest songwriters I know. His take, from a commercial point of view, was that a good song should be written so that the listener does not need to know anything about the artist's life. In a recent conversation with Verlon Thompson on the same subject, Verlon cited Guy Clark as disagreeing with that by saying that we all live the same life, and if you can't relate to a particular song, you just haven't lived that life yet. In any case, these songs were definitely about the life I was living. From "Valley of Tears":

Shake my life don't you leave me here
'Cause I'm lying in the valley of tears
Break my life, it's too much to bear
And I'm dying in the valley of tears
When things ain't going my way
We'll be flying down the highway
That valley holds them back I hear
Tomorrow's brief vacation should provide a new sensation
The same old town I hear

If I was giving advice to myself back then, I'd have suggested making some changes in my life. But this kind of writing was the only way my heart could even come close to my sleeve. Quite simply, it was the best I could do at the time. This one is called "Song for the High Mountain."

You know I need you darling, though you think I lie
If you don't believe I love you look into my eyes
Every day you hurt me, and I don't know why
Though the night will change into the morning

Many years later, these are just songs I can listen to somewhat dispassionately, liking some and passing over others. Whatever emotions I was expressing in my songs at the time resonated in such a way with my fans that they have listened relentlessly over the years, and I shall always be grateful for that! Still, some of the songs call out to me today; "Wolves and Lambs" is one of these.

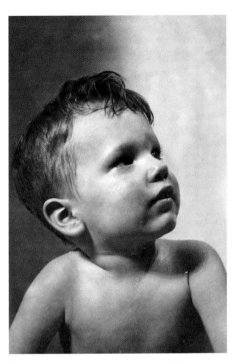

Portrait of me as a baby, circa 1941.
(*Photograph by Jorma Kaukonen Sr.*)

Grandma Kaukonen with Peter in her arms
and me on my trike. (*Kaukonen collection*)

A kid with dreams. *(Kaukonen collection)*

Peter, Beatrice, Jorma Sr., and me out by the house on Drigh Road in Karachi, Pakistan, 1954. (*Kaukonen collection*)

The clear eyes of a Cub Scout. (*Kaukonen collection*)

Me with Dad's Korean clarinet by the family Steinway in the house in Chevy Chase. (*Kaukonen collection*)

The 1961 Christmas regatta at the Manila Boat Club on the Pasig River. Tony Rittenhouse as cox, Vic Niemeyer as stroke, and me. (*Kaukonen collection*)

Me at the Chevy Chase house in 1956 with my first car, a 1950 Studebaker Starlight coupe. I'm wearing Dad's World War II field jacket. A proud moment! (*Kaukonen collection*)

Return to Antioch after my first co-op job at the Department of Health, Education, and Welfare, 1960. (*Kaukonen collection*)

Margareta Kaukonen, 75½ Wabash Avenue, San Jose, 1964. (*Photograph by Jorma Kaukonen*)

Me at the Folk Theatre in 1962 on First Street in San Jose, California. (*Photograph by Marjorie Alette*)

Janis and me at the Folk Theatre, San Jose, 1962. (*Photograph by Marjorie Alette*)

Janis Joplin at the Folk Theatre, 1962. (*Photograph by Marjorie Alette*)

Lowriding in San Francisco. (*Photograph by Margareta Kaukonen*)

Peter, Jorma Sr., and me in front of Steve "The Eagle" Elvin's mural in my living room in San Francisco. (*Kaukonen collection*)

Me at the starting line in Inzell, Germany. (*Kaukonen collection*)

Me, near the old Lone Star Café, in New York City in the late 1970s. (*Photograph by Margareta Kaukonen*)

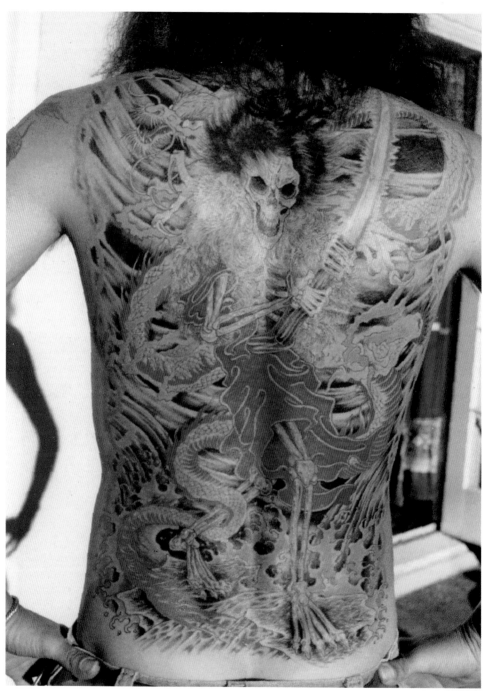

My back piece tattoo by Ed Hardy. (*Kaukonen collection*)

Performing with my band White Gland. (*Kaukonen collection*)

Jack Casady tears it up in the mid-seventies on the Flying V bass Glenn Quan made for him. (*Photograph by Margareta Kaukonen*)

The blues aren't always about tears! (*Photograph by Margareta Kaukonen*)

The psychedelic Gibson ES-345 appears onstage with Jefferson Airplane . . . and me. (*Photograph by Margareta Kaukonen*)

Playing slide with a Stevens Steel over the top of a Fender Stratocaster neck with Hot Tuna in the mid-seventies. (*Photograph by Margareta Kaukonen*)

Portrait of the artist as a young dog. (*Photograph copyright © Barry Berenson*)

Jack and me warming up backstage. (*Photograph copyright © Barry Berenson*)

Me with Hot Tuna and one of my Firebirds in the mid-seventies. (*Photograph copyright © Barry Berenson*)

Sitting in on Bob Margolin's class at Fur Peace in 2017, showing them how he does it. . . . Whatever "it" is. (*Kaukonen collection*)

Me and my current ride, a 2016 CVO Breakout Harley-Davidson. (*Photograph by Vanessa Kaukonen*)

Rob Wasserman, Bob Weir, and me backstage at Sweetwater, Mill Valley, California. (*Photograph by Vanessa Kaukonen*)

My favorite people on the planet: *(from left)* my son, Zachary, my wife, Vanessa, and our daughter, Izze, backstage at the City Winery in New York City, November 2017. (*Kaukonen collection*)

Susan Tedeschi and me goofing around on tour in the summer of 2017. (*Kaukonen collection*)

Winter 2017 at the Fur Peace Ranch is southeast Ohio. A mecca for guitar players and musicians who want to learn and play at one of the coolest places around. (*Kaukonen collection*)

A modern Jorma . . . content and satisfied with my life. (*Photograph by Vanessa Kaukonen*)

When you lie awake, feel your body shake
Come on girl don't let your spirit break
When the life you're in is more than you can take you got to
Once more look away, living for today
Don't satisfy your senseless pleasures
Once more look away and follow with your heart
As the waves come crashing miles apart

Margareta had a book by the Comte de Lautréamont called *Les Chants De Maldoror*. Comte de Lautréamont was the pen name of Isidore-Lucien Ducasse, a Uruguayan French writer who published this dark and nihilistic tome in 1869. Truthfully, this book was too surreal even for me, but some images did stick in my mind. At one time (and I paraphrase) the author said, "Wolves and lambs do not good companions make." Part of me knew as clear as day that Margareta and I were as incompatible as wolves and lambs in the same pen. The writing of this song did not exorcise these demons, but I like the writing in this tune today even more than I did when I wrote it. It's always nice when you can look back on any of your work and find that it is still satisfying.

I needed a couple of more songs to finish out this project, so I wrote some lyrics (which became "Requiem for an Angel") to go with this set of changes that had been dancing at my fingertips.

Wait for tomorrow it'll be a better day than today
Wait for tomorrow child you better heed the words that I say
Well the sun gonna shine, ain't gonna change my mind no way
When that new day comes, I know I won't be seeking no gray

In the early sixties there was a finite amount of available source material for those of us who loved traditional American acoustic blues. All this changed in 1968 when wealthy eccentric Nick Perls started first Belzona and then Yazoo Records. Nick had an immense 78 collection and he was incredibly talented in being able to remaster these gems, which he then pressed and released as LPs. Early on, thanks to the relative dearth of available material it was easy to pick songs to learn. With the many Yazoo albums Nick was putting out, I was hard-pressed to decide where to start with new songs. Instead of sourcing them around guitar parts as I had done in the past, I gravitated to songs with lyrics that just tickled me.

Thanks to Nick Perls and the Yazoo collection, I was able to bird-dog "Vampire Women" by Spark Plug Smith. Then there was that little gem from Finland, "Da-Ga Da-Ga" by M. A. Numminen. Margareta introduced me to this Finnish folk poet and humorist. Though a Finn, he recorded quite a lot in Swedish, and somehow Margareta and I got his LP, *Jag har sett fröken Ellen i badet*, which translates as "I Saw Miss Ellen in the Bathtub." I've never been fluent in Swedish, but I did have enough of the language back then to be able to count money, order food in restaurants, and understand songs. I loved Numminen. "Da-Ga Da-Ga" was this utterly nonsensical spoken-word piece that resonated with me at the time.

With the pressure of studio obligations temporarily out of the way, my life devolved into gigging, training for skating, and the annual trip to Inzell, Germany, to skate for a month. *Jorma* came out in October 1979 as I was nearer to forty than to thirty. These days it is an accepted alternative medical protocol, but in the seventies, even though it was probably at least two thousand years old, acupuncture smacked of witchcraft and magic. Fortunately for us the acupuncture treatments that Margareta got from George Long on Post Street and from John Cole on the road put her hyperactive thyroid back to normal, much to the dismay of her allopathic doctors who, at the time, refused to take acupuncture seriously. Our lives were always teetering on the edge of some disaster. What to do? The answer was always the same: keep trying the same thing over and over again. We were always getting involved in some sort of time-consuming project. Margareta was artistically prolific but she never wanted to do anything with it. She decided to get into photography, so we did. I say we, because I had some darkroom skills I had learned from my friend Marge back in the early sixties. I became Margareta's darkroom technician. It is unfortunate that she never really interacted in the San Francisco artistic community; as an artist she was really something. As a person, sad to say, she was severely damaged and could never seem to get out of her own way. Believe me, I was no better, but for better or worse I had an identity in the real world.

Back in Inzell in 1980 I turned forty years old. We were staying with our friends the Hirschbichlers in their *Gästehaus*. Hubert Hirschbichler was a speed skater as well as a business partner to his dad. We were sitting at the dinner table celebrating my birthday, and Hubert's dad looked at me and raised his glass. "Forty years old, your life is almost over!" He said it with humor, but to me it was like whistling past the graveyard. I did not know it at the time, but within the next couple of years I would make some drastic changes in my life.

Back in the States, as always, it was financial catch-up. More often than not I was broke coming back from Europe, but my long-suffering parents would always come through and help bail me out. I certainly would not have been happy if my children took me for granted this way and I have no idea what I would have done if the shoe was on the other foot. I'm not sure Mom and Dad did me any favors, but I will always be grateful to them for loving me unconditionally.

I owed Grunt/RCA one more project, so I started to think about putting a band together. Bob Steeler and I were still pals and he had been playing with a punk band called the Offs. At the time the bass player was a local cat named Denny DeGorio, aka Denny Boredom. I got to know Denny and we started to do some duet gigs. I took him to Italy for a short tour, and as the final RCA project was looming large, the next band was beginning to take shape. David Kahne got on board again. This time David convinced RCA to let us record and mix at the Automatt, where David still had an office. David had worked with Pearl Harbor and the Explosions, whose rhythm section featured John and

Hilary Hanes, aka the Stench Brothers, on drums and bass. David brought them in. The album would be called *Barbeque King*.

Though I didn't admit it at the time, I was missing the camaraderie and friendship that I had with Jack. I had distanced myself from everyone in the Airplane/Tuna family. My solution to Margareta's illness had been to totally isolate myself from all my old music friends. It was a poor solution, but it was nothing new for me. Faced with another recording project, I was afflicted with a dearth of material. My life with Margareta was becoming more clearly defined by the use of drugs and alcohol to make our waking hours tolerable. I was still convinced that cocaine was an essentially harmless drug. Margareta and I used to call cocaine "the shower drug." We couldn't get out of bed in the morning and into the shower without a blast and a cup of coffee.

The recording sessions for *Barbeque King* found me in an absolutely noncreative space, yet I had to put an album together. I leaned heavily on David and his team. I had always loved the Mickey and Sylvia song "Love Is Strange." Mickey Baker's guitar hook in that tune had been a source of wonder to me since I was a teenager. The twist was that instead of me getting to play Mickey's iconic lick, David planned to have Mike Butera play it on sax. It was actually a great idea but it took me awhile to get it.

This was to be the last project for RCA. Our vanity label Grunt proved to be just that, fruitlessly vain, and RCA was only holding on to the Airplane and what was left of Hot Tuna—by this point, me. I didn't realize how blessed I was to still actually have a record deal at a time when that still mattered. It would be years before I realized the very simple fact that if nothing changes, nothing changes . . . and nothing was changing. From cocaine to get going in the morning to vodka at night to push fear and pain away for a few moments—that was the rhythm of my life.

I still did not have enough material and the project needed more songs. The solution to my problems had not yet been found in heroin, but I was around it a lot. Back in those days, we believed in "chipping"—

occasional use of opiates. We used to think that if you just chipped, you weren't an addict yet. It was the same line of thinking that considered cocaine a "recreational" drug. We were hanging out in an apartment down in the mission and we encountered a junkie who couldn't find dope, so he smoked angel dust. You write about what you know, and even though I chose not to recognize this, my world was becoming a darker place. Enter my song "A Man for All Seasons."

Just a junkie on angel dust
Looking for a man to trust
One good shot, is what he's got
And that's enough

Listening now, these lyrics are incomplete and mutable. They are difficult to understand on the recording and when I listen to live versions on YouTube they are all a little different. I just used to make stuff up with this song. I found it difficult to listen to the recorded version on *Barbeque King*, because I am obviously drunk and sloppy. Good or bad, I have always been honest in the presentation of my music. On this track I hear a lost and unhappy man.

Denny DeGorio, John Stench, David Kahne, and I wrote a rock song called "Starting Over Again." I'm not saying this is or isn't a good song. By this time, on side one of the project, I really didn't have a dog in the fight and my survival did not depend on the depth of my songwriting. James Wilsey and Denny DeGorio did write a cool song for side one, however: "Runnin' with the Fast Crowd." At the time, Jimmy was playing with Chris Isaak, and in my opinion Jimmy was the architect of Chris's sound. The rest of the side had a Kokomo Arnold song, "Milk Cow Blues Boogie," and a rerecording of "Roads and Roads &."

Side two opened with our version of "Love Is Strange." Listening to it today, I find it's not bad. The next tune was called "To Hate Is to Stay Young." My personal frustrations were starting to reflect in my songs and frankly, I'm glad I didn't write more back then. I was not aging well as a human or an artist. It had been fifteen years or so since Jefferson Airplane first flew, and although the momentum of that band was still carrying me, my relevance was dissipating. Playing with younger musicians, talented though they might have been, left me on foreign soil. I was losing the connection to the roots that had always been so important to me as a person and an artist. I was allowing myself to be reinvented by others and it just didn't really work.

It wasn't all bleak. Denny and I had been messing with some changes and with the lyrics I wrote we wound up with a little number I called "Snout Psalm." I like this one!

It's a miserable morning got nothing to do
I wish there was something or someone to sue
There's time on the meter and I'm feeling blue
While I'm busy here
I feel like a piece of shopworn shit . . .

Shopworn shit indeed. At least I got a good song out of that moment. The title song for this album was inspired by two people who were in my life: Bill Thompson, our manager, and Larry "Bad News" Green, our San Francisco boxer friend who was part of the inspiration for "Funky #7." Larry had been around since the early seventies. There was something likable about him, but he was also dangerous and often really scary. Right before I cut the *Jorma* album, Larry had been shot in the back with a twelve-gauge during some sort of altercation in the Mission District. I visited him in the hospital and the doctor told me that the only thing that saved his life was the massive musculature in his back. Needless to say, he never boxed again. He was one of those guys that you're sort of happy to see at first. But before long you realize that things can go south in the blink of an eye, and you don't want to be a part of the collateral damage. In any case, between Bill Thompson's eccentric fashion sense and Larry Green's antics, I came up with "Bar-beque King," which I wrote right there at the Automatt.

The Barbeque King, he's coming to town
With his shiny pants, well, he looks like a clown
And he'll cook your barbeque, any way you please
He's filling up your kettle with every pound
The man can squeeze

Then, as if it never was, the time in the studio was over and things were about to get really crazy.

14

Broken Highway

Barbeque King was recorded in 1980 and came out in 1981. While in Inzell on the next to the last skating "vacation" I had met a man who called himself Eric de Furstemberg, who was in the music business. He decided he wanted to promote a European tour with me and the band that I was calling Vital Parts, which consisted of myself and the Stench Brothers, John and Hilary. We planned for the tour to take place in the late fall of 1981. I've seen different dates for this outing, but this is how I remember it.

John and Hilary and Margareta and I flew to Italy to begin the tour. Eric was there to meet us with his tech crew from Germany. Life is filled with "What was I thinking?" moments. I really had lost my direction in a lot of ways and it is amazing that I was able to keep on going. Part of me missed Jack and my musical life with him, but I had distanced myself from everybody from those days and that was that. In retrospect there was no logical reason for any of these decisions, at least none that could be put into words at the time.

I left the Airplane because for me the excitement and the group creative processes that had always sustained the band were gone. By the time I left, we had refined our MO for recording albums into a system that just didn't work for me. In the beginning we had always worked together in either writing or rehearsing new material as well as recording in the studio. As the seventies ushered itself in, except for gigs, we were rarely in the same place at the same time. I have no idea how the rest of the music establishment functioned but this just wasn't getting it for me. My time with Jefferson Airplane was done. Distancing myself from Jack was another story altogether. As I have said, my dealing with Margareta's hyperactive thyroid, as well as her manifestations of bipolar behavior, required that I insulate myself from the rest of the world and deal with it on my own. I have no idea how Margareta looked at these developments, but I didn't know how to ask for help. It doesn't make any sense to me today, but at the time nothing else made sense. Whatever Jack and I had or didn't have had no place in the small world I lived in with my wife. The same was true for my mom and dad and my brother. I just couldn't deal with someone else I cared about. Today it's hard to say what I was running from or to. I found myself in a situation where I needed to put together another band, and that was that. The band with John and Hilary was a good band, but for me, in a way, it was again marking time.

We played our way through Italy and worked our way up to Germany. In Germany I met this American expat musician named Shawn, who delightfully called himself China White. He started to hang around. Heroin had not yet taken possession of me, but Margareta was delighted that he was in the picture. Life was taking a much darker turn. We played a gig in Hof and drove on the autobahn corridor through East Germany and passed through the checkpoint into West Berlin. This was before the fall of the Soviet empire, so that corridor linked the city to West Germany. We were booked into the Metropole and played a couple of nights. After that, back through the corridor to Dortmund, where we played the Westfalenhalle as part of the Rockpalast series. This concert was recorded and there is a DVD available. I do not look happy. I am wearing an "IMPEACH REAGAN" T-shirt and people who've seen this DVD sometimes ask me about it. Truth be told, I don't remember where I got the shirt, and in a time when I complained about everything and always tried to find someone else to blame for my life predicament, perhaps I blamed Ronald Reagan too.

The accessibility of heroin in Germany and Margareta's love of it was not making me a happy camper. Not that I was really doing any better. I just wasn't doing dope . . . yet. After the Vital Parts tour, Eric had booked a couple of solo dates for me in Austria. We were in Inzell by this time skating, and Margareta was outraged that I would take a job during our "vacation." Her bipolar mood swings were now exacerbated by heroin withdrawals, and I convinced myself that she could not be left alone so I just ignored the gigs and didn't show up.

Shortly after this we were back in Munich so Margareta could score. There was an American guy there that night shooting dope, and I remember his last words as we left that apartment: "The dope ain't made that can put me down!" Gotta love junkie pride. He was dead before dawn and the paranoia that accompanies such moments sent us to Malmö, Sweden, for a couple days while things blew over. Many years later the irony is inescapable. She didn't want me to interrupt the skating by taking a night out to play a gig, but we could take a week off to hide out because someone died at an apartment where she scored. This is insanity at its finest.

Back in Germany we went back to Inzell and continued to skate and train. It just wasn't the same. I couldn't see it, but everything was starting to fall apart. I had a tour coming up back in the States when the season was over. I don't know how or when I came to this decision, but I wasn't going to use John or Hilary anymore. I think I was chasing the magic I always had with Jack. In any case I was without a band, but to fill this vacuum, I called one of the German cats from the Vital Parts European tour who was also an excellent bass player. His name was Alex and he and I rehearsed a little in Inzell, and then I shipped my gear back to New York. I had many friends in Long Island and the word got out through the Long Island network that I needed a drummer for the upcoming Vital Parts American leg. A friend named Ira Stengal got in touch with Joe Stefko, who agreed to do the tour.

Margareta and I packed our bags at the Hirschbichlers' in Inzell for what would be the last time and headed to Munich to the airport. We checked in and headed to Immigration. I showed my passport and the next thing I knew I was being arrested by the German police.

Eric de Furstemberg was having me arrested for my breaking the contract for the Austrian gig. Getting arrested was a first for me, and getting arrested in a foreign country added a whole new dimension to the experience. Margareta and the airport faded into the distance as I was transported back to Munich and processed. I was put in a cell with eleven other inmates. It was an octagon-shaped room with the toilet out in the open in the middle of the room. Going to the bathroom was a real adventure, especially if you had to crap. There were some aggressive souls in that room. There were nine Germans, two Austrians, and myself. The Austrians were real badasses; they didn't like Germans but tolerated Americans. They took it upon themselves to protect me for the few days I was there.

I got my phone call and got in touch with my friends Rita and Dieter, who came and got Margareta and found me a lawyer. I was in that German jail for three days and two nights. Rita and Dieter lent us some money and the lawyer posted bond. After I got processed for release, when I walked out of the jail into the street, there were Rita, Dieter, and Margareta. Margareta's first words to me, loving soul that she was, were these: "Well, did you get fucked in the ass?" I started feeling hurt, but then the surreal nature of the whole thing was so absurd . . . I laughed hysterically.

I had already sold one of the guitars that I had with me on tour to pay for the escape to Malmö. I had borrowed money from Rita and Dieter for the lawyer and bail. I was broke in Germany and broke back in the States. Back at the airport for the second time, Margareta, Alex the bass player, Dieter, and I headed to New York and the little tour, which would at least put some money back in my pocket. I rehearsed for a couple of days with Alex (sad to say I can't even remember his last name) and Joe Stefko and we played a cluster of gigs. Margareta, Dieter, and I went back to San Francisco. Dieter visited for a couple of days and then he went back to Germany, where my trial was getting under way in Munich. There was lots going on in my life and little of it seemed to have anything to do with music!

Margareta and I went back to Munich, where I was to appear in court. We never had any written contract so there was no real way for Eric to win his case. As it was being dismissed the judge spoke to me in German. There was a translator present, of course, and he gave me the judge's words: "Tell Mr. Kaukonen that doing business of this magnitude is not the same as buying or selling a cow in the country with a handshake." And that was that.

Back in San Francisco, music was back on the table again. I needed a band. Jack was busy with his band SVT, and I couldn't bring myself to call him yet anyway. We had really not spoken since I shelved everything in the late seventies to deal with Margareta's illness. As far as I knew Jack's life had also moved on; he was not a part of my world, I was not a part of his. I called Joe Stefko again and grabbed his bass-playing buddy Mike Visceglia, and they flew out to San Francisco and moved into Saint Francis Wood with Margareta and me. We started to rehearse while waiting for gigs to come in. The neighbors must have loved it! I had understood that there would be another Vital Parts album, and the three of us were counting on that. While that dream danced in the air we did our tour old school: in a van, with us, all our gear, and Margareta well armed with her personality and mood swings.

As these things sometimes go, we didn't make the money we were counting on, so in a break in our touring schedule, Joe invited me to come to New York to meet with the attorney Dennis Katz. Joe thought Dennis was the right guy because he had a relationship with RCA, and for the moment I was still an RCA artist. Joe also suggested Mick Ronson as a producer. Mick was a great guitar player who had done legendary work with David Bowie. He had creds way beyond that as well. It all seemed too good to be true, and it was. As we approached the end of the tour on the pier in Manhattan on the Hudson, Dennis came to me and strongly suggested that finishing the run solo was the only way I would wind up with any money. We got one more gig together as Vital Parts at the WLIR show at Fireman's Field in Hempstead, Long Island. Joe Stefko recalls that we each got a thousand bucks for the show. I wouldn't see Joe again for a couple of years.

Skating was done. It was almost never mentioned again. Speed skating gave me an identity outside being a member of Jefferson Airplane. Of course I loved the sport, but there was more to it than that. There was the physicality of it. The getting stronger, the technique improvement, and ability to test your work against the clock—that made it all so appealing. I was always striving for personal bests. There were no subjective artistic considerations. It was a simple and powerful way for me to feel a place in the world outside of the ephemeral considerations of the music business. For almost a decade, off-season training in San Francisco and the winter trips to Norway, Sweden, and Germany to skate on the 400-meter tracks had dominated my life. My professional life rotated around that schedule. Was it dysfunctional from a business point of view? You bet it was, but in an odd way it saved my life. When skating or training, I just didn't drink as much or use as many drugs. Without a performance-oriented goal—speed skating—there was no reason to lead a healthy life at all. It's amazing that I survived the years that were to come either physically or mentally.

I was getting a lot of solo gigs but Margareta hated it when I worked. I just accepted this without ever knowing or understanding why, which was utter insanity. The hole I was digging myself into just got deeper and deeper. I planned tours without her knowledge and at the last minute we would talk about it. Nothing was working for us. One day I got a call from a New Jersey promoter named Michael Gaiman, who suggested that I get in touch with Jack and that we reassemble Hot Tuna. My musical life was starting to come full circle.

I didn't know what was going on in Jack's life, but my professional life was becoming not only stagnant but also toxic. It's hard to imagine, given how close the two of us have been over the last thirtysome years, that we spent half a decade hardly saying two words to each other, but that's the hand I dealt us. When Michael Gaiman gave us what seemed like a commercially viable opportunity to reunite, I jumped at it and picked up the phone!

Without even discussing the fact that we hadn't really seen each other for years, Jack accepted this anomaly as if it were completely natural. We decided to put a band together that we would continue to call Hot Tuna. After all, Hot Tuna was always a Casady/Kaukonen affair! It was great talking to Jack again. On a primal level it was the beginning of an important healing process for me. I needed more time, but at least it was under way. I talked to my friend Michael Falzarano and asked him if he would be part of the project, and he said yes. Michael had his own band, Vauxhall, but he had been accompanying me recently on solo dates, and he and his wife, Claudia, were good friends with Margareta and me. In fact, if it hadn't been for Claudia I never would have met Michael. Claudia had been the receptionist at Mr. Broadways, an eccentric hairdressing salon Margareta and I frequented, and we had become friends.

We needed a drummer, and Michael recommended a guy he had been playing with, Shigemi Komiyama. Here's where the idea started to go south. Genius that I was, I decided that instead of playing the songs that got us noticed in the first place we should play all-new, never-before-heard material: "If they really love us, it won't matter what we play." That was the synopsis of the plan. It wasn't a great idea! Still and all, we were actually goal-oriented after being adrift for so long. We rehearsed while Michael Gaiman put together a crew of techs and staff, and we got ready to hit the road.

It was a good band, but it wasn't the band people expected to see. Jack and I did not fall back into our groove. We were both professionals, so we were able to play together in the same way we probably could have played with anyone. It's hard for me to say the magic was gone, but at best it was dormant. (Even *Pair a Dice Found* in 1990 did not really manage to unearth and resuscitate the truly creative aspects of our partnership.) It was an adventuresome project for us in many ways, but there were a lot of cooks in this kitchen: the intuitive creativity that Jack and I share when it works was largely dormant. Jack and I would work at it relentlessly over the next twenty-plus years to not only revive it, but to truly give it new life in a new century.

Margareta was now a bona fide junkie, and as her enabler it fell upon me to make sure she had the fix she needed. I was also the de facto bandleader, and the responsibility for the tour really rested on my shoulders. At that time I was incapable of making good decisions. We toured as long as we could but the project was ill conceived. When we realized our financial dreams wouldn't be realized, we disbanded and scattered for home. As always, there's plenty of blame to spread around. My part will always be on me.

Margareta and I started home in one of the rented vans accompanied by Michael and Claudia Falzarano. You had to be there to realize how truly insane this all was. We had no money, no credit cards, a rented van that had to be returned at some point . . . I almost can't believe it myself today, and I was there! It was financially touch and go but somehow we made it back to San Francisco. Life was a jagged graph of highs and lows. My creativity was completely worn away; it had been some time since I did anything I thought was really worthwhile. Margareta's behavior was increasingly erratic. We might be driving in the car and all of a sudden, apropos of nothing, she would blindside me with a shot to the face. At my age I have a lot of scars, but there are more on the right side of my face than there are on the left.

Back at home I ran into Tom Buckner, a college friend and an amazing baritone singer. He had a little Berkeley label called Arch Records that specialized in avant-garde recordings. His studio featured the Mark Levinson recording system, which had an unequaled signal-to-noise ratio. I toyed with the idea of playing with some of his heady jazz friends, but it just wasn't who I was. I didn't have those kind of chops and intellectually the music was over my head. The all-encompassing concept of Americana had yet to be invented. I was struggling to get back to basics. I saw myself as a storyteller first and a guitarist second.

Margareta had been writing poetry for years in addition to her relentless painting and graphic art. My mother, Beatrice, had financed a very limited letterpress edition of Margareta's work on handmade paper. The work was aptly titled *Shreds*. I think we both knew things were finally really coming apart, and perhaps *Shreds* itself was there to sound the death knell. I set a couple of her poems to music and started to record at the Arch studios in Berkeley. It wouldn't be finished until a couple of months later in the symphony hall in New Haven, Connecticut. I was actually able to do some more writing and this song, "Broken Highway," came just in time for the Arch project.

> *Broken highway, edge of town*
> *Be my main street when that sun goes down*
> *Broken highway, broken dream*

Wow! If that wasn't me, then I don't know what was!

A year or two before this record was made we had been in Inzell, Germany. It was one of those rare occasions when Margareta could sleep and I couldn't. I woke with wisps of the future in my consciousness and this is what I wrote: "Too Many Years."

> *Well I opened the door and I found I was looking at danger*
> *Well it's been so many years but we're hiding our faces like strangers*
> *She says that she's got to go, but there ain't no way*
> *I'm letting her walk while there's something to say*
> *Too many years just to watch our hearts dying this way*

That was really it in a nutshell. I don't think I have ever been able to say better what I felt back then. Some of Margareta's lyrics certainly spoke her truth too.

. . . she said her name was pain
her body was a cloud,
and her best friend was her vein . . .

We were living in a brittle world that could only be talked about in songs and poems. With Malles Meje—or Margareta, as this was one of her noms de plume—I wrote "Too Hot to Handle."

She's a woman that I cannot afford
Just look into her eyes a thousand bucks just roared
Into her vein

I was starting to drink during the day. Each day became a blur. My circle of friends was changing and I gravitated toward those who lived the way I was living. One day I threw some things into a bag, grabbed my old J-50, and got in my Chevy van. I drove away from our house, my stuff, and Margareta. That was it. I was gone! After twenty years, this long chapter in my life was over. Like leaving the Airplane, like putting Hot Tuna on hold, like so many decisions in my life—if I had it to do over again, I would do it differently. But I could see no other way.

On the way out of town I stopped by the Stone, a club on Broadway in North Beach there in San Francisco. Jerry Garcia was playing that night, and I don't really know what motivated me to stop. He was one of the first people I met when I came to the Bay Area. Maybe I just wanted to say goodbye. One of his handlers brought me to his dressing room. "Where's Jerry?" I wondered out loud. "In the closet . . . go on in," his buddy told me. Inside the closet Jerry was chasing the dragon with a gob of morphine base, or tar heroin. I told him I thought that looked like a lot of dope. "Not really," he said. "I've got it under control." I didn't know much about that stuff yet, so I just took a hit and walked out into the fall night, got into my van, and left California and my previous lives behind. About a decade later Jerry himself would be gone . . . really gone. Forever.

15

The Other Side of This Life

I drove across the country to New York and survived by crashing on people's floors. I cultivated a new circle of friends. I couch surfed in Manhattan for a while and then wound up renting a little house in Mount Tremper, New York, more or less halfway between Woodstock and Phoenicia. I was still employable, although I'm sure my performances were not as crisp as they should have been. Jack and I, having rediscovered each other during the short-lived 1983 Hot Tuna tour, started playing again as an acoustic duo.

Margareta and I needed to sell our house on Yerba Buena Avenue, so I went back to San Francisco to file for divorce and get rid of the property. As my life unraveled toward the end of our twenty-year marriage, I had quit paying the mortgage. It was utterly ridiculous considering what a low interest rate we had, but that's what I did . . . or didn't do. The house needed quite a bit of renovation; we had really let it go in the last years of our marriage. There was a hole in the kitchen wall where she had put her fist through the Sheetrock. With a marker she had written "THE PRICE OF PASSION" next to it. What a sense of humor! The house was not yet in foreclosure so I was able to refinance the mortgage and get it ready to sell. I never planned on returning to California as a resident and Margareta could certainly not afford to keep it, so it had to go. It took some work for the new buyers to make it habitable but they got a great deal! Dennis Katz was still serving as my attorney. Margareta just wanted to sign off but our legal system doesn't allow for this, so I found her an attorney. Her lawyer wanted to nail me to the wall, but all Margareta wanted was to sell the house and split the proceeds. She wasn't interested in anything else. That a relationship so long and so intense could just disappear like a receding tide is more than amazing. It's tragically unbelievable. Years later she left all her amazing artwork to Vanessa. They would become friends.

The house on Yerba Buena was sold. We bought the place for about sixty grand and sold it for about three hundred thousand dollars. It seemed like a lot of money; at the time I guess it was.

We started our life together as friends, learned to hate the space we shared, but in the end we parted as friends. Sad to say, we parted as friends who barely knew each other. How did this come to pass? The friend business, I mean. It was like osmosis. Somehow a moment of truth passed through the semipermeable membrane of denial and in that moment we actually saw each other as we were. We never got together and actually had an adult discussion about our lives—what happened, what didn't happen, who or what did or didn't do this and that. In retrospect our life together seemed like a series of faits accomplis. We always waited for the storms to come and then dealt with the consequences. We just accepted the consequences of the dissolution of a twenty-year relationship by dividing up the pieces and moving on. We never allowed each other to lay our cards on the table or talk honestly about who we were. This many years after the fact it still makes no sense to me. This will always be an unfinished conversation, so many things left unsaid. I will just have to live with that loss.

Margareta took her share of the proceeds from the house sale and moved to New York City, first living in the Gramercy Park Hotel and then getting an apartment until her money ran out. Then she returned to San Francisco. I have no idea what she did in order to survive. She never held a job in the years we were together but somehow she managed on her own once we split. When I heard she actually went through the bureaucracy necessary to qualify for supplemental security income from Social Security, I was amazed. That I considered this an accomplishment is indeed a sad commentary on the state of things.

Back east I had a gig at My Father's Place in Roslyn, Long Island. I was backstage waiting to go on when Jaco Pastorius himself showed up. I was familiar with Jaco because of his work with Weather Report, Joni Mitchell, and others. I was amazed that he would have come to see me play, and frankly I have no idea why he did. He wore a full-length duster and looked a little like a seventies Times Square pimp. He came up to me with a big smile and put out his hand. "Where's the babes and the blow?" he asked. "I thought you brought them," I fired back. That one of the great jazz bass players of all time wanted to play with me was baffling, but true. This chance encounter led to the formation of a band.

We decided to do some gigs together and he enlisted Rashied Ali to play drums. Rashied had played with John Coltrane, the jazz great. As a drummer and a percussionist Rashied was relentlessly creative. He rarely played the same song the same way twice, so his role as a rock drummer was idiosyncratic to say the least. I doubt we even rehearsed, but we got a gig at Jonathan Swift's in Cambridge, Massachusetts. We all checked into the hotel, but by the time we got to the club, Jaco was gone. Jaco's bass tech was a great guy named Steve Sacher, and Steve was there, so Jaco was out and Steve was in. Steve had his bass with him and played the gig and the short-lived band There Goes the Neighborhood was born. We added Steve's roommate Ben Prevo on guitar, and shortly thereafter Steve Farzan, a keyboard player from San Francisco, was added to the company. We played a lot around the Tri-State area and then actually booked a nationwide tour with no record and no national identity. We all traveled from New York to California and back in my 1977 Chevy Sportvan: manual transmission, no air-conditioning. On those days when the trip went through hot parts of the country, we deferred to Rashied as the oldest member of the band and flew him to the gig. The rest of us piled into the old van and drove. This was old-school touring at its finest.

I would run into Jaco a little later in the street drug scene not far from the West Village. It was not a happy time or place for either one of us. He was shooting hoops for spare change. I recall he was playing barefoot. It was yet another example of how fragile one's place in the universe is. I remember one time we went to pick up Rashied for a gig. Rashied lived in a building he owned on Greene Street in Lower Manhattan, and he also had a piece of a little jazz club next door called the Five & Dime. We were waiting on the street for Rashied to come out when the door to the Five & Dime blasted open as Jaco was thrown into the street. He rushed back and moments later he was out again, this time in the hands of a bouncer. We just sat in the van and hoped he wouldn't notice us. It seemed best to not get involved. Poor Jaco had just been bounced from a place where they liked him.

Another time I was at the old Lone Star Café down at the corner of Fifth Avenue and Thirteenth Street. It was in the dead of winter and it was snowing. When I left California in 1984 and moved to New York, the Lone Star would be my living room . . . my home when I had none. Cheers had nothing on the Lone Star. Everyone knew everyone, and everything—and I mean everything—was always going on there, always. Anyway, there was already about six inches of snow on the ground out on Fifth Avenue and there was little if any traffic. I believe Dr. John was playing, but I could be wrong. In any case, Jaco tried to get up on the stage and was turned away. The bouncers tried to get their hands on him but he eluded them by slipping out of his clothes. He then wedged himself in the revolving door at the front of the club and ultimately slipped out. He was last seen that night walking alone down Fifth Avenue, the only living soul on the street, ankle deep in snow—nude. It is strange and somewhat sad to say that events like this did not really seem strange to me back in the eighties.

Back in Woodstock, life was about to take a darker turn. Opiates had never been my thing. I had sworn that I would never do any of the things I saw Margareta do in the final years of our relationship. But I did. Many of my friends in Woodstock were junkies. Like they say, "If you hang around a barber shop long enough, you're going to get a haircut." Margareta used to say that being addicted managed time. Every moment in every day had to be scrupulously scripted. Going up, coming down, or merely maintaining, there was no such thing as spare time. Managing your time was essential if you wanted to keep the wolf from your door. There is no way to describe myself at that time as anything other than strung out.

When I moved upstate to Mount Tremper, I ran into Rick Danko while shopping in Woodstock. Rick and I had gotten to know each other as brother musicians on the road over the years and it was nice to see a familiar face. We also frequented the same bar in Kingston, Uncle Willy's. Willy was a great guy and the times spent in his club were always fraught with grim but delightful debauchery. Nights at Uncle Willy's were legendary! Rick and I started playing at Willy's a lot. Along the way we discovered we both enjoyed some of the same substances, and he had good connections. What a bonanza for a new arrival to the area.

I started to spend a lot of time working with Rick, and in addition to our "social" connection, we also found ourselves with the same agent. As a result of these synchronicities I got to do gigs not only with him, but with Levon Helm and The Band as well. It gave me a chance to not only play with world-class musicians, but also to cash in on their visibility as well as sharing mine.

Thank G-d there are always humorous moments to brighten the day. One time Rick and I went to Albany, New York, to be on an NPR radio show that Artie Traum was hosting. I had just enough dope on hand to get from Woodstock to Albany, do the show, and get home again. At the radio station Artie wanted to interview us separately and I went first. I finished my gig with Artie and came back out to the waiting room, and Rick went into the studio. I looked for my stash . . . and it was gone. Rick was the only guy there; I knew he took it but he denied it vehemently, with an unbelievable hurt look on his face. He was just so lovable in his denials that even under the circumstances, I couldn't get mad at him. He had to drive home. He was cheerful all the way, me not so much.

That's how it was being a friend of Rick's. You would tolerate anything, and no matter what else was going on, when he sang it was always with the voice of an angel. There was more to our friendship than just drugs. We genuinely liked each other as people and we loved to make music together. We frequently showed up at each other's gigs and sat in with each other. We would play acoustic guitars and sing songs together for hours. As previously mentioned, I would often be included in The Band's touring endeavors. It was an honor and a treat. They let me ride on their bus, and believe it or not I had never ridden on a tour bus before. I felt like a star. One time they took me with them on a fairly long Japanese tour. While I was there I also got to do some solo dates, which opened the door for me to start touring in the Far East. Being in Japan with The Band in the eighties was a never-to-be-replicated experience.

Being strung out required meticulous preparation when traveling abroad, especially in countries with draconian drug laws. I signed into a methadone clinic. At the time I didn't know as much about alcoholism and addiction as I do today, and for a brief moment in time, I thought methadone would cure me. In any case, I showed up clean weekly to convince the folks at the clinic that I was a good scout and could be trusted to play by the rules. I then convinced the doctor I needed take-homes to travel, and against all odds he gave them to me. All this pre-supposed that you were convincing and your piss was clean, and at least for the moment, it was. I still needed a safe way to spirit this stuff into other countries. I got to thinking, and what I came up with was dissolving the doses into a bottle of Pepto-Bismol. The concoction was still sickening pink but with careful measuring, it did the trick and made international travel possible.

Let me give you a sidebar on methadone as I see it. This drug and others like it are designed to keep you a slave. If you truly want to be clean and sober, quitting drugs and drinking would seem to be a good idea. If nothing changes, nothing changes! As an author's disclaimer I should say, I am not an expert on recovery and am not going to delve into this much more, other than to say that living what I consider to be a good life is always a work in progress. Being able to play music sustained me in a time when I was spiritually bankrupt. Playing music was all I really loved to do, and having given myself a potpourri of handicaps to deal with, I struggled to live what I considered to be a normal life. Somehow, I made it through.

The guitar never abandoned me. In retrospect it didn't seem like a lot to hold on to, but it was. It was a mutual love affair and is as strong as ever today. I never lost sight of the hope the guitar held out to me as a teenager.

After the ill-fated "reunion" with Michael Falzarano and Shigemi Komiyama, Jack and I got back to basics and started to tour again as an acoustic duo. I wasn't really doing any writing but I never missed a chance to play. Jack and I were starting to find a new perspective on our identity. The friendship was still there, but it took over a decade for the music to start to grow again. At least the pieces were in play.

In the summer of 1988 we toured through the South, through Florida and down to Key West. We checked into the Pier House and went to our second-floor rooms overlooking the hotel beach. I looked out the window, and there right under my balcony was a very pretty girl sunning herself. She was lying on her back, so I could see how delightful she was. In that one happenstance moment G-d opened a window into my future. Jack, our sound guy Ricky Sanchez, and our tour manager Mike Roberts, witnessed this wonder with me. The girl sensed motion upstairs and looked up. We scurried back from the window like rats afraid of the sun. I closed the blinds and thought that was that. This was July 3, 1988, and a great change in my life was indeed about to happen.

That night Jack and I appeared onstage at the Pier House. Normally when I'm onstage I exist only in the world of my music, but on this night I chanced to look toward my left and there, scant steps away, was the girl from the hotel beach. She was backlit in a diaphanous dress. She had nothing on underneath. Wow! We finished the set and I asked Mike Roberts to see if he could bring her backstage so I could meet her. Now that I had gotten a good look, I realized this was indeed a woman and not a girl. We got to talking and I was beyond smitten. This was something I had never experienced before and I really did not know how to handle it. When you meet someone, what is it that makes it "the real thing"? Based on my previous life, I would not have known. But I knew this was special! She introduced herself as Vanessa and that was the beginning.

She told me that if the guys and I wanted to go sailing on July 4, to call her in the morning. With a day off in Key West, the boys and I got up bright and early and decided to take Vanessa up on her offer. We called about seven. She had just gotten in about seven thirty, so we caught her right before she was about to hit the sack. She scurried around to find her friend who had a boat, and before we knew it, on the Fourth of July, 1988, we were sailing in the beautiful water off Key West. She and I took the Zodiac off the stern line, took some fins and snorkel gear, and went off by ourselves. Snorkeling with her in that crystal water in that moment, I was freer than I may have ever been. Just as we were pulling back into the dock, fireworks began to fill the evening sky. Happy Birthday, America! Back at the hotel, Vanessa joined Jack and me for dinner. We talked and talked, and when I took her back to the Truman Annex where she was staying, we had the most amazing kiss goodnight. This was better than fireworks.

It was like coming home.

The next day Vanessa was going to swim with the dolphins, and Jack and I were to fly to LA for some gigs. The Jefferson Airplane was about to rear its head again in the form of the 1989 reunion and we planned some meetings to talk about that possibility. I went to my rental car, a white Pontiac convertible with a black top. Under the windshield wiper was a note from Vanessa: "JORMA . . . IT WAS A SPIRITUAL THING . . ." And in that moment of clarity, it was.

Anniversary

December 2, 2002, 9:38 p.m.

How does this all begin? Vanessa and I have our fourteenth anniversary coming up. I asked her what she wanted. "Write me a story," she said, "a story of us." "OK," I countered. I mean, she's really tough to shop for. Shopping is such a profound activity and she is so focused on the essence of what she likes, it's tough to hit that nail on the head. So hey, a story it is.

How does this all begin? Well, I could start with the third of July, 1988, in Key West, Florida, but in a sense, it all goes way back. December 23, 1940 . . . A child is born and his parents bring him into the world. Having brought him thus far, they then begin to shape his life with their values and in some small way their dreams. This is not to say that parents are responsible for who their children become. I do not believe that for a moment. There are always choices to be made and each individual must make them. That said, in the beginning, our parents deal the cards face up and pick the ones we are allowed to keep. In any case, as we grow, we think we are honing survival skills . . . tools to make our way in the world. Some are survival skills, and some are the tools of destruction, and these we hone as well. And so I was born, and lived and grew. As a child, for some reason it seemed to make sense to surround myself with mendacity and false dreams. Without the slightest idea of who I really was, it seemed easier to submerge myself in smoke screens . . . living as a chameleon, all things to all people.

Well, enough on this front. I'd like to think that I have always had decency lurking in the far reaches of my inner self. Looking for love, well, if not in all the wrong places, at least not knowing what love was to begin with. Writing songs about idealized situations . . . dream goals. There I was, hurtling down a road, being about as proactive as a bullet from a high-powered rifle. You get the picture . . . an average American guy who grew up in the fifties without a clue. Enough background . . . Let's fire ahead to July 3, 1988.

I'm down in Key West with Jack for an acoustic Hot Tuna show. We're

staying at this hotel on the beach, I forget the name. But what I'm not forget-
ting is looking out the window down at the beach and seeing this lovely lady
sunning herself. Well, since she was scantily clad, and quite shapely to boot, I
found myself peeking through the curtains at her for some time. Imagine my
surprise later that evening after the show when my road manager brings her
backstage to meet me. Well, I have to tell you I was immediately infatuated.
Actually, it was more than infatuation. I mean, I was a hurting lunatic back
then, but there was something about this woman that struck an eternal chord
in me. Her name was Vanessa.

Well, Vanessa had an agenda of her own that night, but she foolishly of-
fered to take the gang sailing the following day. At around 0700 on the morning
of the Fourth of July, we called to take her up on her kind offer. Now, what
she had to do to make this happen is her story, not mine. Suffice it to say that
it happened and we went sailing. Now, on this little jaunt a lot of whacko
stuff happened, BUT the most amazing thing that happened was that I found
myself completely in love with this woman. I brushed her arm with my lips
as the fireworks began to start that Fourth of July.

Now, at this time in my life, I was completely unfit to be alone with my-
self, much less anyone else, but I knew I wanted to be with Vanessa. In spite
of the complete unmanageability of my life at the time, obsession was one thing
I could understand . . . and I was obsessed with Vanessa. I wanted to spend
the rest of my life with this woman. On December 7, 1988, we were married
in Key West on the schooner Wolf. In attendance were a large number of our
collective friends, and of course that magnificent specimen of a bull terrier,
Marlo.

Our life together as husband and wife began tumultuously . . . I knew I
wanted to be happy and serene with Vanessa, but I didn't have the slightest
idea how to go about this. I was addicted to drugs and alcohol, and what
was left of my spiritual life was a fortuitous accident. I know now that to
have a life well lived, first you must live life well, but at the time I had no
idea how to do this. I would like to think that I always had the best of inten-
tions, but good intentions and two bits won't even get you a phone call in
Manhattan today. As the years began to unfold, I was never able to give

Vanessa the love she deserved and the honesty she needed. You see, honesty was a quality I knew nothing about . . . just a little-used word. My life was spiraling into a bottomless pit, but the lifeline that sustained me was the thread of love and hope that I always felt Vanessa held out to me over the precipice. My love for her did not wane, in fact it grew . . . but it grew in a window box that only I could see, in a private garden that only I had the key to. I kept her locked away . . . for when or what I did not know. As for my own life, it continued to shrink.

    I would have disappeared, a forgotten footnote, but something made me realize that something was wrong with me. I was with the woman that I wanted to love and be with for the rest of my life, but I had no idea what to do with any of these feelings. I knew I was killing myself, but worse was the fact that I knew I was killing Vanessa's feelings for me. I had lied to her and dishonored her and I was killing the spirit within myself. I had done none of the things that I wanted to do in my heart. I was still the emotional adolescent simply thinking about a good and complete life, but doing nothing to attain it. My inability to get out of my own way was overcome in a cataclysmic way. A son appeared on the scene . . . my son . . . a son with a woman other than Vanessa. Well, this was a wake-up call that could not be denied. I had deeply injured the one most important to me, and it looked as if all my hopes for our future were dust in the wind. There I was, confronted with an undeniable reality, feelings I finally had to deal with. I cannot say what was going through Vanessa's heart, that is her story, but I can tell you that I was now prepared to go to any lengths to become a better man and at least to be able to show her my heart, if she was still interested in seeing it.

    Vanessa bestowed the gift of possibility to our damaged relationship. She was out of the window box now, the walled garden a thing of the past. A new period in our life began. She had decided to stick around for a while, why, I can't really say. I don't know what I would have done had the roles been reversed, but the gift of possibility was still mine.

    I began to learn about living, and this gave me the ability to begin to learn about loving. We're not talking obsessions any more . . . no more quick fixes or impulse buying . . . We're talking about real living. Vanessa had her fortieth birthday this year. When I was forty, I was just about to commit myself wholeheartedly to jumping into the pit. At almost sixty-two, I have learned that I do not even need to walk close to the edge. My path is not without thorns, but at least I am not consigning myself to Hell today.

As Vanessa and I approach our fourteenth anniversary, a number of things have become apparent. I do not know what tomorrow will bring for anyone, but I do know that for today that I am with the woman who is the love of my life. I know that time once spent cannot be recaptured . . . that for some-one to give you their life and time on this earth with honesty and love is the greatest gift of all. Vanessa has given me this with an open heart. She could have made many choices over these years, but she chose to grow with me. You can't wrap this present up, it wraps you.

December 7, 2002 . . . well I guess Pearl Harbor Day might come to mind, but those Historical Memories that only really exist for those of us who grew up in that time cannot compare with the love of those who are surviving the battleground of the heart. Vanessa has given me the timeless gift of her time with me. She has blessed me with so many of her numbered hours on this earth that she might be in my life today so I can write this for her!

To really write the story of Vanessa and myself, I would have to do noth-ing but that for years, so this is but a synopsis. I have written these pages with Vanessa existing in the third person because that is the way the flow of the writing went. But Vanessa, I want you to know this, this story is for you and you never exist in the third person for me in my heart or in our reality. You have given me the gift of yourself for fourteen years. Today, let me tell you that the greatest gift I could give you is my gratitude, love, and honesty. You are the cornerstone of my heart. I know sometimes I do things that irritate you . . . Hopefully these moments are but pebbles being washed smooth in the flowing stream of life . . . Hopefully we will be able to float down that stream together. Perhaps we will reach the sea . . . perhaps not. My fondest hope is that we make the journey together, shielded by love, compassion, honesty, and serenity.

Vanessa, you are the heart of my heart, and I love you!

Happy Anniversary!

Jorma

My life had never really been about doing the right thing, much less the next right thing. It had always been about doing the next expedient thing, and expedience did not necessarily require truth and honesty. In any case, Jack and I flew to California to play some gigs and talk to the remaining Jefferson Airplane principals about the possibility of a reunion.

On March 4, 1988, Jack and I played the Fillmore Auditorium in San Francisco. Grace Slick, Paul Kantner, Papa John Creach, and Will Scarlett joined us. Here is the set we played:

Set 1:
I Know You Rider
Hesitation Blues
Walkin' Blues
The Other Side of This Life
That's the Bag I'm In
I'll Be All Right Someday
99 Year Blues
Mariel
Wooden Ships
Third Week in the Chelsea
Papa John's Down Home Blues
Keep On Truckin'

Set 2:
Keep Your Lamps Trimmed and Burning
Candy Man
I See the Light
Martha
Embryonic Journey
Ice Age
Comandante Carlos Fonseca
San Francisco Bay Blues

Genesis
Parchman Farm
Good Shepherd
Let Us Get Together Right Down Here
John's Other
Vampire Women
Have You Seen the Stars Tonight
Mann's Fate
Put It in My Hands
I'm Movin'
Killing Time in the Crystal City
Water Song
America
Volunteers

This set list is important because it was the first time that Jack, Paul, Grace, and I got together since the band scattered in 1972. This little meeting of the minds set the stage for the Airplane reunion of 1989. It was a helluva show for the audience, and we found we still liked each other and could still make music. I convinced myself that there was gold remaining in those hills. Grace wanted powerhouse management, and she got it from Howard Kaufman Management in the person of Trudy Green, who would be our personal manager. We're talking about big dogs in the music business; this world was completely alien to me. Jefferson Starship, with Grace and Paul, and later the renamed Starship with Grace, attained levels of popular and financial success we never dreamed of with the Airplane.

Looking back on it, I can see that the Airplane reunion was more another incarnation of the Jefferson Starship than an actual Airplane project. The producers, the sidemen, the songs, the videos, almost all of it was geared toward eighties pop stardom. That didn't really occur to me at the time, but that was the reality. I believed I might make as much as a million dollars. How could I say no? In any case, the ball started rolling again with that little meeting.

Back east in my world, I was pursuing Vanessa relentlessly with five phone calls a day. In a pre-cell-phone world this meant pay phones and more pay phones. On July 17, 1988, Jack and I were to play the Cabooze in Minneapolis, and I convinced Vanessa to fly up and join me for the show. It was still magic to see her. She had to get back to Key West where she was working as an interior designer, and after I dropped her off at the airport, Jack said to me, "If you let this one get away, I'm going to punch you right in the face!" I resolved I was not going to let this one get away, but I still had a relationship with a woman in New York. Today that word, "relationship," brings with it a minefield of meanings. The relationship I had was really more about sharing storage space than anything else. I should have slammed the door shut on that one the second I met Vanessa, but I let it drag on. Back in those days, fear of a confrontation could stop my heart. I still don't like conflict, but now I try to deal with it straight on and get it out of my way.

In any case I followed Vanessa to Woodstock, Vermont. Her boss owned quite a bit of property there and she commuted from Key West. Regardless, I would have followed her anywhere. "Relationships make me sick," she would tell me. I was sure that ours would be the exception. I was relentless. She had more than enough work to keep her busy in Key West and New England, but I constantly pestered her to visit me whenever she could. We were driving north on the New York Thruway (that's I-87) and at 3:28 p.m. at mile marker 57 between Harriman and Newburgh, I asked Vanessa to marry me.

She said, "Can I think about it?" I said, "What's to think about?" This was indeed the woman I had always wanted to share my life with. She agreed to marry me and everything started to move at lightning speed. We decided to get married on the schooner *Wolf* out of Key West. My old friend Rocky Williams (of Big John and Rocky fame) agreed to be best man. Jerry Weiner, Vanessa's best friend, was her maid of honor. (By the bye, Jerry is a man, not a woman. We never were very conventional.) It is rumored that Jerry was Meyer Lansky's massage therapist. What provenance! Michael Falzarano flew to Miami, and I drove up on my motorcycle to pick him up and bring him down to the Keys. His wife Claudia followed in a day or so. My dear friend and agent Steve Martin flew down from New York. My oldest friend, Jack, was also there. When I had asked Vanessa to marry me, she was separated from her husband but the divorce had yet to be finalized. The final papers came through six hours before our wedding. Timing is everything.

The *Wolf* put to sea an hour or so before sunset. The sea was almost like glass. There was just enough wind to fill the sails. With the sun setting magnificently, the only sounds other than the voices of the guests were the creaking of the rigging and the water gently slipping by the hull. At 5:39 p.m. the captain brought the *Wolf* around as the minister, Giselle, joined us in marriage. One of the deckhands fired a two-inch black powder cannon as we kissed.

Vanessa has always been a woman with plans and ways to execute them. By the time we got married she had already found us a little conch house about two blocks from the Southernmost Point marker. I kept the house in New York, but moved most of my things to Key West in October 1988. By this time I was off the methadone program, and for a while opiates were not part of my life. I was not, however, clean and sober by any means. There were so many new and wondrous things beginning to evolve in my life with Vanessa. I had indeed found the love of my life but was not quite sure what to do next.

I have not mentioned my parents here for a long time. I see them today as having been long suffering and tolerant of my dysfunctional life. They let me make mistakes and helped when they could without getting too close to the fire. It was time to take Vanessa to California so Beatrice and Big Jorma could meet the new Mrs. Kaukonen. In San Francisco, Dad picked us up at the airport and drove us to his house in Mill Valley.

My mother and father had their own lives filled with anomalies. As

Mom was wont to say when she felt like speaking truth, "Your father was never faithful to me." Back then I would have rather walked on broken glass than have a real conversation with one of my parents about their lives. In retrospect, it was an honor that she felt she could talk to me like that. In any case, Mom really needed to live her life in her own space, unencumbered by Dad and his baggage. She had served him faithfully as the dutiful embassy wife during his career, and she was done holding his hand 24/7. She bought a beautiful piece of property in Talmont in North Lake Tahoe and built a house on the side of the mountain. She lived there for over two decades and became quite a force in the local community. She was an environmental warrior long before it became a well-known concept.

Vanessa and I spent the night with Dad in the Mill Valley house, and then we all set out to drive to Tahoe. It was December, and December through the mountains on I-80 can be treacherous and unforgiving. The snow started falling around Auburn; by the time we got to Truckee it was a full-on whiteout blizzard. Roads were closed unless you had four-wheel-drive or chains. Dad had a set of chains for the front-wheel-drive Honda, so we pulled off the road so I could install them. There was already about six inches of snow on the ground. I lay on my back in the slush until the job was done. Then I took the wheel and drove the three of us over the Donner Pass, down into Truckee, and on into North Lake Tahoe. As we were getting out of the car, Dad looked at Vanessa and said, "You're a Kaukonen now."

Mom and Dad had suffered through my sundry relationships and tended to view them with a jaundiced eye. In spite of her inherently suspicious nature, Mom managed to be better than lukewarm in accepting Vanessa into our family. Mom would have loved it more if Vanessa had been an English major who spoke four languages rather than an engineer and an interior designer, but that's what she got.

We were sitting by the fire in Mom's chalet when we got a call from the Key West Police Department. Crackheads had broken into our little conch house, stolen and sold off everything valuable in the house, and moved in and made themselves at home. So much for the honeymoon. We were at the airport in Reno, Nevada, the next day and on our way back to the Keys.

We had become friends with some undercover policemen down there, and by the time we got in, some of our things had already been recovered. The thieves got a Heckler & Koch P-7 pistol and a myriad of other things. All of Vanessa's clothes had been worn and were filthy. Our K5 Blazer had been hotwired and driven around. The locking gas cap had been broken off so they could put gas in the car and drive it. It was not quite the honeymoon we had planned.

We were not quite done with Key West yet. Soon there was another attempted robbery. Vanessa looked out the upstairs back window and saw the lower half of a human body sticking out of our kitchen window. She called the cops while I came around the back of the house with a twelve-gauge shotgun and racked the slide. It was a real attention-getter for the thief! He was cautiously extricating himself from the window, careful to keep his hands in sight, when Vanessa and the police came around the corner. "Jorma, don't shoot him!" she screamed. "Hold the gun on him while we cuff him," one of the officers said. They cuffed him and threw him in the back of the cruiser while they thanked me for my civic assistance. South Florida in the eighties—you can't make this stuff up.

By this time we were late for the dinner we had planned with some friends and Leonard Bernstein. After a delicious dinner and some convivial merrymaking, Lenny reached his hand around me to pat me on the bottom. What he patted was the Browning Hi-Power pistol I was carrying. He began to laugh hysterically. Good times in Key West in the heyday of the crack epidemic!

The fact that we were about done with Key West coincided with plans for the Jefferson Airplane reunion, which were taking seed. There we were, Vanessa and myself, not even two months married and getting ready to pull up the shallow roots we had put down in Key West. I convinced myself that the money we were promised would come to pass, but I wanted an ally in the project. My brother, Peter, agreed to sign on. Vanessa shelved her job, and she and I packed up our stuff and closed the house. Back to Woodstock we went. Thank goodness we never let go of the rental up there; we had a place to go while we got ready to head to LA for the reunion project. I had found the person I wanted to spend the rest of my life with, and I truly felt like I knew her. I still didn't really know the first thing about myself, though—and navigating the waters of the coming set of storms would take more than I had at the time.

16

Do Not Go Gentle

As the second act with Jefferson Airplane was looming large, I remember what Margareta said to me the first time around: "When you sell your soul to the Devil, it's very expensive to buy back!" How true, how true! In the beginning it seemed like a good career move considering I really didn't have much of a career at that time. We were promised a lot of money and that made sense. After all, we had been big stars twenty years prior. Why could it not happen again? Jefferson Starship, which became the Starship, had more than kept the ball rolling. They had a string of hits and were definitely on people's radar.

I was newly married to the love of my life. I had never experienced an emotion this pure before, and I had no idea how to deal with it. This was compounded by the uncertainty of trying to get clean, if not quite sober. My creativity as a writer was slender to say the least. I don't know what I expected by bringing my brother, Peter, into the fold. I had tried in the past to work with him but the chemistry was never there, and that chemistry has always been necessary for me to make music. That it did not work for me is not my brother's fault.

Grace and her team got Howard Kaufman Management, one of the big companies in the music business, to take us on. Trudy Green was our face-to-face contact. I flew out to LA from Woodstock by myself, with Vanessa to follow shortly after. Trudy rented a Mustang convertible for me and checked me and some of the others into the Mondrian hotel on the Sunset Strip. Someone recently asked me, "How did you hide your heroin habit from Vanessa?" The simple answer is that you can't hide a heroin habit from anyone. Vanessa knew I had been in a methadone program and was trying to get off the juice. Neither of us realized at the time that methadone is far from recovery; it is really just a way to mark time. I was marking time. We were recording at the Record Plant in Los Angeles. Vanessa was back at the Mondrian when a package arrived for me. She opened it, of course, and inside were taped lines of dime bags. She jumped in her Jeep and drove over to the studio. I was in the game room playing pinball. In that moment, I was the Pinball Wizard and I could do no wrong. I was racking up replays, lights were flashing. For about a minute, I was the man! Vanessa walked into that room with the package of dope in her hand. The energy of her rage and disappointment filled the room and even the machine went south on me. I lost all the balls in the blink of an eye. The game was over! "What's this?" she asked, holding the package out. I looked at it and replied, "I don't know. People just send me things!" A dope fiend will say anything and expect it to be believed. "Give it to me. I'll get rid of it." Yeah . . . right! Vanessa knew what was going on and I have no real idea why she continued to stay with me.

The Mondrian is very expensive. Renting convertibles in LA isn't cheap, either. It didn't really register with me that all this money being spent was an advance, and advances must be paid back. We started to rehearse. Paul, Marty, and Grace brought songs. I have no idea if they were written for the album or if they already existed. I brought three songs. The first two were "Ice Age" and "Too Many Years," both of which I had previously recorded. I also crafted a jam tune, "Upfront Blues," which was basically an excuse for me to play lap steel. Fun, but not the stuff of hits! Still and all, I did get three tunes on the project.

We started rehearsing with Ron Nevison, who had produced hits for Jefferson Starship. Without even taking into consideration my glass nerves, things were different than when we had played together before. That shouldn't have been a big surprise to me, but it was, at least in the beginning. Twenty years had elapsed since we had been a band. The family that we were in the sixties had long since grown up—and apart. The magic had been replaced with agendas. There are a lot of ways to make music. The process for me has always been an organic one. I am invited by my emotional environment to participate in the process of creation. At that time my environment was in a state of flux, but there was no time or place for flux in this project. I was truly not ready for the "efficiency" that this production required.

When Vanessa was finally on her way to LA I took a personal advance and bought her a bare-bones 1989 Jeep YJ. This little car cost $8,000 out the door. I passed the Mustang rental off to my brother and started driving the Jeep. Manual transmission, ragtop, LA weather, what's not to like? Trudy Green from HK Management got a real estate agent to look for houses for us. She found one on Beverly Glen Boulevard that belonged to John Rubenstein, the actor and musician. It was a palatial hillside mansion, LA modern. The walk-in closet was bigger than the bedroom in most houses I had lived in. Vanessa and I started unpacking and set about to make this place our home . . . at least for the moment.

The Airplane continued to rehearse and get ready for the album. I was still trying to find my place in this evolving world, and that included being a husband, something I really knew nothing about even though I had been married to Margareta for twenty years. My contributions to the project fell into the "something borrowed, something blue" school of thought. Vanessa and I were lonesome without our bull terrier Marlo, so when there was a break in the action we flew back to New York, snagged Marlo, and started driving back to LA in our 1977 K5 Blazer.

Driving across the United States is always a majestic process. Even the long flat states like Kansas have an eternal magnificence to them. On US 83 in Oakley, Kansas, who can forget the world's largest prairie dog, the five-legged calf, and all the rattlesnakes? This is roadside America at its finest . . . and right across the street is the Colonial Steakhouse. (If you can't get a great steak in Kansas, you're never getting a great steak.) In New Mexico we stopped by the side of the road to watch the sunset over the ancient cliff dwellings. Just before the last sliver of sun made its way to the other side of the world, Lee Greenwood came on the radio singing "God Bless the USA." Corny? Maybe. Extremely moving? You bet. You had to be there!

The air conditioner barely worked in the old Blazer. Mostly it circulated lukewarm air. With the dog on board we had to occasionally get a day room in a hotel with air-conditioning until the sun went down and we could drive comfortably. Before we knew it we were back in our house on Beverly Glen, and the preparation for the album continued.

With the advent of new digital technology and automation, "bricklaying" tunes was the order of the day. Instead of the band playing ensemble the music was built in layers, part by part. I had never really worked in the new environment before. Ron Nevison's vision was his own and I didn't fit well into that scenario. I am not a session player. Sometimes I am invited to play on other people's projects and I always caution them about my shortcomings. I'm a slow learner and at that time I really knew little about bricklaying a song. Overdubs were one thing— we learned about that back in the sixties. But crafting a tune in parts was alien to me. I admit that over the years I have created more than one Frankensolo. It seems to be the adult way to do things these days, but it's just not as much fun.

In the old days we would have pals on a project, but the core of the Airplane always did the heavy lifting ourselves. On this one we had Kenny Aronoff on drums. Kenny is one of the great drummer/percussionists of all time and it was an honor to work with him. David Paich added keyboards. Michael Landau added some guitar work. The wondrous Nicky Hopkins was in the keyboard mix, as well as Efrain Toro on percussion and Steve Porcaro programming keyboards. Steve's brother Mike did some bass playing. My brother, Peter, played guitar as well, and Mark Volman and Howard Kaylan from Flo and Eddie and the Turtles did some background vocals. Of course there was Grace Slick, Jack Casady, Marty Balin, Paul Kantner, and myself from the original core.

Why in the world did we need this massive mélange of musical talent to make an album? Looking back, I totally get that a lot of it had to do with Ron Nevison wanting a crew that he was comfortable with. The Airplane itself hadn't been an active entity for over a decade and a half. We no longer had the unified vision that we had in the sixties. We also no longer had the youth. We could no longer count on the magic finding us. We had to seek it out and this was proving to be difficult.

I always tell my students and my kids that realistic expectations are one of the keys to a happy life. None of my expectations involving the Airplane reunion were realistic. I can't speak for the others, but as simple as it sounds, I just didn't grok our mission. The Airplane had few recognizable hits other than "White Rabbit" and "Somebody to Love." We never had that powerful identity that comes with a string of hits. We needed a healthy splash of creativity, and in that LA world where we found ourselves, we needed to be team players.

I could have said no, but I didn't. I said yes for all the wrong reasons.

With the recording done, we hit the road for the tour. Vanessa and I packed up and got ready to head back to Woodstock. I had two motorcycles in LA: a 1984 Softail, the first year of the Evo-engine Harleys, and a Yamaha V-Max. We had to get these two machines home so I bought a little trailer. This was ill thought out from the beginning. The trailer was really designed for dirt bikes. It was short and had very small wheels. The V-Max and the Softail each weighed well over five hundred pounds and the tires were so wide, they barely fit on the tracks to hold them. The K5 Blazer was a cool 4×4 but it had a short wheelbase and was poorly suited for towing a trailer with two heavy bikes on board.

We shipped what we could and packed Vanessa's Jeep YJ and the

Blazer with everything we had left. With the trailer hitched up and the bikes loaded, we enlisted the help of our good friend Chuck Fadel to help make the transcontinental run. We figured we'd zip up I-5 to the Bay Area, visit my dad, and then head across the Bay Bridge to jump on I-80 for the run to New York. We started driving north on the I-5. I was driving the Blazer with the bike trailer behind it and Vanessa was behind me in the Jeep. Chuck rode shotgun with me. We headed up what was once the Grapevine, and on the way down I started to pick up speed. The trailer had no brakes of its own and I was not experienced in towing. I tapped the brakes and the trailer started to fishtail. One minute I could see nothing but the trailer in the left mirror, and the next it filled the right. I could hear Vanessa screaming at us on the CB radio. The solution was the gas pedal, not the brake pedal, so I kept accelerating. The grace of G-d was with me yet one more time in my travel life. I made it down the north side of the Grapevine and gently allowed myself to coast to a stop. We pulled off into a rest area, got out of our vehicles, and hugged each other.

We continued the drive up to the Bay Area and across the bridge to Mill Valley, where my dad awaited us. We needed a day to get rid of the little trailer and rent a U-Haul. It took most of the day to get that done, and we were back at Dad's place by midafternoon on October 17, 1989. We had the two bikes in his driveway and were about to push them into the U-Haul when, at exactly 5:04 p.m., the Loma Prieta earthquake hit. The road looked like someone shaking a blanket as an asphalt ripple raced toward us. The motorcycles vibrated like toys. Dad looked at the ripples coming toward us. "Jesus Christ . . . Jesus Christ . . ." was all he could say. Moments later, you could see the smoke in the air from the fires in the Marina in San Francisco. The road we had just driven the day before, I-880, was totally destroyed. The Bay Bridge was so damaged that when we left we had to head north and cross the Richmond Bridge to pick up I-80, which we would be on for a long time. We left my father, and San Francisco wreathed in smoke, and headed east.

My life is filled with Roadside Americas. I drive for a living—the music is just an added blessing. America is a large and wondrous place and even after all these years, I never tire of the never-ending panorama. I will say this, however. Towing a trailer coast to coast with a short-wheelbase Blazer is one thing. Driving the length of I-80 in a Jeep YJ with a cloth top is quite another. By the time Vanessa, Chuck, and I got to Woodstock, New York, none of us wanted to get in a Jeep again . . . ever! It was quite a trip!

The Airplane machine was gearing up for the big album tour, and the cast of characters changed from the session crew to the reunion tour. In addition to Grace, Marty, Paul, Jack, me, and my brother, Peter, it was decided that Tim Gorman would play keyboards, Randy Jackson would be added on keys and guitars, and Kenny Aronoff stayed to play drums. They were all very fine musicians, but in retrospect I really can't imagine why they were all there. You might ask, "How many guitar players do you need?" I have no answer for that. One concert review said that I did not look particularly healthy, and indeed I was not. If you should chance to look at the music videos for "Planes" and "True Love," I am obviously in a very dark place, but it was a place I was not quite ready to leave.

The tour proceeded. It is a blur to me. I was there, and then I was not. We were there, and then we were not. The tour ended before all the advance monies were recouped, and there was a lot of money that needed to be paid back. Today, the whole thing smacks of smoke, mirrors, and ill-conceived decisions.

At the very least, the Airplane deal made us all visible again, and Hot Tuna was able to pick up some of the pieces. The Airplane album was on Epic, which picked up Hot Tuna for a one-record deal. I was still not writing, so I found myself in the same situation I had been in for the Airplane project. I recycled some of my old tunes, snagged some Americana chestnuts, and leaned heavily on Michael Falzarano for songs. Michael is a great writer and he came through in spades for us. We also bird-dogged some songs from Randall Bramlett and others.

By the time Jack and I got ready to record *Pair a Dice Found* we were accompanied by Lenny Underwood on keyboards, Michael Falzarano on guitar and vocals, and Harvey Sorgen on drums. We did some tracking at the Dreamland studio in Woodstock, New York, and finished up at BearTracks studio in Suffern, New York. We had our good friend Ricky Sanchez as an engineer and mixer. He had done sound for Tuna for years and he knew us well. Harvey and Michael joined Jack and me for a nationwide tour. Our first tour bus was an old Eagle that was filled to overflowing with people and gear. In addition to the band and support techs, Vanessa; her sister Ginger; and our two bull terriers, Marlo and Zola, were on board the charter bus. Sometimes Jack's wife, Diana, would come. There were a lot of people and animals on this bus, and we were all together across the continent and back.

I was moving back into the opiate world. For a while I hadn't done any dope, but I was by no means sober. I had no idea what that idea meant back then. I didn't know any other way to live. I still had music and the guitar, and that kept me going, but the drinking and using prevented much creativity from emerging. In the beginning alcohol and drugs seemed to work for me. Those days were long gone. I simply survived. That my marriage to Vanessa survived as well was quite simply a miracle. That's just the way it was. Anyone in recovery will know exactly what I'm talking about.

In the spirit of the right things often happening at the right time, before we left on the tour another miracle occurred. I was in our kitchen in Woodstock when the phone rang. "Jorma!" a voice bellowed from the phone. It was my old friend Big John Clark. I hadn't heard from him in years. "I've got this piece of property in Meigs County, Ohio. I want to sell it. Are you interested?" I had visited John in the eighties when I played Athens, Ohio. I knew that Meigs County was famous for pot and I suspected that this piece of property might have had something to do with that industry. The property had belonged to one of John's friends, Scott Cooper, a famous Florida body builder. In fact, he was Mr. Florida in 1967. He died a drug-related death in the eighties and left the property to John.

"Yeah, man," I told John. "I'm interested. When can I see it?" "How about tomorrow?" John bellowed. He was always very loud. Now, I'm having two conversations, one with John on the phone and one with Vanessa in the kitchen. "Hang up the phone," she whispered sotto voce. "We're not moving to Ohio. You're losing your mind! We're not moving to Ohio!" I heard her, but I had a good feeling about this. "Let me just go take a look at it," I said. The next day I was at the Albany, New York, airport on my way to Ohio.

I had a good friend in Columbus, John Hurlbut. We had met through the music in the early eighties and remained friends ever since. John met me at the airport and we drove down to Athens, Ohio. Rocky Williams flew up from Florida to join us. We drove down to Meigs County together, picked up Big John at his farm, and headed over to the property.

The piece of land had been uninhabited since Scott died. The road had grown over with weeds and the only building there was a ramshackle A-frame. It was just before Christmas. Winters in Southeast Ohio can go a lot of different ways. Mostly it's what we call "wintry mix," which is a euphemism for cold, muddy, and nasty. On this visit though, there was snow on the ground and the little Shade River had water and ice in it. As I walked through the forest with the crunch of the snow under my feet, listening to the creaking of the frozen trees, I felt this was going to be a good place to put down roots. It's funny how you feel things. I had lived many places in my life, and home to me had become a moveable feast. I never felt that I would ever have a place to come back to.

I closed the deal with Big John Clark with a handshake. I found a pay phone and called Vanessa collect to tell her about my hazy vision. It's amazing that something so life changing for Vanessa and myself happened in such a casual way. G-d definitely had plans for us!

When we got back from the Hot Tuna tour, Vanessa, her sister Ginger, my friend Ira, and I drove to the Ohio property and camped out by the decaying A-frame for two weeks. With no livable buildings on the property, we needed a place to live while we thought about what to do with our new real estate. We rented Hillside Farm on Kingsbury Road, about ten miles away from what would become the Fur Peace Ranch, and got ready to move. Out of this moderate chaos, some order was to come. Without really thinking about it in three-dimensional terms, we joked that the property where the Ranch exists now would be a great place to teach and grow guitar players. Out of the blue the name Fur Peace Ranch came to us because it's a "fur piece from anywhere." It would be half a decade before these dreams gained substance, but in our hearts they already existed. Today the first thing that seems to follow an idea is a website. Back then it was letterhead stationery and T-shirts. Either way, it's always good to look ahead.

All this humor aside, to say that Vanessa was not excited about these prospects would be an understatement, but to her credit she went the distance and more to make them all happen. I don't know if her vision was gaining clarity or if she just wanted to support me. In any case, she made up her mind to give this opportunity her best shot. We had a yard sale at our place in Woodstock, enlisted the help of some friends, and rented a U-Haul truck. We were definitely not planning on coming back. Fate was taking the wheel for us now. With two cars, a pickup, and the U-Haul, we left Woodstock for good and moved to Ohio.

17

Too Many Years

Despite the possibilities of the Ohio property, in the parallel universe of my heart I was still living in self-inflicted pain. Why do we do these things? I haven't the slightest idea, but my spirit had yet to come out into the sun. Someone said to me recently, "You didn't look that miserable." I could only say, "You weren't inside my head!" We had made the move to Ohio, but there is no such thing as a geographical cure. In 1993, I finally was able to admit that I needed help. This was no surprise to Vanessa or most of my friends, but for me to say it out loud to another human being was a giant step. Vanessa and I scraped our meager savings together. I went to Hazelden for a twenty-eight-day rehab. I was so dense that I was almost through the program before I realized that the Hazelden logo contained five steps and referred to the first five steps of a twelve-step program. Sometimes it's hard to see the forest . . .

At first I couldn't sleep. I thought I would never sleep again, but one day I did. It seemed like a miracle to me at the time. I remember calling my father, who was struggling to recover from a series of strokes he suffered in the early nineties. I told him where I was and what I was trying to do. I had just hung up the pay phone in my unit when it rang. It was Dad. "Are you sure you need this, son?" he asked. I told him I was sure . . . very sure.

It would be nice if I could say that I came back from treatment "cured" and could now live life like an earth person . . . or a nonalcoholic. This was not the case. One of the counselors at Hazelden told me, "Jorma, you're going to have to change everything but your name!" I didn't get that then, but in time I would. I was able to stay sober for three months, and that seemed like an eternity. I had taken the substances out of my personal equations, but the "-isms" were still alive and well. I chose to ignore the fact that alcoholism is progressive, and that the disease, untreated, was under the skin just waiting to bloom again. As they say, alcoholism is cunning, baffling, powerful, and I will add patient! In my case, it didn't have to be too patient. I started drinking and using again—and of course, lying about it and pretending to be sober.

In spite of this I was able to accompany Dad back to Ironwood, Michigan, for his last trip to that the place of his birth.

February 5, 2001

An amazing thing happened the other day. I got a letter from my friend Gerry up in Duluth. Gerry was one of my dad's pen pals and he sent me a note that Dad sent him about seven months before he died. As I have said before, I carry those who have moved on . . . those I love, in my heart. However, occasionally they speak in tangible ways. I include Dad's words here simply because I like what he has to say, and I thank him for it:

Wednesday, August 7, 1996

It is a gray, cool autumnal day, and I am devoid of inspiration and energy. I have overslept and I have come back to consciousness to find Chuck here. Beatrice has just awakened and is about to embark on her daily rounds. She had a pretty bad night and we cursed her so-called cardiologist. Bach partitas in the background, serene lovely sounds as background for a day in which I have no talent for consecutive thought. Except this. It is August and the year has grown old, its high point rounded off as it moves toward winter. I remember the eagerness with which I have looked forward to seeing Jorma—way back in the Heroes tour, then the guitar summit, then the recent Furthur tour. Each of the year's early tours were followed by visits, joyous reunions. The wait for Furthur to bring him here was tedious, the reunion joyous, as I have written. Now I wonder when we will see him again. He is probably home again, the gauntlet run, and he can rest for a while. And for us? Beatrice is not well and it is clear she will not be able to travel for a while. We had thought briefly that we would go by train to Columbus and then by car to Pomeroy, but there is no way we can put a date to this. As for me, I have an appointment with an ear doctor next week and sometime later in the month my annual physical, which will put in medical terms the extent of my physical deterioration since the last one. It is clear to me that I will never be as vigorous as I was two years ago when Jorma and I made my homecoming return to Ironwood. In the background there is the ineffable, eternal beauty of Bach. Across the centuries, Bach speaks to me, marking time's passage. Beatrice has looked in, on her way to marketing, and I marvel at the constancy of her devotion, as I have been marveling at it in recent years. On this autumn becoming day she personifies the life force to me, the power that is born, that grows gradually to a powerful flame, and then gradually diminishes until it is extinguished. I feel very much that I am in the period of the flame's gradual extinction. So on this gray, quiet autumnal day, my melancholy is not sad, but a quiet review of my blessings. Here are some of them. I am 86 years old, an old man. As Yeats said, "An old man is like an empty coat hanging on a stick." The attempt to recall the quotation is inexact and I will find it later. But, as an old man. There is another poet, a sixteenth-century one, which is pertinent to me now. He writes, "My mind to me a perfect kingdom is," and mine is because I remember, I remember—sometimes more than is comfortable. So, with an active mind, I am old and live actively each and every day. But there is also Beatrice—frail, indomitable, working all the time, devoting herself to me, but not just to me, her sons and young people all over, buying them books, keeping in touch, writing to them and encouraging them. She is central to my life. The poem by Yeats I was looking for has the word "Byzantium" in its title.

We derive sustenance from youth—other people's youth, Beatrice's relatives and her protégés, but also the people who come into our home and into our lives. There are Chuck and Donna. And it occurs to me that some of the young people who enrich our lives do so because of Jorma. We are legatees of his ability to make long-term friends. There is Bruce Wagman, a lawyer, Hot Tuna fan, an unexpected friend. There is Donna Rudolph and her husband Robert, the gift of Dianne Ochletree, who makes her living finding young people to help old ones. And Anne Ochletree came to us through Peter. Our lives are enriched by the warmth and vigor of a host of young people. So, it's been a kind melancholy day, a day of quiet contemplation of life. But melancholy is not sad. Paradoxically, I see a quiet joy in melancholy recalling the blessings, thinking of people loved, now dead, but still alive in memory.

[Note from Jorma: The poem is "Sailing to Byzantium" by William Butler Yeats.]

An aged man is but a paltry thing
A tattered coat upon a stick
Unless soul clap its hands and sing
And louder sing, for every tatter in its mortal dress.

In 1996, I experienced one of those odd interludes that people think define your life. Jefferson Airplane was inducted into the Rock & Roll Hall of Fame. There we were at the Waldorf in New York, joined by David Bowie, the Shirelles, Pink Floyd, Gladys Knight and the Pips, the Velvet Underground, Tom "Big Daddy" Donahue, Little Willie John, and Pete Seeger. The Airplane played "Volunteers," and I got to play "Embryonic Journey" as a solo. I am still amazed at the long legs this little piece has grown and that I was able to create it. I also got to play "Goodnight, Irene" with Pete Seeger. How good can it get? As heady as this experience was, it was really a sidebar in my life—I was still struggling to stay sober.

Vanessa was tending to her own spiritual condition and staying out of my life as much as possible, lest I drag her down too. "Alcoholism and addiction take no prisoners, destroy all in their path!" I saw this on

a T-shirt. It made a lot of sense to me. There is no need for a drunka-
logue here; there is nothing new in my story. I know today that Vanessa understood what was going on in my life. Why she chose to stay
with me under these conditions is her story to tell, not mine. The important part for me is that she did choose to stay. I had been cheating
on Vanessa by sleeping with a woman in the DC area. I had known
Stephanie for a number of years. She had worked for some of the ven-
ues that hired me and Jack; she was one of the girls about town and was,
through her boyfriend, a go-to source for the things I needed to be able
to kill the pain of each day. The relationship was symbiotic: I got what I
needed, and she got to be one of the gang backstage.

The detritus that my life collected in the eighties was hard to shake.
One day I decided I could no longer live like this. I had no desire for a
new life with someone else. There was still so much work to do. I was
used to living and acting with no regard to consequence. This time
though, there was a consequence I could not ignore. I found out that
Stephanie was pregnant, though I didn't tell anyone. In this moment I
truly realized that my life had to change. This was the wake-up call that
ultimately led to true honesty for me. A child does not just disappear.
But, in typical Jorma fashion, I chose to ignore this news and hope that
it went away. Of course it did not, and G-d had other wake-ups in store
for me, but it would take a little more time. I had been a liar and a
cheater for what seemed like all my life. It's just what I did.

Sunday, January 7, 2007, Meigs County

*Ten years ago this morning I was over at my studio on the property where
the Fur Peace Ranch is now. I remember I was standing by the island in the
kitchen area. I was going to string some guitars, do some email . . . I don't
remember. What I do remember is that the phone rang and when I answered
Vanessa said, "Your father died this morning. You need to go to California."*

*A week before we had been in California visiting my folks and my brother.
My dad's health had been declining since his stroke in 1992, but even in his
infirmity he was vital . . . His life force was always strong. I look at my folks'
life today with the distance that years have given me and I am able to see*

them as the ordinary folks we all are. They followed the path of their life with the same tentative steps that we all do . . . seeking the right path. Sometimes successful, sometimes not so . . . that is the way of things and there are no grades given on our progress.

Anyway, the last time I saw my father alive, Vanessa and I were driving away from their house in Mill Valley. It never occurred to me that this would be the last time I would see Dad alive. We exchanged hugs inside the house and then walked to the car. This time as we were backing out of the driveway the door opened and Dad came out on the porch. He never did this before . . . but he did it this time. He came out and his body language said goodbye one last time.

"Your father looked different today," Vanessa said. "One of the last things he said to me was, 'Is the kid all right?'" (He still referred to me as "the kid" from time to time. It was always thus.) "Your father is saying goodbye," she said. "His eyes are already looking at a place we can't see." He did have that distant look, but I wasn't tuned into it yet. I have seen it in others since then, but this was the first time I was really made aware of it. As I looked in the rearview mirror he was still standing on the porch, watching us. He grew smaller and smaller, and then he disappeared as I drove around the corner. That was the last time I saw him alive.

You know, I have always considered myself a typical guy of my time. Whether this is really true or not, today I do not know. I do know that my path alienated myself from my family and for this I take responsibility. Today I believe that I was driven by ego and fear for many years. Something lucky happened to me though. The last four or five years of my dad's life we became friends. I was no longer afraid of his ephemeral moods, or my own for that matter. I don't know whether he changed or I did. It really doesn't matter. A change had occurred between the two of us and we became equals and friends.

He was always a funny man. Even as a sullen child I found his somewhat cynical worldview humorous and enlightening. The way he would turn words and phrases into spoonerisms and malapropisms still makes me laugh when I think of it today. I have inherited a little of this. When my son was visiting last week, I thought how he would have loved his granddad and how his granddad would have loved him. It was not to be, but the possibility still dwells in my mind.

I went to California, and as I held my mom and my brother, we mingled tears. My grandparents and my uncles had been gone for almost a quarter of a century by this time. When they passed I was so consumed with self that I never really gave myself time to grieve. It all started to come together for me in that January of 1997. I really think I expected Dad, and all of us, to live forever. I know it was totally different for my brother Peter. Peter was our parents' caregiver at the end of their lives. He made it possible for them to live out the end of their lives at home. He was bathed in their human frailties on a daily basis. I have nothing but love and the deepest respect for the great sacrifices I know he made on their behalf.

They had Dad laid out on a gurney or something, I don't remember. It was in some funeral parlor in Mill Valley. I remember seeing him there still . . . a white sheet drawn up to his chest. I remember thinking, "Your ears look larger than I remember." There was a bruise on his face from where he fell as he died. "Your father always was an inconsiderate bastard," Mom said to me on one of the days I was there. Apparently he had dropped dead at her feet. Dad's sense of timing sometimes left something to be desired.

There was no movie magic done to Dad's remains. He lay there as he fell . . . as he left the hospital for the funeral home. He was cremated and then that last vision was gone. There was a memorial at Jeanie Patterson's Sweetwater in Mill Valley. Many people came, and many memories were shared. I remember Mom sitting there stoically. I don't remember if she was crying. My brother and I played some songs. We told stories . . . the evening came and went. I remember thinking at the time, "Is this all life is about . . . a memorial?" I know today that memorials are for those left behind. It helps us clear the air. It makes us part of the flow. Many touching things were said that night, most of which I could not quote today. I do remember this one thing, however . . . and I can quote it. I believe it was a gentleman named Werner Johnson . . . one of Dad's brothers in the Kaleva Lodge, one of the Finnish-American things Dad was involved in during the last twenty years of his life.

Werner spoke and said some nice things as I recall. He finished with "Fair weather and following seas, Brother Jorma!" Brother Jorma . . . that really touched me then . . . and now. I was glad to know one of his "brothers" if only in this superficial way. It made him more human, more real.

He would not be buried immediately, but I would come back to California for the service. My brother and I and my friend Chuck and cousin Dan and his dad Joe . . . we were there that day at Inglewood Cemetery. He sleeps near his mother Ida, his father Jack, his brother Pentti, and a year later he would be joined by my mother Beatrice. He sleeps in the approach pattern to LAX. He would have had some choice words to say about that.

We got to take a trip together to the Upper Peninsula of Michigan to his home place in 1993 or 1994 . . . I forget. He was born in Ironwood, Michigan, in Gogebic County in 1910, in another world and another time. I think that trip was when we really started to get to know each other. I got to meet some of his childhood friends . . . see where he was born, where he played as a kid, meet his first girlfriend. The memories he shared with me about the old Finn Hall rustle through my memory like a spring breeze in the pines.

He is gone ten years now . . . a decade has passed. I used to wish he were still alive . . . selfishly . . . so I could share with him that my family and I are doing well. Even if he had not gone that morning in January ten years ago, he would be gone now. No one lives forever, it would seem. He will always live in my heart. Sometimes as I walk in the woods here on the farm I can feel him with me. I remember the trip he and my brother Peter and I took in 1963 to Kiruna in northern Sweden. We camped together. There were many volatile moments as there always were in our family life, but I remember that trip fondly. Sometimes when I'm riding my motorcycle I feel him riding next to me on his old Lambretta scooter.

We are all in the river together and time has no barriers. I will always miss him but I rejoice in being part of his journey. It is an honor to be his son and I will cherish this thought as long as I have thoughts.

Vanessa and I spent the entire weekend home together. We rarely do this, but we did this weekend. It just happened and I welcomed the serenity.

Family, that is what it is all about for me today. Fair winds and following seas, Dad. What is ten years for those who love? Bless you!

Back in the present that was 1997, Mom was stoic, my brother was inscrutable, and I was truly confronted for the first time with the fact that no one lives forever. Somehow I just felt that my parents would always be there. A couple of weeks later we all went to LA to bury dad next to Jaako and Ida, around the corner from Pentti. Dad's work as a father was done. I know my parents worried about me a lot when they were alive. I hope, if these things mattered to them in their moments of passing, that they knew that I was going to be all right.

The Fur Peace Ranch was already in the works. I might drag my feet and procrastinate, but Vanessa does not. Vanessa had convinced the bank to lend us the money that we needed to build the Ranch; plans were drawn and ground broken. In spite of whatever turmoil surrounded me, the dream of the Fur Peace Ranch was strong and tangible. Vanessa and I both felt that it was more than the right thing for us to do . . . it was something we *had* to do! All that being said, we were about to embark on a life-changing adventure and I should have been excited and breathless. My life was still shrouded in lies and whatever breathlessness I had was a function of fear. There was always a cloud behind my eyes.

Vanessa and I found ourselves at the Hotel Triton in San Francisco in late December 1997 for some end-of-the-year Hot Tuna dates when we got a phone call. "Margareta just died." This was not totally unexpected, but somehow I still found myself surprised that we do not live forever. She died of renal failure and cirrhosis of the liver. Lena Margareta Kaukonen (née Pettersson), September 23, 1943–December 28, 1997. She was fifty-four years old. When we told my mom she just nodded her head and accepted it like the fact that it was.

In the year following my father's death, Mom hung in there, but we could see she was developing issues as well. She had always been the rock in our family. She could be opinionated and on occasion single-minded, but she was always a warrior for those she loved. It was painful to see her diminished as we were swept into 1998. My brother devoted his life to her care in that last year, as he had for my father. I guess looking back I did the best I could, but I really had no true awareness of what was transpiring in their world. I called Mom often to talk. "How are you?" I would say. "I'm still here" would always be her answer.

Back in Meigs County, Ohio, we were consumed with the opening of the Ranch. Our first workshops were in April 1998 with Rory Block, Roy Book Binder, and me. At that point we had only the cabins, the library, the workshop, and the kitchen. The grounds were still muddy from the construction and the spring rains; hay covered the ground everywhere. We were navigating uncharted waters for sure. As that first week rolled by I talked to Mom every day and the conversations were always very similar. As that first week approached its finale, I called Mom in Mill Valley and Sara, her other caregiver, answered the phone. "Can I talk to Beatrice?" I asked. "Oh no," Sara said. "She can't talk anymore." The next voice I heard was Peter's. "If you want to see Mom, you better get out here now." I was stunned. I went down the hill to my little A-frame studio and immediately wrote a song.

April 27, 1998
Fur Peace Ranch
Meigs County, Ohio

Strength unto my life she was before I was a man
Daddy's off to fight a war in some far off distant land
He don't come around much just at special times of year
But Mama always holds our hands and puts away our fears

"Come and take a walk," she'd say, "down by that old Pierce Mill
And listen to the water passing by the rocks and rills.
That old gray goose will bite you, but you can feed the ducks,
Trust your heart in all you do, you won't have to trust in luck."

Mama tried to teach us to be strong
And keep walking against the wind even though your hope is gone
It don't matter how alone you are today
'Cause if you keep on walking hard, you'll find a better way

Many years have come and gone, now that I'm a man
My bro and I are all that's left in this part of our clan
Daddy won't be coming back, he's fought his final war
And Mama's eyes look far away, for some distant shore

She wanders in her mind now to that old tobacco farm
When she was just a girl at play in my grandfather's arms
He strokes her hair with loving hands and sends her on her way
To walk across this century, which brings us to today

My brother sits beside her bed and holds her hand so tight
He looks upon her shuttered eyes, will she make it through the night?
The what she is remains today, the who she is, is gone,
But what she's done in both our lives I know will linger on

Her favorite books are closed now, her favorite song's been sung
For her boys who stay behind her, she's done all that can be done
She's going to see her friends now that have vanished for so long
She's on the road beyond the stars . . .

She's going . . . going . . . gone

"Song for Our Mother" just poured out of me. There was no artifice, no creative agony. It was in my heart, and then it was in the air. Vanessa made arrangements for me to fly to California as soon as that first camp was done. Rory Block played a set on our little stage in the workshop and she asked me to sit in on "Mama's Blues." Tears ran down my face as I played that song with her. And then that first weekend was over.

The Ranch had been born that spring in Ohio mud and passion for the future. When I got to my parents' house on Underhill, Mom was in a hospital bed in the living room. Dad's old stereo was tuned into an FM classical station and soft music gently filled the room. We could talk to her, but there was little or no response. The hospice nurses who came by daily told me that at the end of life the ability to hear is the last sense we lose. Peter and I never stopped talking to her. "It's OK to go home, Mom," he would say. Her breathing became labored and there was a tinge of blue at the base of her nails. Peter showed me how to give her the palliative meds she needed and I did the best I could to help, which wasn't much. We changed her sheets and bathed her. In the end it was the least we could do for her. One morning as I sat by her bed, she opened her eyes and grasped my hands with a strangely powerful grip. "My dear one, my dear one," she said. Her hand relaxed and her eyes closed again. Those were the last words she would ever say to me.

The hospice nurse told me that Mom would probably hang on as long as Peter and I were around. In moments like this these are just words, but it did come to pass. Mother's Day was coming on the tenth of May. On the morning of May 8, Peter and I drove into Mill Valley to buy Mom some flowers and when we came home, she was gone.

Wednesday, May 8, 2002

Four years ago today at 1400 West Coast time, my mom finally went home . . . for the last time. My father never anguished vocally the passing of his two brothers, his father, and his mother. My mother held the memory of those gone close to her heart. "It would have been your grandfather's 100th birthday today," she would say and light a candle.

Dad was gone much of the time as we were growing up. Mom was my den mother when I was in Cub Scouts. She taught me outdoor skills, love of nature . . . an early lesson in being in the moment . . . one with the universe. She was something of an intellectual snob, but she was proud of her education. As an educator, she was proud of her ability to pass knowledge on. She loved kids.

It has taken many years for me to see my mother and father as plain folks, trying to make their way in the world. Two more lives with the threads of success and failure running through the fabric. Looking back on their story today, I would say they shared more success than failure. I hope they knew that. I can now let them be themselves and see them as people, not just my mother and father.

I miss them . . . Today I am missing Mom especially. It is such a selfish longing. I would like to tell her that I am better than all right. I would like to share a little of my world with hers . . . I would like to give her one more hug. For a while after her death, I remembered her that last week I was there as a dying person. I have not forgotten that . . . it was quite a lesson she gave us all, but today I remember her as a lively and vital person. In different memories she is different ages . . . a young mom in her thirties . . . the mother of growing sons in her forties and fifties . . . a struggling wife in a difficult but not impossible marriage . . . and always a woman trying to find her place in the universe. She has found it now.

My brother was so strong in those last years. I know it was difficult for him but he was there for them twenty-four hours a day. He and I were never close and now it has been some time since we have spoken. On this day I think of him and wish him well . . . wherever his path takes him. And you, Mom . . . I will always love you and cherish your memory. May the poetry of the universe fill you with verse.

Mom's final lesson to me was how to die with grace and dignity surrounded by family. I can only hope for the same. Mom was gone and indeed my brother and I were now orphans . . . like it says in the song, "Sometimes I feel like a motherless child . . ." Mom joined Dad and the other Kaukonens in Inglewood Cemetery and I returned to my life with Vanessa and our evolving Fur Peace Ranch in Ohio.

I always seemed to require pain and deadlines to get anything done. I knew that my son, Zach, existed but I had never come to grips with this reality. That would have required rigorous honesty, and I wasn't yet capable of that. Zach had been born on September 6, 1997. Stephanie had tried to bring him by a gig at the Birchmere in Alexandria when he was born, but I refused to see her. To say that denial ain't a river in Egypt would be the understatement of a lifetime. The year before, in 1996, Vanessa and I were at a hotel again in San Francisco. We were there for a Hot Tuna date and we were still in bed one morning when I got a call from Stephanie, Zach's mom. "Who was that?" Vanessa asked. I came up with some lame bullshit excuse and I'm sure Vanessa didn't believe me, but she let it go. I had known that Stephanie, the woman in DC, was pregnant, but I said and did nothing. I guess I expected the situation to resolve itself . . . and it did, in its own way. In October 1998 we were pulling into the end of the first year of the Fur Peace Ranch. Stephanie had gotten in touch with my friend and agent Steve Martin and he contacted me. "You have a son," he told me. I was terrified. I had no desire to leave Vanessa for this woman. Vanessa was the love of my life . . . the source of my truth. But I had no truth yet. Everything in my life had directed me to this moment. This seemed like the last chance I would have to come out into the sun.

It was a beautiful fall day. I'm sure Vanessa knew something was going on with me. I'm the most transparent person in the world. We had driven to town and taken a walk together on the bike path in Athens. We got a bite to eat and returned to the Beatrice Love Kitchen at the Fur Peace Ranch. We had both walked back into the kitchen. It was a moment of truth I think I had been waiting for all my life. "I have to tell you something. I have fathered a child." "Who's the mother?" she asked. "Stephanie," I said.

To be truthful with you all out there, trying to tell this story honestly has proven more difficult than I could have imagined. Vanessa asked if the baby was a boy or a girl, and then she punched me in the chest. More words were said but I cannot recall them. In silence, we drove back to Hillside Farm on Kingsbury Road, and she threw her things in a few green garbage bags and left for Cabin One at the Ranch. Within a month Vanessa rethought her position. Why should she be sleeping in a tiny cabin at the still nascent Fur Peace Ranch? She returned to the farm with her things and I found myself in Cabin One. I was alone with myself for perhaps the first time in my adult life. I had no idea what was going to happen next to any of us. Looking at my situation from a twelve-step point of view, I had finally done a fourth and fifth step: making a searching and fearless moral inventory of myself, and admitting my wrongs to myself and to another person.

I don't remember the order in which these next conversations happened, but they happened. Vanessa asked me what I was going to do. I was prepared to do anything to save my marriage. "You're going to be a father to that baby!" she said. "He's your son and whatever happens to us, you need to be there for him as best you can!" This is truly an amazing woman!

I got in touch with an attorney in the DC area. She got in touch with Stephanie, who also got an attorney. In Virginia, Stephanie, Zach, and our attorneys met and I got to see the boy for the first time. Stephanie looked at me and said, "What did you have to get a lawyer for?" "Because that's what adults do in a situation like this," I said. Zach took a look at me and started to cry. In this inauspicious way a path of healing began. My attorney, being an attorney, recommended a DNA test. We did one and indeed I was Zach's dad. Today Zach looks so much like I did at his age that, looking back, that DNA test was superfluous.

At home, there was much that I needed to do. I had no idea what was coming next for Vanessa and me. I had dishonored my wife and my vows. In a way I felt I had dishonored the gift of life itself, but like the Bible says, "Faith without works is dead," and I had a lot of work to do. Vanessa insisting that I be a father to Zach was good advice on a molecular level. Vanessa and Stephanie and I started this new journey by seeing a counselor together in the DC area. This wound up not serving everyone's needs so that petered out. What it led to for Vanessa and me was a relationship with an amazing psychologist in the Columbus area. We saw Dr. Al for a number of years. These sessions were an important part of the healing process, and those conversations would be instrumental in my opening the door to myself.

All this was certainly more than just stones in the road, but I had had finally gotten the message. If nothing changes, nothing changes . . .

and I was ready for change. I got sober right after Stephanie got pregnant. Early sobriety was difficult for me. It was a totally new mode of existence. My nerves were like stripped wires, showering sparks on myself and anyone near me. It was the first time I had ever tried living life on life's terms and it wasn't easy for me. The Fur Peace Ranch had just concluded its first season, Vanessa and I were trying to find our way together, and I was a father. Everyone's plate was more than full.

Dealing with Zach's mother has never been easy. She's had her own row to hoe so I can't comment on that. Things would have certainly been easier for all of us if she had not chosen to be so adversarial toward Vanessa. In a very real way Vanessa was always in Stephanie and Zach's corner, but it was never easy for any of us. Stephanie never gave Vanessa any respect and always treated her as an enemy. That was unfortunate, but that's just who Zach's mom was.

In retrospect the next couple of years went by in the blink of an eye— but not at the time. Stephanie was Zach's custodial parent and I was a "vacation dad" for many years. It was the best we could do. The Ranch was quickly becoming highly respected and kept on growing. "Focus on the things you love, listen with an open heart, and the music will speak for itself" would be our mission statement and our mantra.

In the midst of all these emotional earthquakes, 9/11 happened. I had decided to seek counseling. I truly knew that I needed real help if I was to continue to grow. The morning of September 11, 2001, Vanessa and I were driving up Route 33 to Columbus to have a session with Dr. Al. At a little after 8:45 I was parking at the doctor's office when we got a call from Michael Falzarano in New York. "The Twin Towers were just attacked! They're burning!" This was impossible to process. "Listen, Michael, I'm just parking at the doctor's office, I'll call you back." I hung up and parked the car. The reality of Michael's call suddenly hit me. I called him back almost immediately but the phones in the New York City areas were already down. We went to our appointment and by the time we were back in the parking lot, the world had changed. The second plane had hit the second tower. We were driving out of Columbus when the Pentagon was hit. We tried calling Stephanie and Zach in Virginia, but their circuits were already down. On the way home we stopped at a Sam's Club to buy some things for the Ranch and walked by a wall filled with hundreds of flat-screen TVs all tuned to the same station. We saw the first tower fall at 9:59 a.m. By the time we got home we knew that our longtime friend David Weiss was one of the many who died that morning in Lower Manhattan. Over a decade and a half later, we are still processing all these things. It certainly made my problems seem insignificant in that moment.

I found that the truth really does set you free. If you're not living a life of lies, you never have to remember to keep your stories straight. There is only one to remember.

18

Heart Temporary

Thursday, November 14, 2002, Hillside Farm

The thread of the past reached out and touched me today. I was coming from the gym early this morning and I stopped by Donkey's, our local coffee-house, to get some beans. The last time I saw my ex-wife, Margareta, was in 1989 as I was winding up the Airplane reunion tour. She didn't look well . . . I probably didn't either, but that's another story for another time. She met my wife Vanessa, and she liked her. She was in the process of dismantling her life and I think she realized that her years were numbered. Margareta was an artist . . . always drawing, painting, sketching . . . At the end of our relation-ship, I was making three-dimensional wooden frames for her work and then she would paint them as an extension of the picture. Anyway, Margareta told Vanessa that she was giving her all her work to do with as she pleased. Van-essa had all the paintings in our barn waiting for the right moment. Mar-gareta died in 1997 right before the New Year. She died alone in a transient hotel in the Mission District of San Francisco. The cause of death was listed as liver disease. This didn't come as a surprise, but it was sad nonetheless. Margareta and I were married for twenty years . . . in some respects we grew up together . . . in others we never grew at all. Still and all, when we were young we were filled with hope and sense of destiny. Our destiny was to grow ever further apart and to sink into our own individual sense of despair.

But she was an artist . . . and she left Vanessa with her work as proof that she had ever been here at all. Vanessa put together an exhibit of Margareta's paintings at the Donkey, our Athens coffee shop. These were the ones with the 3D wooden frames that I had crafted over twenty years ago. Mitered, dadoed, routed, glued, and painted . . . a part of the work. There were earlier works painted on Corrasable Bond . . . gone with the advent of the computer. I walked into the room where the paintings were hanging and I was touched. In one sense it was sad to think that someone's life would be measured by twenty or so works of art, and on the other hand it was nice to have it measured at all.

When I was young, it was hard to take measure of anything. I was like a leaf in the wind and it was shear luck that I didn't wind up in someone's burn pile. I am certainly a more serene person today than I was 38 years ago . . . and yet that spark of youth . . . there is such power in that! Sometimes the committee in my head deludes me that it would be nice to live in an "if I knew then what I know now" scenario . . . fortunately that is just smoke.

There were Margareta's paintings on the walls of Donkey. They looked great! She would have appreciated the moment. She used to tell me that her work would be her legacy, and thanks to Vanessa, that is the case today. Would that the legacy had been larger . . . or happier or . . . well . . . It will have to be good enough.

This morning, there was a bittersweet moment for me in the gallery. "This is really something," I thought. I was moved . . . moved by touching that thin thread to the past . . . seeing that out of the dark years, some light still shown . . . Moved by Vanessa's sense of love and compassion to give life to these things today.

Moved . . . and a little wistful. Before my mother died, when I would call her, I would ask, "How are you today, Mom?" And no matter how she felt, she would say, "I'm still here." I too, am still here, and there is a little smile on my face.

Things were beginning to happen with the Fur Peace Ranch that we could have never envisioned. The sense of musical community that we embraced has become very real. In a time where there really are no safe zones for anything, there is still the Ranch, where it is safe to be with like-minded spirits. It is a place where music is the ultimate haven. If you focus on the things you love and listen with an open heart, the music speaks for itself.

My career was also about to change in a most positive way. In 1999, I had an amazing publicist named Diane Connal who introduced me to the record executive Yves Beauvais. Yves was working for Atlantic Records when we had our first interview. "If you could do a dream project, what would it be?" he asked. This was simple. It was something I had been thinking about since I first played MerleFest in the late nineties. "I'd like to do an acoustic project with some of my bluegrass heroes. I'd want Sam Bush on mandolin and fiddle, Jerry Douglas on Dobro and Weissenborn, and Byron House on bass." I wanted to source material from the Great Depression era that featured white country artists who played blues-based material. I realize that music knows no color, but these were the masters I wanted to honor in this project.

Yves was interested and said he'd run it by the label. I didn't hear from him right away, and frankly I didn't expect to. I was flattered to be asked, but I thought nothing would come of it. Some months later Yves called again. "I'm with Columbia now," he told me. "If you're still into it I think we can get this project off the ground." I absolutely was into it and I went back to New York for a meeting.

"Why do you want to work with a major label when you could do this project on your own?" he asked. At the time the Internet meant little to me. "For the cachet," I told him. I never thought I'd have the opportunity to be on a major label again. "Talk to the guys and see if they'll do the gig," he said. I called Jerry, Sam, and Byron and they all signed on.

Yves started sending me hundreds of songs from the period and I began bird-dogging tunes. Yves got Roger Moutenot to produce the project and we planned to record in Nashville. Sony was the mother company for Columbia then, so we also got a chance to use Sony's new high-definition audio system, Super Audio CD (SACD). I listened for months to all the material that Yves sent me and picked out enough songs for an album.

March 24, 2001, Nashville, Tennessee, 7:07 a.m.

This whole trip has been evoking strange emotions in me. It has been so long since I came down to Texas, and Louisiana and Nashville, that I have had a chance to reflect on the changes in my life since the last time I traveled these roads.

Yesterday we drove up from New Orleans through Mississippi and some wondrous things occurred. We took I-59 out of NO and picked up I-65 north into Mississippi. Through Hattiesburg we went until we got hungry in Meridian. We pulled off the road and wandered into a Wendy's for a grilled chicken sandwich (eating healthy) and on the way out I saw a sign for the Jimmie Rodgers Museum. It hit me then that were indeed in THE Meridian, Miss., home of Jimmie Rodgers, the Singing Brakeman, the Blue Yodeler. My dad liked Jimmie and had some of his recordings. There were even 78s in the house before LPs. I remember wandering around the house as a kid singing "T for Texas." Something about Jimmie made me feel even then that he was The Man!

We asked a local gentleman for some directions. He paused and allowed that as he had lived in the area for 65 years, he could probably help us find the place. Find the place we did and what a treasure trove of stuff. We wandered around for about half an hour, bought a pile of great memorabilia, and went outside to take some pictures. On one of his monuments was a great Jimmie quote that I could really relate to.

"I'm no better than the bottomest dog, and no worse than the toppest dog." Good stuff!

In Nashville at the hotel I ran into Jerry Douglas and got to hear him play at the Association of Stringed Instruments Artisans evening. Nashville . . . Music . . . the kind I love.

At the time I had no idea that many of these tunes had also become modern bluegrass classics by such artists as Tony Rice. I realized that Jimmie Rodgers's "Waiting for a Train" was more than a chestnut, but

I had to do it anyway. My mother used to sing that tune around the house when I was very young. Out of deference to my listener's sensibilities, I have vowed never to yodel in public, so we did the yodel with instruments. I fell in love with Jimmie's "You and My Old Guitar" the first time I heard it. It was a new one for me and I loved the sentiments. "Tom Cat Blues" was credited to the great Jelly Roll Morton, but the version that I sourced was by Cliff Carlisle, one of the early innovators of the Dobro. I picked "Just Because" . . . just because. I first heard that tune in a version by Elvis. "What Are They Doing in Heaven Today?" was on a Washington Phillips album called *I Am Born to Preach the Gospel*. I had first heard Washington's "Denomination Blues" back in the sixties, but I knew nothing about him or his instrument, the dolceola, at that time. I heard my buddy G. E. Smith play that tune at a gig we did together at the Sweetwater in Mill Valley, California, around 2000. He gave me some important insights into what would become my arrangement.

There were many amazing aspects to this project. Yves and Roger would not let any of us rehearse together. I had picked the songs and shared that info with the guys but that was it. This was to be a live recording without any digital magic. The night before we were to start recording Byron came by the hotel. I wanted to do the Delmore Brothers tune "Big River Blues." When Doc Watson did it he called it "Deep River Blues." "How do you do it?" Byron asked. When I showed him he said, "Doc didn't do it like that." "Well, how did Doc do it?" I asked. Byron took my guitar and picked the Doc version. I was amazed. Byron is a bass player. I checked out what he was doing and stole a couple of things for my arrangement. The folk process is always enlightening that's for sure!

The next day we all headed over to Masterlink Studio. Sony sent over the new SACD gear with some techs and we started recording immediately. Jerry, Sam, Byron, and I started to play "Waiting for a Train." In the beginning we all made an effort to be respectful in our performance. After the first take, Yves got on the talkback. "Quit being so

nice to each other. Be more aggressive. And Jorma . . . shame them!"
We all laughed and got with the program. From that point on we just
jumped in and played. If arrangements needed tweaking, we did that.
The last day or so in the studio the great banjo player Béla Fleck came
and played on two songs. I was knocked out. In a little over a week the
tracks were done. We mixed at Seventeen Grand in Nashville and Ted
Jensen at Sterling mastered the project. Sad to say, SACD is another
lost format along with Betamax video; it did sound unbelievable though,
and if you're fortunate enough to have an SACD player around, give it
a listen. If not, it still sounds great as a CD!

This whole project turned out to be life-changing in a lot of ways. In
those moments in the studio I was able to simply play music with
friends—for the joy of it. I felt every moment in the studio in a way
that, truly, I never had before. I listened to the entire project when it
was mixed, sequenced, and mastered, and I was so excited I said, "I'd
sure like to take this band on the road!" Lynn Bush, Sam's wife, just
laughed. I got it. That was a pipe dream indeed; the guys already had
plenty on their plates. But I started to think about who I could take on
the road to play and support the album.

I needed a Dobro player, a mandolin player, and maybe a bass player.
I called my old pal Sally Van Meter, one of the finest Dobro players
around, and asked her if she was interested. She was. We had an endless stream of dates coming up over the 2002 season. Sally could do
many of the dates, but not all. I got in touch with another old friend,
Cindy Cashdollar, one of the finest steel guitar players on the planet,
and she signed on for most of the dates Sally couldn't do. I needed a
mandolin player but I didn't yet really know many people in the wooden
music world. Strange to say since I started out as an acoustic player, but
I had been sidetracked by rock and roll for many years.

I called Sally again. She was in England doing a bluegrass camp. "I
think I have just the person for you. His name is Barry Mitterhoff and
he's standing next to me." Barry got on the phone and we agreed that
he and Sally would come out to the Fur Peace Ranch when they got

back from England. When we all got together in the workshop at the Ranch it just worked. Barry and I became dear friends and colleagues, and we have toured and recorded together for more than a decade.

Back in the business part of my world, Diane Connal, my publicist, was pulling out all the stops to help make the new album, *Blue Country Heart,* a success. We had a lot going for us that year. The project was an event and people were starting to take notice of it. The Fur Peace Ranch was evolving too. Thanks to Rusty Smith at WOUB out of Ohio University, we had a syndicated public radio show. This was the year Vanessa built the Fur Peace Station Theater, a 220-seat venue where every seat is golden. Up to this point our shows were held in the little workshop across from the Beatrice Love Kitchen. Now we had a real venue! Vanessa was busy growing the Ranch and guiding my career alongside Diane Connal.

All things considered, I had already had a lot of professional and artistic longevity, but this was different. We really wanted to get on the charts, such as they were, and we hoped to at least get noticed by the Grammys. I always work my ass off, but in 2002 it was relentless. Press, radio, in stores . . . all that stuff. *Blue Country Heart* peaked in the top ten of the Americana Charts. The Airplane had charted, but I never had as the leader of a project. It felt good! The Grammy process began and I wound up getting a nomination in the Traditional Folk category. Today that category is gone, and there is so much talent under the Americana umbrella that I never would have gotten noticed. Awards and the like never occurred to me as a younger musician. That is not why I played music. That said, the Hall of Fame and the Grammy nomination were both amazing honors and I am grateful for them.

Vanessa and I went to the Grammy ceremony, which was in New York that year. Doc Watson won the Traditional Folk category that year—well deserved. After the award ceremony I got a call from Byron House. "Who won?" he asked me. "Doc," I told him. Byron was quiet for a moment. "That's OK. He's Doc Watson." Byron was quiet again for a moment, and then said, "but darn him anyway." For Byron, modest Christian that he is, that was almost acting out. Later that night at the after-party I ran into one of Byron's Nashville buddies. I related the conversation to him and he thought about it for a minute. "Boy, Byron must have really been mad." We both laughed a lot.

The trickle-down blessing from *Blue Country Heart* kept on coming. The decade or so I spent playing with Barry Mitterhoff was like being part of an ongoing master class. Ultimately Jack and I co-opted him into Hot Tuna and we became a bass, guitar, and mandolin band. Some folks like it. Some folks don't. I love it. The process of conscious learning had become so important to me that I soaked up as much as I could. Later, when Izze came into our lives, Barry, a father of three girls, gave me some of the best advice I have ever been granted. "Don't get used to anything!" Words to live by indeed.

Back in Ohio another life-changing event was stirring in the wind. When I was married to Margareta nothing could have been further from our collective minds than children. I had a wonderful son in Zach, but I was not his custodial parent; in fact, I didn't even have joint custody. Vanessa always made him welcome . . . he was my son and her stepson. We saw him as much as my schedule allowed and as much as his mother would allow. It was difficult but we did the best we could.

One day Vanessa and I were talking and she asked me, "I had the weirdest experience yesterday. I heard the universe whisper in my ear that our daughter was waiting for me. What would you think about adopting a little girl?" For some reason it all made sense to me. It was absolutely the next right thing. At the time I knew nothing about the Chinese proverb of the Red Thread: "An invisible red thread connects those who are destined to meet regardless of time, place, or circumstance. The thread may stretch or tangle, but it will never break." I always believed in destiny, which I have come to call G-d's will. The proverb talks about newborn babies being connected by invisible red threads to the people who will be important in their lives. These threads shorten as the people, bound from birth, get closer together. I did not yet know that the threads that touched our lives would find their source with a little girl in China.

Vanessa's and my collective age made adopting difficult. International adoptions have become increasingly chancy over the past decade. They were tough enough when we embarked on that journey in the early part of the new millennium. A friend whom we met at the Fur Peace Ranch was an attorney who specialized in adoptions. He put us in touch with an adoption agency in Rochester, New York, and also interceded strongly on our behalf. The Red Thread was stronger than our age or other bureaucratic entanglements.

When I told Zach and his mom about our plans she was livid. Stephanie did everything she could to stop our adoption. This made an already contentious situation even more flammable. I felt this was absolutely none of her business, that she had no right whatsoever to meddle in the plans that concerned me, Vanessa, and our family to be. There was a time when I would have done anything to avoid a situation like this. This time, however, I truly believed that G-d wouldn't give me more than I could handle. It was an unpleasant time, but I did my best not to let it color my relationship with Zach. All this turmoil could not help but affect the life that Vanessa and I shared, but share it we did. One foot in front of the other, we got through this chapter. Stephanie would always be Stephanie, but over the years we learned to tolerate each other on some level. In September 2017 Stephanie would succumb to cancer. Whatever conflicts our families may have endured no longer mattered. Zach was with her to the very end. She did a fine job raising this boy to a young man, and I can think of no greater compliment than that! As for me, I would like to think that I was becoming a better friend, a better husband, a better father, and in general a better man.

Back in 2003, Vanessa and I were sitting at the dining room table at the old Hillside Farm on Kingsbury Road one morning. She felt that I was not being responsive enough to her, and she was probably right. She said, "I have self-inflicted holes in my heart!" We both stopped in our tracks as she shifted gears. "That's a great idea for a song. Go write it now!" Immediately I went to my little office above the garage and wrote "Heart Temporary."

Blue skies in the morning,
Stars they fill the night
Fall wind rustling through the trees,
Sings a song, of great delight

On such a day, you think you'd say,
Exactly what you mean . . .
But in G-d's perfection, things ain't always
Just the way they seem

When the best you have to offer
Falls short of the mark
Self-inflicted holes are piercing
Deep within your heart

I am not a tunesmith but I write songs, and the impetus for this writing has come from many places over the years. Being in the moment for this little piece was a gift. "You'll never be able to sing this song without crying," Vanessa told me. "Yeah, I will," I said. It would be the leadoff song for *Stars in My Crown*, the album I recorded in 2006 at Seventeen Grand in Nashville. My level of acceptance was improving, and I was starting to write again.

I had also written three instrumentals: "Fur Peace Rag," "Living in the Moment," and "A Life Well Lived." These were about five years old, but I had never recorded them. Byron House produced the project, and he crafted some amazing arrangements and got great people to play. It went over budget, of course, but I listened to it again today, and it was certainly an adventuresome project for me. In addition to the songs I wrote, I picked material that was normally way outside my comforts. My version of "The Man Comes Around" by Johnny Cash is an example of this. *Stars in My Crown* came out in 2007.

In 2006 our Izze was born, and for the Kaukonens in Ohio, our immediate family now had three members. Our adoption process took so long, it seemed like an elephant pregnancy. We knew we were getting a daughter and we knew her name would be Israel Love Diana Lucy Kaukonen: Israel after Israel "Iz" Kaʻanoʻi Kamakawiwoʻole, the great Hawaiian singer; Love after my mother Beatrice's middle name; Diana after Jack Casady's amazing wife; and Lucy after John Hurlbut's mom. They were all powerful names from powerful people . . . all of whom are gone now. This would be an amazing legacy for our daughter.

You never know when you're going to get the call that you are ready to meet your daughter. I had planned to go to China with Vanessa but as fate would have it, I was on tour when the call came. Vanessa made the China trip with her sister Robin and I participated from Italy with my iPhone. The first time I saw a picture of Izze as an infant it was overwhelming. I had been doing my best to be as good a father to Zach as I could, but so far I had pretty much been a vacation dad. We lived four hundred miles apart; scheduling visits was always complicated. Now I was going to be part of a full-time family.

One of the most humorous conversations that Vanessa and I had while she was in China went like this. (Keep in mind, I was still in Italy.)

Jorma: Where are you right now?
Vanessa: I'm in Walmart with Lady Robin and Izze.
Jorma: What does it look like?
Vanessa: It looks like Mason, West Virginia, except that it's a high-rise and things are cheaper because they don't have to ship them to the States.

Good times in the global twenty-first century!

I came back from Italy in time to pick the girls up at the airport in Columbus. When I got there I found that weather had rerouted their plane to Cincinnati so I started driving down I-71. The Cincinnati airport is actually in Kentucky but in an hour and a half, there I was.

I was so glad to see Vanessa and meet our daughter for the first time. I got a good hug from V, and Izze took one look at me and started crying just like Zach did the first time I met him. I love you, sweetheart! People have been raising kids for a long time and this is not a treatise on child rearing. Like Barry had said, "Don't get used to anything!" Nothing like having a kid around to teach you about reality! I was no longer just a vacation dad.

Being a touring musician is not for everyone. It's not even for every musician, but I had been doing it all my life and it was all I knew. Because of World War II, and later my dad's postings, the Kaukonen family was used to moving. I had never lived anywhere so long in my entire life and I cherished having an anchor point. I continued to tour relentlessly as Hot Tuna, and as a duo with Barry.

In the fall of 2008 I decided it was time for another solo Jorma project. Red House Records OK'd the deal and I got in touch with Larry Campbell to see if he would produce it. We decided to track and mix at Levon Helm's studio up in Woodstock, New York, on Plochmann Lane. I had recorded "Been So Long" on the second live Hot Tuna album, but I always wanted to do it as a truly acoustic number, and this was my chance. With Barry Mitterhoff playing tenor banjo, mandolin, and tenor guitar, and Larry Campbell playing guitar, baritone guitar, tenor guitar, resophonic guitar, fiddle, Dobro, mandolin, cittern, and percussion, it was set to be a great project for me. Levon himself played drums on two tracks, and Lincoln Schleifer played bass. My longtime friend and guitar tech Myron Hart played a little upright bass, and Teresa Williams lent her beautiful voice to the mix. Justin Guip, who was engineering the session, also played some drums. Justin would become Hot Tuna's drummer and percussionist in subsequent years.

Some years before at a gig in California, I had met the sister of my long-departed Hells Angel friend Badger. This chance meeting started a flow of memories and later that night I had a dream. I dream from time to time, but I can almost never remember the dreams and tend to put little stock in the ones I do. This time, however, I dreamed Grandma Ida came to me and said in her Finnish-inflected English, "We're all here floating in a river of time." When I woke up I called Vanessa immediately. "Write it down," she said. "You'll write a song about it some day."

Tuesday, June 26, 2002, San Francisco, California, 7:24 a.m.

I had a dream last night. Usually I don't remember my dreams, but this one circles my head even now. Much of it is lost, an epic . . . but what remains concerns my uncle Pentti. Pentti has been dead now for almost thirty years, but in this dream I went to an apartment complex to visit him. It was the kind of place he would have lived in, simple, but efficient. Of course instead of being in some little community down the peninsula like Belmont or San Mateo this building was filled with elder folks and was down by the Hyde Street Pier on the Bay near Fisherman's Wharf. Anyway, I went to see him and he was gone and there was another name on the door. I rang the doorbell and a young man answered the door. "Where's Pentti?" I asked. "Oh, he's gone," the young man said. "Passed away . . . a while ago." "Don't you feel so strange being so young and living amongst all these old folks?" I looked through the door into the living room and could see that some of my uncle's things were still there. "It's not strange at all," he said. "They're nice folks and the place has a great view."

Then my grandmother Kaukonen, Ida, was there. She outlived Pentti, but not by much . . . but there she was, outside the apartment. "Grandma, you're alive," I blurted out . . . stunned by the apparition. "Oh no," she said. "I'm gone, your uncles are gone, your parents are gone, we're all gone." She paused. "But we surround you in the river of time." Her English was imperfect in the dream as it was in reality. It had that strange lilt of irony that I always thought I detected in her when she spoke. I looked around . . . across the street the San Francisco Bay glistened with dancing sunlight. I turned back to her and she was gone, and as my eyes opened back in the world I was in my hotel room in San Francisco.

I lay there for a while floating in the wake of my dream and jumped up to write about it while it still lived in my memory. Last night I played a show with my pals G.E. and Sally. We were in Santa Cruz. As I sat there looking out at the audience I was reminded that I used to have a little place down there on Sunset Beach. My comment out loud was that there was less traffic back then but it was more than that. After the show, a woman came up to me and said, "Do you remember Badger?" "Paul Mumm!" I said. "I remember the last time I saw him on Yerba Buena Ave. in San Francisco. It was back in the early seventies. I remember it like it was yesterday." She looked wistful. "He has been dead for twenty-seven years." To her I could see that those years were as the turning of a page. We spoke for a moment and then she left. A few minutes later she came back and thrust a photo into my hand and then turned away. I looked at it . . . it looked as if she had carried it in her wallet for many years. It was Badger, young . . . in his colors . . . alive. In my memory, he has aged as I have. We are equally old. In the picture he was still young, as he was when he died. I had to look hard to recognize him. I found him in my memory and in that same place I found myself.

The winds of time vanish like smoke and those of the present come and whirl all these thoughts away. It is 2002, real time. I often describe my memories of things past as if they were almost a dream. Sometimes they are a dream . . . and sometimes, like this morning, they are more than that. I bathe in their pool . . . climb out, dry myself off, and have a cup of coffee.

Before Myron and I got up to Levon's place to record, I had already decided that *River of Time* would be a song and the title of the album. The session went as planned and the next to the last day I realized that I had yet to write "River of Time." At the end of the evening's session I grabbed my guitar case and dove back to the hotel. When I got to my room, I looked at the case; it said COLLINGS. Now I don't own a Collings guitar, but I figured it would do. When I opened the case, it was empty. It was now three in the morning. I was alone in my hotel room and Levon's studio had long since been shut down for the night. I sat down and wrote a poem.

The river of time, it marks our line
From birth to death there is no rhyme

A chance to meet along the way
Will we go or will we stay
There is no sound of tolling bells
Our task on earth is living well

When I write songs I usually start with a melody or some cluster of moves on the guitar that call to me. This time I needed a melody and chords. While Larry and the guys were getting ready in the studio for the morning of the last day, I went into the woods behind Levon's house with my guitar (which was waiting for me at the studio) and in half an hour I had this tune. When I'm giving songwriting workshops I point out that this is probably not the best way to write, but by the Grace of G-d, this time it worked for me. Folk Alley named "River of Time" folk song of the year. It was another great musical year for me.

I had been writing another tune inspired by having an infant in the house for the first time. The waters we were navigating as new parents might have been filled with sand bars and shoals, but we loved every moment of it. Spurred by these experiences, I wrote this song, "Simpler Than I Thought."

I never thought that I would ever feel this way
Your tiny hand would press to mine as we would spin
Circles round the day

It's simpler than I thought
Your smile unties the knot
There is no time like now to learn
The lessons we forgot

This is definitely a song written by a guy who is a hands-on father for the first time. Barry looked at me wryly. "Does she really go to sleep without a fight?" Not often, I had to allow, but I took some sentimental poetic license.

19

A Life Well Lived

Tuesday, June 25, 2002, San Francisco, California

Visiting San Francisco is always such a bittersweet experience for me. It was home to me for almost a quarter of a century, and yet I was never at home here. When I come here to do anything, the streets swirl with my ghosts. Of course when I split up with my ex-wife, Margareta, and headed back East in 1984 I didn't realize that we never lose our baggage, we just learn to arrange it in neat little piles that are easier to handle. On the one hand, my memories of San Francisco from the early days of the sixties are dark and somewhat mysterious . . . very noir, very high-contrast. I had forgotten those golden days in Northern California where the sky is impossibly blue, the landscape is sheathed in burnished gold. Well, yesterday when I left the hotel to walk around, it was one of those days. I went down to Chinatown, walked through North Beach, through the Cannery and out onto the Hyde Street Pier and the Maritime Museum. The tall ships of my memory from back then were there. The C.A. Thayer and the Balclutha greeted me like old friends. I stood on the stern of the Balclutha and looked out toward the Golden Gate. I remember that spring of 1962 when my mom and dad and I sailed back from the Philippines on the Golden Bear. *Captain Sven Rogenes was the Master . . . I'm sure he is gone today, as are Mom and Dad. The skyline of San Francisco was so exciting to see as we passed under the bridge! There were no tall buildings then . . . The Port of San Francisco was still a working port . . . Oakland was filled with ships loading and unloading. I knew I wanted to move there . . . to walk those streets . . . it was one of those golden bright days.*

Back in the present, I left the Balclutha saying goodbye to her like an old friend. As I walked back to the hotel, the day was still beautiful. The San Francisco in which I began my plunge into darkness vanished like a puff of smoke and I was able to enjoy its loveliness today. Very nice, this letting time pass gracefully . . . there is so much left to do and no place for shackles.

As my friend Chuck says, "Wings, not anchors."

Amazing things kept happening, though the economic crash of 2008 certainly affected us. We could no longer afford to have as many instructors each session, and there were other cutbacks. We never cut back the quality time we offered our students though. Our little community of like-minded people continued to grow. Over the years I became a better teacher, and as I became a better teacher I also became a better player.

I consider my teaching method to be anecdotal. I teach songs but there are always overriding principles contained in those songs. Over the years at the Fur Peace Ranch I have come to know what I am doing in a way that I can consistently communicate to students. Also, in that communication I do things really slowly and precisely. It is an exercise regimen I never would have thought of on my own. I also began to understand some of the principles I would have learned if I had taken a music theory class in college. Better late than never I say. I have come to realize that each note means more to me today than it ever did when I was younger because I am so aware of them as contributing entities.

I was no longer a prisoner of any self-inflicted misery. Sure, some days were better than others, but catastrophe was no longer looking over my shoulder. I was working on building my place in this world brick by brick, stone by stone. Vanessa had converted to Judaism after we met and this gave me an opportunity to connect with roots in my life that I had never really looked at before. I was born Jewish but my family was never really observant. As a much younger man there is no question that I was an assimilationist. Jews were the outsiders in the neighborhood when I was a kid and we were not a part of the Jewish community. Now I was a part of a community within a community, and I liked the sense of belonging regardless of how limited my Hebrew was.

Vanessa is always a body in motion, and her motion always yields more fruit than you can imagine. The Fur Peace Ranch has never ceased to be a work in progress. We built our Company Store, and not long after that our Psylodelic Gallery, dedicated to the art and culture of the sixties and early seventies. If you're not busy growing, you're busy dying. My life was now filled with growing children. Zach was navigating middle school in Arlington, Virginia, and Izze was at the Child Development Center at Ohio University.

As a parental sidebar, the great teachers at the CDC certainly laid the groundwork for Izze's development. She entered first grade at East Elementary School in Athens, Ohio, and she did well. When she was in second grade, though, we began to feel the negative effects of the Common Core approach to education. Izze is a very smart girl and she was getting bored. She realized that if she finished her work, they just gave her more of the same, so she started to slack off. We couldn't have that, so we pulled her out and started homeschooling her. You think playing Woodstock was an adventure? Think about homeschooling your kid. We were lucky to find Shannon Arnett, a student at Ohio University, who became Izze's learning coach. My world was certainly filled with different adventures now, but the common thread of the guitar and the music always remained true and pure.

In 2005, I started playing with a truly great drummer, Erik Diaz. Jack and I felt it was time to start bringing back Electric Hot Tuna. I had met Erik at MerleFest in the early 2000s when he was playing in a band with Howard Armstrong. Howard was a former member of the Tennessee Chocolate Drops, and back in the 1930s he was part of Martin, Bogan & Armstrong. Howard was still brilliant and when

I heard Erik in the backing band, I remember thinking that if I ever decided to go electric again I wanted him as a percussionist. His Americana sensibilities were impeccable.

Jack, Barry, Erik, and I started rehearsing at the Ranch. We worked out an acoustic set followed by an electric set. We started to tour extensively in that format. It was nice to be standing up and rocking again. I was playing an Epiphone Jorma Kaukonen model JA ES-335, in the color red, of course. At the time I used a Carr Slant 6V. All musicians know it is always inspiring to get new gear. I owned a 1968 Fender Deluxe that was not vintage to me. It was just old. I had bought it new. Owsley had modified it back in the day with what was then an experimental master volume. I had Pat Cahill up in Canton restore it to original specs. It's a very cool amp, but it just didn't have the horsepower we needed for the Tuna gig. (I still have that amp. It lives on the stage at the Fur Peace Station where it frequently gets used.)

It's always important to find the right guitar for the right job. Back in the nineties my friends down at Gibson Guitars in Nashville gave me a Chet Atkins SST. The Chet was sort of a solid-body guitar with special electronics to make it sound more or less acoustic. It was perfect for Hot Tuna and me. I got it in 1993 and I still use and cherish that guitar today. I had settings for the Chet that didn't drive, and settings for the 335 that did. We toured for five years in the acoustic/electric format.

In 2009 Columbia Artists Management put together a Guitar Blues tour with me, Robben Ford, and Ruthie Foster. Robben was playing through a Dumble amp, which developed some problems early on the tour when we were still on the East Coast. My old friend Louis Rosano was waiting in the wings and lent him a Louis Electric KR12 head and cabinet. I was playing through the Carr, which I really liked, but when Robben got his Dumble back I tried the KR12 and loved it too, so I added it to my arsenal.

I was really enjoying the electric stuff again. The Epi 335 was my main electric axe for the rock part of the show. For the acoustic part I was playing a David Bromberg signature Martin guitar. David had picked this guitar out for me himself and I loved it. When I flew out to join the Guitar Blues tour, the Bromberg developed a small crack up by the nut. It was a fixable wound, but I was not happy. When a guitar is going to break it's usually the neck near the headstock. The guitar repair gurus always tell you, "It will be stronger than it was before you broke it." That may or may not be true but to me once it's broken, fixed or not, it's still broken. I called my friend Dick Boak at Martin Guitars and lamented the damage. He had me send back the Bromberg and lent me what he called an M-5. There were seven of these M-5 guitars made. They featured an Adirondack Spruce top, a one-and-three-quarter-inch neck at the nut, enlarged sound hole, forward bracing, mother of pearl herringbone marquetry, and a Fishman Matrix pickup. I had been with Fishman as an endorser for years. I love their gear. As soon as I picked up that M-5, I knew a great change was coming. I called Dick and told him that I had to have this guitar, and we made a deal.

Hanging out with Robben Ford was inspiring too. I was good at what I did with the guitar, but the learning process is never over . . . if you're lucky. Robben had turned me on to some chord shapes that were new to me and I was on fire. I wound up building those chords into changes and all of a sudden the words to "Things That Might Have Been" came to me in a rush.

When I was young, on the street where we lived
My brother and I were two distant kids
We shared the same house, we shared the same name
But out in the street we played two different games
Momma and Daddy were fighting wars of their own
They left their two boys, to go it alone
We looked for a harbor, safe for the heart
Like ships in the night, our lives drifted apart
Sometimes I think of things that might have been

This song came to me backstage in Newark, Ohio, on the Guitar Blues tour. To be in touch with yourself at any time is a blessing. To put it to music was the frosting on the cake. But there was more on the table too. Dick Boak, my friend at Martin Guitars, had often talked to me about a signature Jorma model. With the M-5 in hand, I was starting to realize what I really liked and wanted. I stopped off in Nazareth, Pennsylvania, to talk to Dick. We went across the street from the Martin factory, and over pizza the Jorma M-30 was born. The original notes and designs were done on a napkin in that pizza joint. For all the guitar geeks out there, here's what we came up with.

M-30 JORMA KAUKONEN CUSTOM ARTIST EDITION—
    SPECIFICATIONS
MODEL: M-30 Jorma Kaukonen Custom Artist Edition
CONSTRUCTION: Standard Series, Dovetail Full Gloss
BODY SIZE: M (0000) Grand Auditorium, 14-fret
TOP: Solid Bookmatched Italian Alpine Spruce
ROSETTE: Style 45 with Select Abalone Pearl Rosette
SOUNDHOLE: Large Soundhole (No Inner Ring)
TOP BRACING PATTERN: 5/16" Width, Forward Shifted,
    Scalloped
TOP BRACES: Solid Bookmatched Italian Alpine Spruce
BACK: East Indian Rosewood, 2 Piece
BACK PURFLING: Style 30 Colored Wood Marquetry
CAUTION STAMP: None, "C. F. Martin & Co., Nazareth,
    PA"
Stamping Between 1st & 2nd Back Braces
BLOCK TO READ: (Lasered Decal Logo)
Custom Artist
Jorma Kaukonen
Serial #
SIDES: East Indian Rosewood
RIBBON: Spanish Cedar

END PIECE: Grained Ivoroid with .0325" Black/White (Black Faces Ivoroid)

TOP & BACK BINDING: Grained Ivoroid

TOP INLAY STYLE: Style 30 Multi-colored Wood Purfling

SIDE INLAY: .0325" Black White Black (Black Faces Ivoroid)

BACK INLAY: .0325" Black/White (Black Faces Ivoroid)

NECK: Genuine Mahogany

NECK SHAPE: Modified V-Shape with Diamond Volute,

NECK WIDTH: 1 3/4" at nut, 2 1/4" at 12th Fret

TRUSS ROD: Two-way Adjustable

HEADSTOCK: Solid Square Tapered

HEADPLATE: East Indian Rosewood with "C. F. Martin & Co." (Less "Est. 1833") in Mother of Pearl. Modified Torch Inlay in Select Abalone nested below logo

HEELCAP: Grained Ivoroid

NUT: Genuine Bone

FINGERBOARD: Black Ebony

SCALE LENGTH: 25.4" # OF FRETS CLEAR: 14 # OF FRETS TOTAL: 20

FINGERBOARD POSITION INLAYS: Maltese Diamond & Square Long Pattern,

Select Abalone, "Jorma" Signature in MOP Between 19th & 20th Frets

SIDE POSITION DOTS: White, 3rd, 5th, 7th, 9th, double at 12th, 15th, 17th

FINGERBOARD BINDING: Mitered Grained Ivoroid with .0325" Black/White Inlay

FINISH BODY: Polished Lacquer

FINISH TOP: Polished Gloss Lacquer, Aging Toner (Mask Pearl Only)

FINISH NECK: Polished Lacquer Complete

BRIDGE: Black Ebony BRIDGE STYLE: Belly

BRIDGE SPACING: 2 5/16" Bridge Spacing

SADDLE: Genuine Bone Drop In, Compensated, 16″ Radius

TUNING MACHINES: Waverly Nickel #4065 with Oval Ivoroid Buttons

STRINGS: Martin SP 4100 Light Gauge Phosphor Bronze

BRIDGE PINS & END PIN: Bone with Abalone Dots

PICKGUARD: Delmar Tortoise Colored Nitrate, Polished & Beveled

CASE: #570 "Geib Style" 5-Ply Vintage Hardshell Case, Cabernet Interior

INTERIOR LABEL(S): Personally Designed and Signed by Jorma Kaukonen

Numbered in Sequence Without Total, i.e., #1, #2, etc.

Secondary "Fur Peace Ranch" Label

EDITION SIZE: Custom Artist Edition, Open Ordering

This was pretty exciting stuff for me. It's still the guitar I play to this day. I know I'm not the only guy with an Artist Model, but it was a real honor for me nonetheless!

Life is never boring when you take the time to look at it. The Fur Peace Ranch was still evolving in spite of the economic downturn. People still seemed to need what we could offer. Gigs kept coming in and we all kept on working. We stopped playing with Erik Diaz in 2009, and Skoota Warner came on board. We quit splitting the evening between acoustic and electric and it was an all-electric evening again. We started to co-opt some of our buddies into the shows. G. E. Smith was in and out of the touring band as his schedule allowed. Larry Campbell and Teresa Williams did the same. Our shows were always filled with friendship and hot licks!

When 2010 rolled around we had a huge celebration of my seventieth birthday at the Beacon Theater in New York City. The old haunts are long gone, but the Beacon still reigns in Manhattan. There was an almost endless series of guests for two days of shows. Playing music with my friends in front of a full house was wonderful indeed. Bracketing this was another amazing event. Jack and the Hot Tuna gang and I went into Levon's studio in Woodstock and recorded our first Hot Tuna studio album since 1990. On this project I had a part in writing six songs. It all started with this tune, "Second Chances," I wrote (with Barry Mitterhoff) in my little office over the garage at Hillside Farm.

We all want second chances, a chance at being free
A chance to take, our measure here, and see what we can be
The dance it isn't over, till the last note has been played
We bow with thanks; we walk back home, to see what we have made

I had the lyrics and most of the music to this tune, but I needed a little instrumental bridge. While I was crashing over at Barry Mitterhoff's house in Scotch Plains, New Jersey, one night, he came up with that bridge. It was a good song, but Barry's artistic input made it a great one.

"Things That Might Have Been" was already in the queue but I needed more. Again, back up in my little office I came up with this tune, "Mourning Interrupted."

Went out early this morning, took a walk in the street
The silence was broken by the sound of my feet
There was nothing before me, no one waiting at home
There was no one around, I faced the future alone

When I first showed this song to Vanessa, she said, "Are you all right?" She thought it was depressing. I replied, "I just chased that rabbit down the hole until I caught him. That's what I came up with." There is certainly truth in this tune—that's what makes the song—but it's not who I am today. It was sort of a "been there, done that" moment, which I was able to capture from a little bit of emotional distance.

Larry Campbell had written a great tune called "Angel of Darkness." The verses weren't quite finished so I had the honor of being a cowriter on this one.

> *What kind of evil baby*
> *I don't wanna know*
> *Would poison pure waters*
> *Just when they begin to flow*

For the next song, Jack Casady had written a set of changes on the bass. Together with Larry they forged it into a tune and I wrote the words. We were staying at what used to be the Holiday Inn in Kingston, New York, off the Thruway. It was right by the Esopus Creek and there was an active train line nearby. You could hear the whistles. I sat down with my guitar and their charts and wrote "Smokerise Journey."

> *Morning thoughts, and mist on these hills*
> *The sound of song, in rivers and rills*
> *Begins my day, wrapped in the grey*
> *Smokerise highway, take me home*
> *Carry me home today*

I was actually bathed in all those images while writing these words. That's what was happening outside my window there in Kingston. The universe sure gave me that one! We also got a chance to showcase Barry Mitterhoff's virtuosic mandolin playing on "Vicksburg Stomp," an old tune by Papa Charlie McCoy. We always loved the old stuff from the masters.

With this project in the can, we hit the road to promote it. Whenever Larry Campbell and Teresa Williams were available we pressed them into service so we could play all the songs on the project live.

In late summer of 2012 the Hot Tuna family set out on a long coast-to-coast tour. Jack's wonderful wife, Diana, had been fighting adenoid cystic carcinoma, a rare cancer, for more than a decade. They gave her a couple of years to live. She fooled them all and made it thirteen years. She and Jack are the strongest people I have ever met. Diana's strength was a thing unto itself. Diana made her final journey with us on the tour bus that summer. I have never seen anything like it. She had been the inspiration for "Smokerise Journey," and a model to all of us for righteousness and fortitude.

As the tour crossed the continent and headed north from San Diego to San Francisco, we pulled into Mill Valley for a gig at Sweetwater. The day after the show Jack and Diana called me into their hotel room. "Jorma," she said in her impeccable British accent. "Jorma, I'm dying." I remember just sitting there. "Then you need to go home," I said. We all hugged each other. We canceled the last couple of dates on that run and we all went home. It was Sunday, July 21, 2012. Zach came back to Ohio with me and all the others scattered to their home places. The month of August flew by and on September 8, 2012, she was gone.

There are those events that just shake your sensibilities with the truth that in the end we are so fragile. My friend John Hurlbut's mom Lucy was already gone, and so with Diana's passing, all three of those powerful women whose names my daughter, Izze, bears had gone home for the last time. There's nothing like a life well lived as a source for spiritual treasure.

Strange and wondrous things are always happening in my life. Wally Pfister was making his directorial debut with a dystopian science fiction thriller, *Transcendence*. He contacted me about using my song "Genesis" not only as background music in the movie but as an important piece of the plot. Now, we always pitch our stuff hoping that someone, somewhere will pick it up, and nothing ever happens. This just fell out of the blue!

After the movie came out my son, Zach, was visiting us at Hillside Farm. "I've got a song in a movie, son. It's pretty cool. It's a science fiction movie. I think you'll like it."

We sat down to watch the movie. As it was unfolding Zach noticed Johnny Depp. "That's Johnny Depp, Dad!" he said.

"Well, yes, son. It certainly is," I replied.

A couple of more minutes went by. "That's Morgan Freeman, Dad!" He was surprised.

"It certainly is, son."

"Wow," he said, "it's a real movie!"

My ego was pricked. "What . . . did you think I shot a Super 8 in the backyard?" Kids are tough to impress.

In 2014 I decided it was time to make another album. I didn't even owe Red House another record. I just felt it was time and would have done whatever I had to do to make this project.

I got Larry Campbell on board again of course. Our pal Justin Guip engineered and played drums. Teresa Williams sang with me, and my friend and guitar tech Myron Hart played bass. Larry, being Larry, would sing and play all manner of instruments really well. He also lent his voice. We decided to record at the Fur Peach Station at the Ranch, and Justin and Larry brought a "studio in a van" to our doorstep.

Jack and I had been in Stroudsburg, Pennsylvania, at the Sherman Theater in 2013. I was shaking off the tendrils of sleep when a line ran through my mind: "We never seem to age in my dreams!" Bang, I was up in a shot and headed for the desk with a pencil and paper in hand. When I write songs, I like to start with a pencil and paper. Too many diversions are available with the computer, and electronics can really be a spirit killer. Anyway, I sat down and wrote "In My Dreams."

Won't you come with me
We'll go running through mountains
Just in time to set the morning free
Our hearts are young and strong
You're moving like an angel
We never seem to age in my dreams

I never took my time
I took it all for granted
The gift of life is never what it seems
Let's run like we did then
Like spirits in the morning
We never seem to age in my dreams

This song lived in my stage repertoire until the fall of 2014, when we assembled at the Fur Peace Ranch to record it.

This project is yet one more example of the gifts the Fur Peace Ranch has given us. One of our peerless "campers," Jim Eagan, played a song he wrote at the student performance on Sunday. It was called "Ain't in No Hurry" and Jim hadn't even played the last chords when Vanessa turned to me and said, "You must record this song!" I was on board immediately. Sometimes you hear a song and it becomes part of the soundtrack of your life immediately. This was definitely one of those times. You don't have to be an "old guy" to love this tune. I think it's universal.

I know I'm waiting, waiting in line
I know I'm waiting, waiting in line
But I ain't in no hurry, gonna take my time

Some time ago Nora Guthrie, one of the gatekeepers of the Woody Guthrie legacy, asked me if I wanted to set one of Woody's unpublished poems to music. As I was putting songs together for this project, I remembered Nora's offer and talked to Larry about it. Larry and Nora had had this same conversation, so it was apparent to both of us that this was the moment. Nora sent me several poems and we picked this one, called "Suffer Little Children to Come Unto Me."

There once was a man in the holy land
Had nails in his feet. Had nails in his hands.

Said mother and father I say unto thee
O' suffer little children to come unto me

This surrealistic little item resonated with me on many fronts. It's hard to pick a verse I relate to the most, but if I had to, it's the one about going to college and buying a degree. With college as expensive as it is today, this is a hard one to ignore. Woody—what a writer he was!

The last tune in this project, "Seasons in the Field," was really a poem I wrote. I had a set of changes for the evolving lyrics, but Larry Campbell helped me polish it up.

We thought we had it all, all grown up inside our skin
A tank of gas and my guitar . . . bring it on, let life begin today
Life was no more simpler then it was just another time
We tried to find conviction without losing peace of mind

I measured time that summer with songs and sets of strings
Duty seemed so far away, one more song before the summer ends
Seasons keep measuring, the time we spend on earth
None of that made sense back then and no one saw the worth

We completed the album in 2014 and it came out in February 2015. I finished up a Fur Peace Ranch on the Road winter teaching gig in San Diego with Larry Campbell and G. E. Smith toward the end of February, and then Larry and Teresa and I hit the road together to promote the new project. I had Larry and Teresa on board for a couple of weeks and then I continued by myself. I found myself traversing the great spectacle of America yet one more time.

20

Stars in My Crown

By the time 2015 rolled around, I couldn't even begin to tell you how many times I had driven back and forth across the United States. I had driven cars and I had ridden motorcycles. The first time I ever rode in a bus was on the Airplane reunion tour in 1989. People asked me sometimes, "It must have been great riding around in tour buses." Tour buses didn't exist for rock bands back in the early days. We tried to rent Ford LTD wagons, but if we couldn't get them, any full-size car would do. The Airplane equipment truck was a bread delivery truck with sliding doors. On a promotional tour of Texas, RCA magnanimously rented a Dallas city bus complete with the scissor doors. That was one of my few bus experiences until 1989.

Driving around the United States has never ceased to awe me. I never get tired of it. I was always at home on the highway; I always felt the power and majesty of the land! On this tour, I worked my way across the Southwest and up through the South, winding up in Long Island. At the end of that long run I flew down to Austin for the South by Southwest Music Festival, and then finally home. Every corner of my life was full and all the things that were important to me were blossoming. My son was more than halfway through his senior year of high school, Izze was finishing fifth grade, the Fur Peace Ranch was growing and I found myself learning more about the guitar than I could have previously imagined.

As I have gotten older I have realized that I didn't need to put so much pressure on the strings, and that an ersatz classical position with my left hand was much gentler on my old joints. I still use the thumb of my left hand a lot. That's an important part of fingerstyle guitar playing. Some of the things that Barry Mitterhoff showed me could not help but surface in my brain and fingers. My guitar harmonies were getting a little more complex. Is this a good or a bad thing? That's not for me to say. One aspect of building a relationship with the guitar is maintaining a repertoire. Another is keeping the journey alive. One of the great blessings of my collective fan base is that they have always allowed me to change and to experiment. It might not always please them, but they tolerate it with respect. I have no plans to try to re-invent myself but I try to keep my mind open to creative change.

In January 2015 Jack and I were in San Francisco for a Fillmore date. I decided to give Paul Kantner, my old friend and bandmate, a call. We had become adversarial in the nineties—frankly, I cannot even remember why. I was twenty-one when I first met Paul. We had spent so much time together when we were young, and it meant so much, that it seemed absurd to ignore each other in our old age.

I took him to dinner at the Mifune noodle joint in Japantown. We slurped noodles together and talked. We chatted about our old manager Bill Thompson, who had died the previous year. Toward the end of Bill's life we all had issues with some of his business decisions, but these became moot when he passed. He was one of us. To be alive in that moment with Paul was nice. The next night he came to the Fillmore to hear Jack and me play. I had no idea at the time that I would not see him again . . . that in a year he would be dead. And there it is for all of us. I should know better by now but I am still surprised when a person important to me dies. We should all live forever and our stories should never die! But that's not the way it is.

Jack and I had been booked to put together a show at the Lockn'

Festival on September 11, 2015, to celebrate Jefferson Airplane's birth fifty years earlier. This was a challenge and an honor. I got G. E. Smith to play Paul's twelve-string parts. Paul's idiosyncratic guitar style was an integral part of our sound. The whole is always greater than the sum of the parts where bands are concerned, and none of us could have done it without each other. G.E. nailed Paul's parts. Our drummer and partner in crime Justin Guip played drums. Larry Campbell was in the mix on guitar, as was I. Jack Casady on bass, of course. My hole cards were our vocalists. Jeff Pehrson was Marty Balin's voice and we had Rachael Price from Lake Street Dive as well as Teresa Williams singing Grace's parts. What a band we had for this gig.

We kicked the set off with Jeff Pehrson singing Marty's tune "3/5 of a Mile in 10 Seconds." Rachael Price took center stage for the next song, Grace's "Greasy Heart." The third number was the Jimmie Strothers tune "Good Shepherd" that I sang with Rachael, with Teresa singing harmony. We had been playing "White Rabbit" with Teresa for some time and she killed this song. What would an Airplane set be without "White Rabbit"?

The next tune brought Rachael back to center stage with Grace's "Law Man." Jeff came back with Marty's "Plastic Fantastic Lover." "Somebody to Love" was another Grace tune that Teresa had done with Larry and us for some time. She owns this song! "Eskimo Blue Day" is one of those songs that I hear as being part of Grace's Erik Satie period. Rachael ruled with this one. Fire-eating people indeed! "Come Back Baby" was a Walter Davis tune I learned in New York back in 1960. It's one I never let go of. An Airplane night also has to include "Volunteers." Jeff fronted this one with the ladies singing backup and Bill Kreutzmann joining Justin Guip for a drum duet. Last but not least, we finished up with "Feel So Good." I had Teresa and Rachael singing alternate parts. I loved it, and so did the audience.

I was really proud of what we accomplished with this one. We were able to do it one more time at the Beacon in November. This lineup may never happen again, but we did it twice and I loved every moment about it. It was amazing that after all those years the spirit of the Airplane soared again!

As 2015 slid into 2016, I got the news that the Airplane was going to be honored by the Grammys with a Lifetime Achievement Award and a stand-alone event later in 2016. They were going to announce it at the 2016 Grammys in February. To be recognized by the Recording Academy was an honor indeed! Those on the West Coast planned to be at the ceremony. In late January I heard that Paul had suffered a serious heart attack and was in a coma. He never recovered, and on January 28, 2016, he passed. Another dear friend made her final journey on the same day. Signe Anderson, the first singer in our young band, also passed on January 28, 2016.

We had already lost Spencer Dryden to cancer on January 11, 2005. In my opinion, Spencer was the most creative of percussionists in the Airplane. The artistry of his playing on those early recordings was unmatched. I was fortunate to be able to reconnect with him shortly before his death. Life and death is a dichotomy that simply cannot be ignored.

Marty and Jack were able to attend that 2016 Grammys show when they announced that the Lifetime Achievement Award show would take place on Saturday, April 23, 2016, at the Dolby Theatre in Los Angeles. We were all psyched about this. Also getting lifetime awards that year were Ruth Brown; Celia Cruz; Earth, Wind and Fire; Herbie Hancock; Linda Ronstadt; Run DMC; John Cage; Fred Foster; and Chris Strachwitz. We were in grand company. As the old folkie I am, I was particularly thrilled to see Chris Strachwitz in our company. His Arhoolie Records provided hours of listening and source material!

April 23, 2016, Los Angeles

Yeah . . . the Grammy Lifetime Achievement Award! Sorry Paul Kantner and Spencer Dryden couldn't be there. It's not up to us to decide when our ticket gets pulled, and sad to say, they caught an early train out. Signe too . . . may all their memories be a blessing!

With all this Jefferson Airplane stuff going on, when I think back . . . it was almost like a dream. I certainly hadn't planned my participation. I'm not sure what, if anything, I had planned. I could have worked in a music store as I had worked at the Benner Music Company on Stevens Creek in San Jose . . . I could have hung out my own shingle . . . I could have moved to Europe. I could have done all these things, but I didn't. It was decreed that I go to San Francisco at Paul's behest . . . it was decreed that my next schooling would be with my brothers and sisters of Jefferson Airplane. I would grow with the band . . . I would make choices, some good . . . some not so good. I would survive all of this and life would carry me in its embrace.

The things we endured together when we were young would forge us in its fire. Some would be consumed and some of us would survive the daily tests of life. Youth is not wasted on the young. It is not only the privilege but the duty of the young to fly toward the sun. The earth is always waiting for us, always.

My ex-wife, Margareta, is gone. Her life choices were indeed too hot to handle. We spent twenty years together and yet that time is a distant memory. The good times, the bad times . . . youth would help us endure it all, and then one day . . . I was no longer young and each moment would become more precious than the one before.

A Lifetime Achievement Award is a momentous thing indeed and we are honored by our peers. As a member of the human family, we should all be honored that we have made it this far.

I am so grateful.

Yet, what was that moment all about? What did it mean, if anything? At the end of life will I say, as Marlon Brando did, "What just happened?" Perhaps. For today, the needs of my family swirl about me, and mine about them. I have been gifted by being allowed to be an artist. I have traveled around the world more than once and seen more than some and less than others. I have today . . . and it is a good day.

As for the rest . . . it is indeed almost like a dream, like so many things.

When that day in April came, Izze, Vanessa, and I joined all the other surviving Airplane members and sundry families. Marty had some health issues and had to sit this one out. Grace, G-d bless her, never lets us down. I wondered at the time how they were going to process her message to make it family-friendly, but with a little editing magic, they did. We all had only minutes to deliver our thanks, but I had time to tell my daughter from the stage: "See what can happen when you follow your dream, sweetie?" As a dad, it doesn't get too much better than that. Well actually, it kept getting good. My son graduated high school and Phil Jacobs, our tour manager, joined Myron Hart and me in DC for the ceremony in Constitution Hall. Hot Tuna was banned from playing that venue back in the seventies. I returned incognito. It was a thrill to see Zach in that cap and gown. The day before the ceremony we went out to dinner and I noticed he had an impressive band tattoo on his bicep. He wasn't a kid anymore, that's for sure. His mom was having some health issues and he had decided to go to college near home and be her caregiver. He went from being a high school kid to being a man. It was another moment where the passage of time smacked you in the face! I certainly am proud of that young man!

Friday, December 13, 2002, Chicago, Illinois

I had such a funny feeling when I got up this morning. I had the alarm set for 0545 . . . I wanted to be awake when Vanessa called me from Hillside Farm. We didn't talk long. She had to walk the dogs and then get over to the Ranch for the Holiday Faire. Still, it was a wonderful way to start the day! I will be home in a couple of days, and with the sound of her voice and the touch of her heart, I felt like I was already there.

I reached over to the nightstand and picked up my watch to see what time it was as I finally dragged myself out of bed to make some coffee. The weight of the watch in my hand started a cascade of memories and thoughts. When we were in Pakistan in 1953, my dad bought a Rolex watch in Hong Kong for $85.00. When he got this magnificent watch, he passed his old Longines down to me. I remember that timepiece. It was rectangular . . . in rose gold. I loved it . . . it was like wearing a piece of him. The Longines has long since vanished in time, swirled away with so many of the things of youth . . . scattered by the winds. But the Rolex . . . that's another story. Dad wore it for many years. When its self-winding mechanism became problematic to maintain, he got a Pulsar, and the old Rolex retired to a drawer in his desk, in its original box, with its original receipt. I used to ask him about the watch . . . I wanted it. It was a Rolex, of course, and I couldn't afford to buy one for myself, but more than that, it would be like wearing a piece of him. He would tell me, "You can't have it. It's mine," and the subject would be closed. "You never use it," I would tell him. "It doesn't even work. I'll fix it and wear it." He would simply say, "It's mine."

At the time I didn't understand. I didn't realize that in holding on to the Rolex, he was holding on to a piece of his younger life. When we were having the "It's mine" conversation, it was in the early nineties and he had already had a stroke and was beginning to decline physically. The watch was a link to the vigor of youth. In his mind, I think he dreamed of hitting the tennis courts in his sparkling whites, the watch on his wrist . . . racket in hand.

In 1995, he finally gave me the watch along with the entire provenance. He had kept everything in his desk drawer all those years. I took it home and sent it to New York to a friend of mine who saw to it that a Rolex authorized repair center put it back into working condition. The next time I saw Dad, I had the watch on my wrist. "Is Rolex time better than Pulsar time?" he would ask. "You bet it is," I would tell him, and for me it was. I would wear the watch non-stop . . . that is until I realized that a forty-something-year-old watch is a fragile thing. It would go back to Rolex more than once to keep it in working condition.

Less than two years later, my father would be dead . . . felled in his own home by the rush of his infirmity, he would fall at my mother's feet. It is now just a month short of six years since Dad headed off to the big tennis court in the sky . . . more than half a decade ago. It is almost five for Mom. The Rolex rests in my nightstand at home. Occasionally it ventures forth on my wrist for a day or two. It is not as accurate as it once was. I fear another trip to the folks at Rolex is in order.

When I turned sixty, Vanessa bought me a Tag Heuer Chronograph. It looks very much like the old Rolex. It is a heavier watch, so much heavier that when I picked it up this morning it felt as heavy as the old Rolex did *when we were both fifty years younger. Its stainless steel band crinkling in my hand opened the doors of memory one more time and the hot, desert winds of time brushed my face . . . Is Rolex time better than Pulsar time, or Tag Heuer time? You bet it is! It's the stuff of dreams. Perhaps one day, a younger person in my life will ask me, "Can I have that watch? You don't use it anymore." I will probably say, "No, it's mine," and hold a lifetime of memories close to my heart. But then on another day . . .*

When Zach crossed the stage in Constitution Hall in 2016 to get his diploma, his grandfather's Rolex was on his wrist. Now it is his to do with as he wills.

A little later in the summer Vanessa and I gave Zach a Jeep Grand Cherokee Laredo to begin his college adventures. I dropped Zach's car off to him in Hagerstown, Maryland, on my way up north to start a tour. He took the car and headed down to the Tappahannock area to visit some friends. This was not far from where I used to spend my summers with my best friend Bill Haile and his family. Zach's mom is now gone too, but he has her eyes and her spirit.

The pace of my life is sometimes faster than others, but it is never still for anyone. The rest of the year passed in the blink of an eye. Zach started his first year of college in the fall and Izze was already working her way through sixth grade. We closed out the year at the Fur Peace Ranch with a concert at the Station featuring Jack Casady, Barry Mitterhoff, and myself for an acoustic evening. We toured as an electric trio after that with simply Jack, Justin Guip, and myself as Electric Hot Tuna. I think on all levels, it was time to go back to basics. I started playing lots more solo shows. I have always loved performing for audiences. When I was a kid I probably played in front of people when I shouldn't have, but I just had to. To sit with my guitar onstage and tell my story to an audience that is actually listening is an amazingly fulfilling experience. Playing and performing was my first true passion and it lives with me still! There is more balance in my life, though. The guitar, the music, the gypsy lifestyle have all found their measure in the composition of my life.

I suspect we all want the same things in life. Here in the United States it is easy to sum up our desires as life, liberty, and the pursuit of happiness. We all want our children to grow and be safe and to be given the tools necessary to find their way in the world. All of my problems have been first-world problems. I have never gone hungry a day in my life, and much of the pain I have experienced has been self-inflicted. Sometimes I take a moment to rest in a cool corner of my memory and think of those who are now gone that I have shared important moments of my life with.

I never considered myself a Californian. I've always been an East Coast kid. That said, the twenty years or so I spent in California defined my life in so many ways. Jerry Garcia, Ron "Pigpen" McKernan, Janis Joplin, Tom Hobson . . . they are all gone now but when our world was still young, we were friends. Neil Cassady, who flipped his hammer in my Divisadero Street apartment many times, is gone. Ken Kesey, while not one of my buddies, was still part of my life. He is gone too. Hunter S. Thompson, who scared the pants off me riding me from the Matrix on his BSA Super Rocket to my apartment on Divisadero in 1965, also gone. Without my time in California and my friendship with these folks, we might not be having this conversation. The magic of youth is a thing unto itself. Combined with fortuitous relationships, it can be transcendental.

Recently my dear friend Larry Coryell passed in his sleep after a gig at the Iridium in New York City. Gregg Allman, who I got to share a stage with more than once, gone. So many of my heroes who I was fortunate enough to get to know are gone also. Hubert Sumlin, A. C. Reed, Johnny Copeland, Reverend Gary Davis, and Brownie McGhee are all playing in that heavenly band. The ongoing tale of blues and gospel will spread their story as long as there are ears to listen. My best friend through high school, Bill Haile, is also gone. Bill was not a musician but I sat in the backseat of his father's car on my first double date. My beloved grandfather Ben, long gone, reached out to me from the grave in a typed note I found in an old folder a decade ago.

Sunday, September 9, 2007, Hillside Farm, Meigs County

So let's see . . . For me that old summer in San Francisco was just another page of colorful self-indulgence in my story. But let me think a little bit about what my real Summer of Love might be. 5767 (2007) was our first summer with our daughter Izze in our life. Yeah, I know, she was a little cranky this morning, teething . . . a little cold and whatnot, but even with all that she is quite simply, a love. In August we had my son Zach with us for a week and we rented a beach house up in Maine. Yep, the first Jorma Kaukonen II family vacation ever. Our vacations as well as our lives in general were punctuated with anger and frustration. That's just how it was. But that's not how it is in our house and that's not how it was on our vacation. There has been love in my life this summer and if I'm lucky and continue to do the things I need to do, I will be able to walk this path through the rest of the journey and into the last mile.

My son, who complains about having to go to school from time to time, actually told me that he liked his new fourth grade class and found his teacher interesting. Now I realize that this is only the first week of school and that a lot of things could happen as the year unfolds, but what a way to start. Izze is in the Child Development program at Ohio University and as her "school" year starts, at fourteen and a half months old, she is the oldest kid in her class and will be moving up the toddler ladder soon. This is love that lasts.

With Rosh Hashanah and Yom Kippur around the corner it is a time for reflection. I have been cleaning my barn yet one more time, a good metaphor for living to say the least. In this process I have been going over box after box of my mom and dad's correspondence and have been getting rid of missives that mean nothing to me. As I have been doing this over the past couple of days (and I'm not done yet) I have been able to go back into a Kaukonen family place filled with love and not fear or pain. I found my grandparents' birth and death certificates. I found Grandmother Kaukonen's applications for American citizenship and the citizenship certificate itself. Izze just got her citizenship so I found this especially touching. There are people who would fight and die for this piece of paper . . . and there it was. There were Pentti's service records . . . his battle medals, his footprints in the Pacific. From Timor

*to the Battle of Leyte Gulf and the liberation landings in the Philippines . . .
there were his tracks.*

*And then, I found some papers that my Grandfather Ben wrote some days
before he died. Ben and Vera were my mother's parents and in some ways,
they were more of a mom and dad to me than Beatrice and Jorma Sr. I lived
with them many times in the course of my life and in 1958/1959 they let me
come home to our house on Northampton Street in DC and live with them as
I finished my senior year of high school at Woodrow Wilson High . . . out there
on Nebraska Ave. I took their love for granted in my thoughtless adolescent
way and pretty much did as I pleased regardless of how they felt. It's not that
I didn't love them. I loved them as much as I was capable of loving anything.
I just ignored their feelings and indulged Jorma . . . or Jerry as I was known
back then. These attitudes certainly set me up to enjoy the hedonism of the sixties but more about that another time. Anyway, I have read my maternal
grandparents' letters to Mom and Dad (yeah, I've got them too) and they
took me to task for being a thoughtless, selfish jerk and they were right. Even
though I try not to replace hope with regret, sometimes you just regret things
and I have to say that I wish I could have made amends to them while they
were still alive. Anyway, I'm looking through this envelope of things Ben
wrote from the rehabilitation home after they amputated his legs and this
is what I found:*

Sholom

A poem by

Benjamin S. Levine, Ph.D.

In lieu of a last word

Dedicated to my two grandsons

Jorma Ludvik Kaukonen, Jr.

And

Benson Lee (Peter) Kaukonen

*I have been reading the poems of
The Canadian Jewish poet, A.M. Klein
And in GLOSS BETH of series—SECOND SCROLL*

Have come across the following cry of his soul:
"Death may be beautiful, when full of years,
Ripe with good works, a man among his sons,
Says his last word, and turns him to the wall . . ."

This hit me hard, in the mind and in the heart . . .
I feel that my life is now full of years,
And had I felt its ripeness with good works,
I among my grandsons might turn to the wall . . .
But, I'm not judge of the ripeness of my life,
Nor of its fullness with good works,
Nor of the essence and the meaning of good works
Done by others appraised by myself as judge,
Particularly as it pertained to works of
Younger generations personified by my
Grandsons. I judged them harshly, especially
In their intentions, knowing now that I was
In error with regard to their coming home
At the hour later than commended, and with regard
To associating with types and "activities" thought
To be undesirable for reasons of my own, and
Completely disregarded by them, which caused
Friction and uncompromising disagreement and
Poison in (and) of the family unity and morale.

In the ultimate youth had won, with no harm done
To themselves and to the oldsters, which bolstered
My confidence and trust in youth's decision
Regarding their own future plans of life . . .
. . . .
No matter how full my years, I will not
Turn me to the wall when come my time to die,
But I will shake the hands of my two grandsons,

And, looking straight into each one's face,
I hope I will say: "Well done, my boy,
Well done, my son, I hope you will continue
Doing well long after I have gone . . ."
PAX–VO–BIS–CUM

Bethesda–Silver Spring Nursing Home
September 5, 6, 7, 1970

As I finished reading this unexpected discovery yesterday I was moved by a physical force that forced the air from my chest. I gasped for air through the sea of raw emotion and memory and I truly felt that I was sent to this old box, this old envelope, and this old piece of paper to read a message that my grandfather Ben knew that I needed to see today! I have no recollection of ever having seen this poem before. It has been waiting there for me for thirty-seven years to surface now in the closing days of 5767. I am, of course, embraced by what I perceive to be my grandfather's forgiveness and blessing to my brother Peter and myself, but more than that, I am called to task for my own lack of ability to forgive. I shall have to work harder on that.

So there it is . . . my Summer of Love, 2007. My family both alive and dead reach out to me with loving arms and today I am able to receive that embrace. I hope there are many summers filled with love for all of us and that our favorite years are not confined to distant memories alone.

In a normal world, at my age I would probably be a great-grandfather, at the very least. Now I tend to spend time with people who are considerably younger than I am. It wasn't planned that way. At the time of this writing Vanessa and I will have been married almost thirtysome years. I have a young daughter who is a pistol and a son who is a fine young man. I am so proud of both of them.

Who can script a life—and who would want to? When someone asks me if I ever think about retiring I always say, "Why, so I can spend more time playing the guitar?" Both my kids play music. Both my kids will occasionally go to the range with Dad and go shooting. They both like to ride motorcycles with me. But I see both their lives evolving without being submerged by who and what their parents are and do.

My dad used to say that getting older was a series of successful adaptations. I'll try to keep that in mind. As for me, I am so fortunate that I get to look forward as well as back. I will never forget one of those last conversations I had with my mother when she looked wistfully at me and said, "I wish I could believe." At the risk of putting words in the mouth of someone who can no longer dispute them, I sensed a lack of fulfillment. I like to think that I am still seeking and finding fulfillment.

I keep finding a large measure of this fulfillment in the Fur Peace Ranch. When we started thinking about the Ranch in the early nineties, when we started building it in 1997, we had the most distant of visions. It was almost as if we could see a hidden world through a fog . . . but not quite. There was surely some unseen guidance here. I doubt we could have conceived of it this way at the time, but we created a haven for like-minded spirits. We find ourselves surrounded with the joy of spirit that only the music can provide, and to be a part of this is indeed transcendental.

As for the road . . . does it go on forever? We'll just have to wait and see how long forever is.

Epilogue

Thursday, August 3, 2017, West of Billings, Montana
Those of us who live on the road share an interesting bond of experience.
It is 0550 right now and we are an hour west of Billings, Montana. The sun
has yet to peek above the horizon and the majesty of this American road as
we climb toward the next pass is undeniable. I sit shotgun with our driver
Ross for a while and we talk about not the tours we have been on but the
roads we have traveled. The light isn't everything; the road itself wraps me
in its world. Cities and towns rise in front of us and fade behind us like
specters in the mist. The brotherhood of the road musician brings the never-
ending tell of where we've been and where we're going. We all know the truck
stops and restaurants and vistas and roadside rests. We all know how we felt
after our last show and how, as glad as we are to be heading home, how we
already look forward to the next show. If this occasionally makes me feel con-
flicted, that's OK. It is all a blessing. I-90 bends gently as it climbs toward
another pass. The smoke from the mountain fires near Bonner is gone and it
is a crisp 48 degrees outside. We stop at a rest area and I fly my drone and
take some great pictures. Back on the road we wind our way to Dickenson,
North Dakota.

We make Minneapolis the next day and Jack and I play two acoustic duo shows at the Dakota Jazz Club. After the second show we drive

to St. Charles, Illinois, and play another acoustic show at the Arcada Theatre. We have been out for over five weeks and it is time to go home. We scatter to our homes, where a different segment of our lives awaits us. Some to LA, some to New York, and my friend Myron and myself come back to our farms in Ohio—and that is that for now.

So when all was said and done, did I fly into the light? And what was that really all about? It's not about Icarus flying too close to the sun, I didn't get burned . . . this has always been the reward. At the time of this writing Hot Tuna has just finished touring for five weeks with Susan Tedeschi and Derek Trucks as well as the Wood Brothers. Seeing the lights dance on the audience almost every night has transfixed me in this moment, where we the musicians dance into the stars along with the crowd. There is no feeling in the world like it! The music seeps into the spaces between the molecules of my soul and I am part of a universe far greater than myself. We are able to fly every night! Was I meant for this? Hindsight muddies the water with false prescience. This is not all of who I am, but it certainly is a large part.

These are moments that do not share easily in the verbal medium, try as I might. The whole is always greater than the sum of its parts, and the music will always fill a vacuum in the heart. So I will come back from this trip and rejoin my family at home. I will be merely Dad again for a while and that's OK. I have missed my family. I look forward to being a part of their every day. I will teach at the Ranch and I will play music with my friends back in the county and that light will have to suffice. In time, another tour will call my name, and I will seek the source again one more time to tell another story.

The process is the reward in and of itself. Everything else is frosting. If life is designed to humble us in the face of time, there is joy in that humility. I shall do my best to respect and care for my gift and to share it along the way, and that will have to do!

Afterword

As I write this, a winter storm is subsiding and the first rays of morning sun splash over the snow-covered fields, spreading its life-giving warmth and promise of renewal. I have just finished reading Jorma's three-quarter-century telling of my oldest and best friend's life story. Jorma has been my friend and fellow music traveler for over sixty years now . . . and counting!

You would think I would know much about someone during all this time, and perhaps I do somewhat. I have always been drawn to Jorma's ability to tell a story and put so many to song. However, here is the chance for me to really absorb some of the deep aspects to this man's life and feelings, from childhood to present. What a privilege for me to have shared some of these pages, but an honor that he has shared his life with all of us. The musical journey is of course mainstream to this telling, but he graciously allows any reader to grasp and perhaps identify with the so-many-layered aspects of his growing years and this search to better ourselves. There is always a solid thread of purpose to Jorma's writing, but here in these pages is his story of redemption, renewal, and the power of love and friendship.

I have always been in awe of Jorma's power, strength, and endurance, but now with this book, we get to understand some of the motivations and meanings to his actions, and sometimes nonactions. You have taken me on one great adventure, Jorma, and I look forward to another quarter century or so of your continued quest!

—Jack Casady

Lyric Appendix

Jorma Kaukonen's Songs
(Lyrics appear chronologically)

THE LAST WALL OF THE CASTLE

BY JORMA KAUKONEN

From *After Bathing at Baxter's*, Jefferson Airplane, 1967

Gone swirling tears came,
She went today
Down falling years go by
No grace in learning how to cry
I went astray
Understanding is a virtue, hard to come by
You can teach me how to love, if you'll only try
So please, don't give up so soon

Sorry, that I hurt her
I went astray
Hurt her mind and broke her heart

But there's no stopping once you start
She went away
Understanding is a virtue, hard to come by
You can teach me how to love, if you'll only try
So please, don't give up so soon

I never knew you
The way you are
The blinded bird is not sincere
His flying's done from only fear
He's lost his star
Understanding is a virtue, hard to come by
You can teach me how to love, if you'll only try
So please, don't give up so soon

ICE CREAM PHOENIX

BY JORMA KAUKONEN AND CHARLES COCKEY

From *Crown of Creation*, Jefferson Airplane, 1968

You don't know just
When to stop and when to go
City streets in the dead of winter
Stop your mind with dirty snow

Walk at night and
Touch your hand to the golden lights
And let them show
Feel the shadows disappearing
I'll smile and say
"I told you so."

Baby . . .
Tell me why, if you think you know why,

People love when there's no tomorrow
And still not cry when it's time to go
And still not cry when it's time to go
And still not cry when it's time to go

The wall of your memory
Still echoes your sorrow;
The pictures of sadness
Are not what they seem
So hold out your smile
Take my hand and be happy
These pictures of sadness
Are not all they seem

Are you so old that you've no childhood?
Is your timeline so unreal
That all your sunsets
Come in the morning?
Baby tell me . . . how you feel

Shelves of books in your mirror reflected,
The sidewalks and alleys that you've seen,
The colors change as the images fade in
The magical vanishing memory machine

Baby . . .
Tell me why, if you think you know why,
People love when there's no tomorrow
And still not cry when it's time to go
And still not cry when it's time to go
And still not cry when it's time to go

STAR TRACK

BY JORMA KAUKONEN

From *Crown of Creation*, Jefferson Airplane, 1968

If your head spins round try to see the ground if you can
My busy eyes missed her path through the air as she ran
My sensory mind is too old to cry
Not ready to live and too strange to die
So stop your doubt push the world on by
With your hand

It takes time to love and open minds to love
And who's got time on their hands
Well life can be hard when you're holes in a card
In some electronic hand
You'll wander around from place to place
Disappear without a trace
And someone else will take your place
In line

You can fool your friends about the way it ends
But you can't fool yourself
Take your head in hand and make your own demands
Or you'll crystallize on the shelf
The freeway's concrete way won't show
You where to run or how to go
And running fast you'll go down slow in the end

Running fast you'll go down slow in the end

TURN MY LIFE DOWN

BY JORMA KAUKONEN

From *Volunteers*, Jefferson Airplane, 1969

When I see you next time round in sorrow
Will you know what I've been going through?
My yesterdays have melted with my tomorrow
And the present leaves me with no point of view

When I see you next time round, look into my eyes
Where we'd be we never could decide
My borrowed moments they cannot fill the moments of our lives
And wishful thinking leaves me no place to hide
No place to hide
No place to hide

I see the shadows softly coming
Taking me into a place
Where they turn my life down
Leaving mourning with myself
And nothing to say

GOOD SHEPHERD

JAMES STROTHER

From *Bark*, Jefferson Airplane, 1971
This is an old-time spiritual/rock song. It was collected from the aging blind blues player Jimmie Strothers as "The Blood-Strained Banders," by Alan Lomax and Harold Spivacke on behalf of the Library of Congress in 1936.

If you want to get to heaven, over on the other shore
Stay out of the way of the blood-stained bandits
Oh good shepherd feed my sheep

One for Paul, one for Silas
One for to make my heart rejoice
Can't you hear my lambs are callin'
Oh good shepherd feed my sheep

If you want to get to heaven, over on the other shore
Stay out of the way of the long-tongue liar
Oh good shepherd feed my sheep

One for Paul, one for Silas
One for to make my heart rejoice
Can't you hear my lambs are callin'
Oh good shepherd feed my sheep

If you want to get to heaven, over on the other shore
Stay out of the way of the gun-shot devil
Oh good shepherd feed my sheep
Oh good shepherd feed my sheep

One for Paul, one for Silas
One for to make my heart rejoice
Can't you hear my lambs are callin'
Oh good shepherd feed my sheep

THIRD WEEK IN THE CHELSEA

BY JORMA KAUKONEN

From *Bark*, Jefferson Airplane, 1971

The music was certainly a product of what I was up to in the finger-style world. The words came straight from the heart. Some were true, and some were wishful thinking.

Sometimes I feel like I am leaving life behind
My hands are moving faster than the moving of my mind

Thoughts and generations of my dreams are yet unborn
I hope that I may find them 'fore my moving gets too worn
If only I can live to see the dawning of the dawn

So we go on moving trying to make this image real
Straining every nerve not knowing what we really feel
Straining every nerve and making everybody see
That what they read in the Rolling Stone *has really come to be*
And trying to avoid a taste of that reality

On an early New York morning, a mirror in the hall
Showed to me a face I did not know at all
Lines were drawn around a pair of eyes that opened wide
And when I looked into them there was nothing left inside
So I walked into a little room that whistled like a sigh

As dawn light closed around me, my head was still in gear
Thinking thoughts of playing more and singing loud and clear
Trying to reach a friend somewhere and make that person smile
Maybe pull myself away from that old lonesome mile
That often comes to haunt me in the morning

Bridge:
All my friends keep telling me, that it would be a shame
To break up such a grand success and tear apart a name
But all I know is what I feel whenever I'm not playing
But emptiness ain't where it's at and neither's feeling pain

Well what is going to happen now is anybody's guess
If I can't spend my time with love I guess I need a rest
Time is getting late now and the sun is setting low
My body's getting tired, from carrying another's load
And sunshine's waiting for me a little further down the road

NEW SONG (FOR THE MORNING)

BY JORMA KAUKONEN

From *Hot Tuna*, 1970

Looked outside my window,
fog came up to play
That gray outside is around my head,
Looks like it's there to stay
Looks like it's there to stay
Looks like it's there to stay
Can't you see I love you, I want you more and more
I see you here most every day
I don't know where you are
I don't know where you are
Time goes on, and I get older
What am I gonna do?
My mirror face keeps getting colder
My eyes still look for you . . .
My eyes still look for you
Said my eyes still look for you
Sun came out this morning
Highway showed my way
Cracks in the sand
Pulled me into the sea
Washed my cares away
Washed my cares away
You know I want to touch you
My vacuum gives me pain
Your smile releases all my life,
Like flowers under rain
Like flowers under rain
We start to live again
We start to live again

SEA CHILD

BY JORMA KAUKONEN

From *Burgers*, Hot Tuna, 1972

Daily games run off like water
Falling down like summer rain
We see each other in confusion
And wonder why we came today

Sitting lonely in our prison
Looking out for ways to say
What we mean without confusion
In our less uncommon way

Through your hair, across my eyes
The twilight shafts in soft surprise
Reminds me once again how nice
It is to be with you . . .

HIGHWAY SONG

BY JORMA KAUKONEN

From *Burgers*, Hot Tuna, 1972

Rolling down the highway
Living in the spring
It's raining somewhere down the road
That don't mean a thing
If I knew where I was coming from or going to
I might make you happy little girl
Living here with you
Till then I'm gone . . . little mama
'fore the dawn light comes my way

I'll be gone . . . ain't got time to stay
Here with you

When I get to Washington
Gonna take you by the hand
Walking the street of your fair city's
Like being in another land
Up and down, all around
Everywhere I go
What tomorrow's gonna bring to me
I guess we'll never know
Till then I'm gone . . . little mama
'fore the dawn light comes my way
I'll be gone . . . ain't got time to stay
Here with you

Bridge:
Rolling down the highway
Trying to head home someday
Don't look back till I get home
Don't worry bout tomorrow
Don't let it bring me sorrow
Down on me . . .

Maybe one day while I'm moving
I might find the end
Comin' cross the desert
Could be coming round the bend
Maybe while I'm at the seashore
It might come to me
I'll go down for the last time
Now just you wait and see

Well I'll be there with you little mama
When the dawn light comes your way
You make me feel so new
And you know I'm here to stay
Here with you

Rolling down the highway
Living in the spring
It's raining somewhere down the road
Now that don't mean a thing
Now I know just where I've been
And where I'm going to
I won't go there with another
If I can't take you
Well I'll be there with you little mama
When the dawn light comes your way
You make me feel so new
And you know I'm here to stay

TRIAL BY FIRE

BY JORMA KAUKONEN

From *Long John Silver*, Jefferson Airplane, 1972

Gonna move on down the highway, make this moment last
Till it closes with the future, leaving out the past
Rolling 'long and doing fine now, what do you think I see?
That bony hand comes a beckonin', sayin' buddy come and go with me

Cause that engine just ain't strong enough to get you round the turn
Lie on your back in the middle of a field and watch your body burn

Chorus:

Don't try to tell me just who I am when you don't know yourself

*Spend all your time running out on the street with your mind home
    on the shelf*

*Looking at me with your eyes full of fire like you'd rather be seeing
    me dead*

*Lyin' on the floor with a hole in my face and a ten-gauge shotgun at my
    head*

Well you can leave me here, but I won't tell

Things I know about you and know so well

The way you smile at me, try to set me free

And keep me wondering what the future will be

Rolling on, won't be long

I won't leave here till I sing this song

Chorus

GENESIS

BY JORMA KAUKONEN

From *Quah*, Jorma Kaukonen, 1974

The time has come for us to pause

And think of living as it was

Into the future we must cross (must cross)

I'd like to go with you

And I'd like to go with you

You say I'm harder than a wall

A marble shaft about to fall

I love you dearer than them all (them all)

So let me stay with you
So let me stay with you

And as we walked into the day
Skies of blue had turned to gray
I might have not been clear to say (to say)
I never looked away
I never looked away

And though I'm feeling you inside
My life is rolling with the tide
I'd like to see it be an open ride
Along with you
Going along with you

The time we borrowed from ourselves
Can't stay within a vault too well
And living turns into a lender's well
So let me come with you
And let me come with you

And when we came out into view
And there I found myself with you
When breathing felt like something new . . . new
Along with you
Going along with you

SONG FOR THE NORTH STAR

BY JORMA KAUKONEN

From *Quah*, Jorma Kaukonen, 1974

They gave me money to find the sky
And I took it with no questions, didn't even ask them why

But days are open and skies are free
And the time it took to learn that didn't leave its change on me

I lived in shadows, away from the sun
And the trembling in my mind kept my heart and body on the run
Then freedom called us, called out our names
And the beckon of its highway saw through all our useless games

The love we wanted was lost in lies
And the chances slipped on by me like the flashing sorrow in her eyes

Bridge:

Then we took the rise together for the first time in our lives
Feeling just like one is better than wasting time on fearful strife

Our time is open for us to see
And our freedom skims on upward like the seagulls soaring at the sea
And our freedom skims on upward like the seagulls soaring at the sea

FLYING CLOUDS

BY JORMA KAUKONEN

From *Quah*, Jorma Kaukonen, 1974

Say there's gonna be some sailing on the morning tide
The breakers clear your ears, the ocean's here to take you on a ride
Building houses made of paper, living for the day
That one way ride, on gravel slides, begins to fade away

Chorus:

I'm singing everybody knows it's true
Way I feel 'bout you
Got no mind for wasting time
Feeling like I do

Now I feel like only smiling, living by your side
Our course is clear, we see it here, there's no more lonesome rides

Heading for our destination, the past is out of sight
Your eyes in mine, their fires entwine, we've finally reached the light

Chorus

Heading for the sunshine country, going with the wind
The love we know, can't help but grow, as life comes rolling in
As life comes rolling in

I SEE THE LIGHT

BY JORMA KAUKONEN

From *The Phosphorescent Rat*, Hot Tuna, 1973

In this world I'm living in, I see the light
Sins are gone and now I know what is wrong and right
Morning came on slowly, pushing back the night
Good times now that I can see the light

On this road I'm walking on, I see my way
Paradise I'm living for, each and every day
'Bout the crossroads of the past, nothing more to say
Good times now that we can see our way

In this sea I'm moving through, feel my life complete
With the one I'm living for, time is oh so sweet
Feeling us together, living in the bright
It's good times now that we can see the light

In this world I'm living in, I see the light
Sins are gone and now I know what is wrong and right
Morning came on slowly, pushing back the night
Good times now that we can see the light

LETTER TO THE NORTH STAR

BY JORMA KAUKONEN

From *The Phosphorescent Rat*, Hot Tuna, 1973

Winter's been a long, long time
Summer's here again
I've been trying to make you mine
Since I don't know when

Way your soul can let you fly
Makes me love you more
You're spirit flowing into mine
What I'm living for

So don't hold back little baby when I reach out to you
I'm doing my best to bring you round
And swing you into view
So I can better see your face and you can look at mine
And we can feel each other move together down the line

One more time I'm asking you to let this moment be
All our lives can intertwine till eternity
Please don't let your pride run free and make me pass you by
There's a place out there for us, if we only try

With what we got together now, the rest ain't hard to do
You can see it ain't no jive, all my love for you

EASY NOW (ORIGINAL VERSION)

BY JORMA KAUKONEN

From *The Phosphorescent Rat*, Hot Tuna, 1973

Chorus:
I got the ridin' pneumonia today
Well the weather's too fine to stay
Now I wanna go down to Mexico
Got a feelin' we'll be heading that way

By this time tomorrow, who knows where I'll be
Highway lines keep marking time, riding by the sea
Ain't no cop says I can't stop, moving on my way
Future's bright, pass the lights, leaving Monterey

Chorus

Movin' in the mountains, snakin' through the pines
That lakeside light on summer nights makes you feel like flying
Passing through this morning dew, nature gives a roar
There's motion on the highway, you can see my spirit soar

Chorus

Look out of the window, tell me what you see
I hear someone calling, reaching after me
Starting to slide on the mercury mile smoothing on the side
The world that's gray just fades away, lets your body ride

Chorus

LIVING JUST FOR YOU

BY JORMA KAUKONEN

From *The Phosphorescent Rat*, Hot Tuna, 1973

I've waited all my lifetime for a moment like today
Our love is really real and really here to stay
And now I know what's happening, this starting all anew
I've been living lately just because of you
People on the sidewalks of the city passing by
They don't know how high we fly
Now I know I've found you, the world all around
Is filled with sounds of smiling from the heavens to the ground
It takes a long time to be free
I want you there with me

Don't want to live my life away, without you
That kind of living now, just won't do
There's been too much wasted time feeling blue
In the morning when we rise, the sparkle in your eyes
Reminds me that I'm living just for you

SOLILOQUY FOR Z

BY JORMA KAUKONEN

From *The Phosphorescent Rat*, Hot Tuna, 1973

Fog rolled in from the ocean yesterday
The beach had disappeared within the gray
And tomorrow almost drowned at sea
Without a trace of living that's to be

Can't you hear me calling out your name
Sun's a halo shining on your face again

And I know that time will never cease to be
For us to be together you and me

Chorus:
Whatever's gonna come can't help but take us further
Down the road of life we call our home
Time keeps moving on, like a river in the dawn
Still we'll never be alone

Yesterday, the way was dark as night
If you look within the road comes into sight
And our love is sharper that a surgeon's knife
We'll be together all our life

SLEEP SONG

BY JORMA KAUKONEN

From *America's Choice*, Hot Tuna, 1975

Shoreline's smaller, every day wonder why we feel this way
You don't know that I got nothing left to say
I been blown across the water, like a ship ain't got no sail
That ain't no way to be

I feel that longing, loud and clear
Dead end streets an alley here
When you're flyin' you got nothing left to fear
Unless you're blown across the water, like a ship ain't got no sail
That ain't no way to be

Winter wind keeps blowing through the trees
But life keeps breathing gaily as you please
Silver birches lying by the road
Branches lined against the winter snow

We left the shelter, yesterday
Had to meet a place someway
You can't find it I got nothing left to say
If you're blown across the water, like a ship ain't got no sail
That ain't no way to be

I been blown across the water, like a ship ain't got no sail
That ain't no way to be

FUNKY #7

BY JORMA KAUKONEN AND JACK CASADY

From *America's Choice*, Hot Tuna, 1975

Walking talking breathing trying to smile yourself to death
With your finger on the pulse of time there ain't no time to rest
It's just a simple component to keep you walking the line
Just trying to get back for what you borrowed in time
The moral of the story's for a limited crew
But we're going to be there in the chosen few

But meanwhile tomorrow tryin' to find me a scheme
There's got to be an easy way to turn my money green
With such a promising future there ain't no way to go wrong
But the line that I'm walking just keeps taking too long
There'll be a rainbow on the morning of the following day
But how we're going to find it I just can't say at all

If I live tomorrow, like I'm living today
There ain't no way to borrow room for me to stay

INVITATION

BY JORMA KAUKONEN

From *America's Choice*, Hot Tuna, 1975

Come along with me my lady, gonna ride this road together
You can see my love for you ain't dependent on the weather
Living with you by my side such an easy road to follow
With the future as our guide as we ride into tomorrow

Chorus:
Though the world keeps turning round
Don't you know we're here to stay
Tired of living underground
The time has come to dance and play
Can't you hear the forest sing
About the things that we have seen
We'll take our chances on the wing
Or lose them in the dream machine

With your body close to mine, can't you feel my heart beat stronger?
Fingers linger on my spine and the hour is getting longer
What a way to spend the day climbing mountains to the sky
On narrow trails that disappear in the spiral of your eyes

Chorus

HIT SINGLE #1

BY JORMA KAUKONEN

From *America's Choice*, Hot Tuna, 1975

Every time I touch your face I get a feeling in my shoes
Marking time ain't the way to race you got to make some headline news

Jump back now don't let your feet go slow, you got to let your body sway
Won't you tell me what I want to know, there's time enough to play

Here we go down we got to slink and slide like a serpent in the sea
In the magic circle we spin and glide, you know my mind is running free
Keep your hand on my shoulder don't get lost in the ride
There's loving left to show
And there ain't no explainin' what I feel inside
Let that motion roll

SERPENT OF DREAMS

BY JORMA KAUKONEN

From *America's Choice*, Hot Tuna, 1975

Flowers today, blooming by the pathway
Lining the edge of tomorrow's grave
Bright shining way, living in the shadows
Trying to be the master of tomorrow's slave

Down in the mine, circled round a diamond
The serpent of your expectations sleeps a nervous dream
Circled so fine, like a velvet palace
He whiles away the passing hours, not being what he seems

Then he creeps into the light
Speeding up like fireflight
Out he moves into the forest floor
Sinew moves the pace of time
Leaves behind the lonely mine
And the diamond shining on the floor

We cannot stay by the crystal mountain
The serpent of dreams, has left his shadow lair

The diamond remains, brilliant in its cavern
With no one to see, and no one left to care

The serpent's friends have come and gone,
Down the road they're moving on
To the lakes and valleys in the dale
They will find tomorrow's rise, brings them all the bluest skies
Frees the lonesome banshee and his wail

I DON'T WANT TO GO

BY JORMA KAUKONEN

From *America's Choice*, Hot Tuna, 1975

Up this morning saw Death coming cross a field far away
"I've been looking all night long, I'm coming for you today"
I looked up, all around . . . hiding I don't know
Lots of things I got to do so I don't wanna go

Chorus:
I don't wanna go
I don't wanna go
Lots of things I got to do and living's most too slow

This time when the demon calls gonna look the other way
See the clock keeps moving . . . too much left to say
The moon is sinking slowly and the raven's flying low
Lots of things I got to do so I don't wanna go, well . . .

Chorus

The singing rain calls out to me and tells me how to fly
An angel slips between the trees and reaches for the sky

Imagination spins me round and wind begins to blow
Lots of things I want to do so I don't wanna go

Chorus

Morning rises slowly and reaches for the sky
The angel from the forest, just seemed to pass me by
The black marauder missed his chance and light began to show
Lots of things I got to do so I don't wanna go

I don't wanna go
I don't wanna go
I've got living left to do and living's most too slow

FREE REIN

WORDS BY JORMA KAUKONEN

MUSIC BY JORMA KAUKONEN AND PAUL ZEIGLER

From *Yellow Fever*, Hot Tuna, 1975

Tell me why you look so free
Looking back, you don't see me
I don't know if I can stay
Living in the world this way
One fine day gonna jump and shout
Ain't nobody turn me out
While that freeway drives me down
That old highway round

Chorus:
Hear an angel say, living ain't so gray
With each passing day, sunshine turns me round

And it seems to me that smiling's fine again
Well it seems to me that smiling's fine again

If you see me riding by
Ain't no time to stop and cry
A merry race is often lost
The lonesome highway's crossed
In the passing friends of life
The greedy morning story sighs
The situation long ago
And timeless rivers flow

Chorus

SUNRISE DANCE WITH THE DEVIL

BY JORMA KAUKONEN

From *Yellow Fever*, Hot Tuna, 1975

Time will come you're gonna see things my way
And maybe you won't mind
When a heavenly spire eludes you're seeking
And grabs you from behind

Chorus:
You're gonna wake up in the morning 'bout a quarter to four
And the thoughts that you been thinkin' won't keep making you sore
You'll find your personal ballroom's got a parquet floor
And the devil's got a new pair of shoes
You're gonna strut around that corner gonna shake your behind
Although the company you're keeping thinks you're losing your mind
You got to overlook the madness cause your spirit is blind
And your feet don't seem to know what to do

Well the sound keeps rollin' and the band plays on
Somebody's favorite tune
And the rough's in your ears obliterates your fears
And you can't get off too soon

Chorus

BAR ROOM CRYSTAL BALL

BY JORMA KAUKONEN

From *Yellow Fever*, Hot Tuna, 1975

Early this morning someone hot on the line
Said me and my friends are downtown, drinking wine
They're trying to help me but they ain't got time
To see which way I've fallen

Chorus:
Well this sawdust's feelin' fine, and my body sure don't mind
This solitary flying,
Past summer's stare again,
I don't remember when

This morning feels as if it's still a part of night
And the dream I had before the last is out of sight
But what I feel between us now gives you the right
To see how far I've fallen

Chorus

One more line before me gonna see me pass
Into the realm of pure imagination last
Before the unsung shower of a lightning blast
Around the house that's fallen

Chorus

Now I see the form that's silent on the floor
And nothing's gonna be the way it was before
Still I feel the shadow from the pistol's roar
Above the head that's fallen

Chorus

WATCH THE NORTH WIND RISE

BY JORMA KAUKONEN

From *Hoppkorv*, Hot Tuna, 1976

Well up in the morning watch the north wind rise
Bringing fire down from the sky
Hey we got a long way to go
So keep on lovin' and make it slow
We're going home, won't be long
Hear in my song,
That lovin' you ain't never done no wrong

Nighttime falls like the crack of doom
Fills the sky with a shining moon
Silver siren just got to please
Feelin' your lovin' down in my knees
We're going home, won't be long
Hear in my song, that lovin' you
Ain't never done no wrong

Chorus:
Well baby mine, one more time
Run your hands down my spine
If you say you got to go
Take some time for just one more

SONG FROM THE STAINLESS CYMBAL

BY JORMA KAUKONEN

From *Hoppkorv*, Hot Tuna, 1975

Get down child; you've got to find another way
Stop running in the alley now, that ain't no way to start the day
I hear people talking 'bout the time that you spent living in the clouds
You know I ain't no fortune teller still I hear your future singing loud

Walking through the shadows with a thousand shiny mirrors all around
Down an endless cavern like some princess in a rainy underground
Waiting for tomorrow and you traded with a never mind today
In a world that's filled with sorrow you're a winner now that anyone
    can say

ROADS AND ROADS &

BY JORMA KAUKONEN

From *Jorma*, Jorma Kaukonen, 1979

Walkin' down that lonesome road
Set my soul on fire
Thinkin' back before I left
The passions I desire
Can't you help me anymore
To live my life more freely
Instead of twisting like a rope that's falling at your feet

Chorus:
Well all right the future paved the way
Still I could not follow
Blindness caught and made me slave
Serving royal sorrow

You could free my captive soul
From hesitation madness
For my life just ain't nowhere
When all I see is sadness

Well all right, all right
Find my blindness changed to sight
Well all right, all right
Still wait for you in the night

Walkin' down that lonesome road
Flying with feet of fire
Looking for that windy place
Searching ever higher
High up on a mountaintop
A fortress beckons fondly
With thoughts about a brighter day together in the sun

Chorus

VALLEY OF TEARS

BY JORMA KAUKONEN

From *Jorma*, Jorma Kaukonen, 1979

Shake my life don't you leave me here
'Cause I'm lying in the valley of tears
Break my life, it's too much to bear
And I'm dying in the valley of tears
When things ain't going my way
We'll be flying down the highway
That valley holds them back I hear
Tomorrow's brief vacation should provide a new sensation
The same old town I hear

Wake my life 'cause the dream is real
And I'm sleeping in the valley of tears
Time is right though I'm bleeding here
And there's screaming through forgotten years
Though it's death the twilight's dealing
Can't decide just what you're feeling
The moment flies too fast this year
When you're through deliberating
And you're trying for escape
You're wandering alone out there

Take my life if you think it's fair
'Cause I'm sinking in the valley of tears
'Sake my life if you really care
And you want to show some sunshine here
Through the messages I'm thinking
I can feel my spirit sinking
Won't come till the end is near
So into the pit I'm falling
I can hear some voices calling
Join me in the valley of tears

SONG FOR THE HIGH MOUNTAIN

BY JORMA KAUKONEN

From *Jorma*, Jorma Kaukonen, 1979

You know I need you darling, though you think I lie
If you don't believe I love you look into my eyes
Every day you hurt me, and I don't know why
Though the night will change into the morning

Say you're walking on a road that don't lead anywhere
And you don't know where you're going and you just don't care

Got to be at least one thing that makes your life worthwhile
If you live you'll find it in the morning

Bridge:

Well I don't know just what to say to help you find a way
In a world that's governed by your sorrow
Well I don't know just what to do I'm being here with you
Wasting time it's hard to climb but still I'm trying to

Well babe you know I need you, here before I die
If I fail on this time round, guess I'll always try
For I missed your loving, reaching for the sky
I'll be waiting for you in the morning
Well I'll be waiting for you in the morning
Well I'll be waiting for you in the morning

WOLVES AND LAMBS

BY JORMA KAUKONEN

From *Jorma*, Jorma Kaukonen, 1979

When you lie awake, feel your body shake
Come on girl don't let your spirit break
When the life you're in is more than you can take you got to
Once more look away, living for today
Don't satisfy your senseless pleasures
Once more look away and follow with your heart
As the waves come crashing miles apart

A ravenous love, celestial from above
Soars on high above the hunter's glove
Fills an empty heart with beggar's blood
Oceans screaming in the storm, waiting to be born
Like wanted children out on Sunday convinced there's

More there standing at the shore
Where their lives once promised so much more

A heartless mate, a creature you could hate
Well take some time and let your conscience wait
And search for vengeance deep within a murky lake
Sorrows crying in the night, sighing from the fright
Of hungry dogs and waiting widows looking for the
Time once spent in the candy store
Where their lives once offered so much more

REQUIEM FOR AN ANGEL

BY JORMA KAUKONEN

From *Jorma*, Jorma Kaukonen, 1979

Wait for tomorrow it'll be a better day than today
Wait for tomorrow child you better heed the words that I say
Well the sun gonna shine, ain't gonna change my mind no way
When that new day comes, I know I won't be seeking no gray

Chorus:
Well everybody's trying to make me change my mind
My friends tell me I'm just wasting my time
Well I don't care cause I really ain't blind or crazy

I won't lose my mind though all I can find is trouble
Though the going gets rough I just slide on by on the double
And though that highway calls I'll fly through the sky like a bubble
And when that new day comes I'll be feeling like driving alone

Chorus

Repeat chorus

MAN FOR ALL SEASONS

BY JORMA KAUKONEN

From *Barbeque King*, Jorma Kaukonen, 1981

Just a junkie on angel dust
Looking for a man to trust
Well I said one good shot is what he's got
And that's enough

Lord I got to take my time
Tomorrow don't never mind
Watch my life slow down
While the world goes round without me

Don't care 'bout the ladies
The world outside just makes you lazy
Don't mind if I flip while I'm on this trip
I'm going crazy

Going up and down
Watch the world go round
Can't touch the ground if I want to
Going in and out, I can't jump and shout

Can't control my promise
Can't control my car
With a shot so small . . .

SNOUT PSALM

BY JORMA KAUKONEN

From *Barbeque King,* Jorma Kaukonen, 1981

It's a miserable morning got nothing to do
I wish there was something or someone to sue
There's time on the meter and I'm feeling blue
While I'm busy here

Chorus:

Outside of the circle not a great place to be
Familiar secrets of past ecstasy
I'm starting to feel but I'm failing to see
I'm an anachronistic cosmology

It's a miserable morning for thinking with fools
The handyman genius has lost half his tools
And time and temptation's got the family jewels
Still I'm busy here

Chorus

It's a miserable morning to greet with a shout
The financer's itching his quivering snout
Like a stick in a carrot he's on pouring clout
And I'm thinking here

Chorus

It's a miserable morning got nothing to do
I wish there was something or someone to sue
There's time on the meter and I'm feeling blue
While I'm thinking . . .

I feel like a piece of shopworn shit

BARBEQUE KING

BY JORMA KAUKONEN

From *Barbeque King*, Jorma Kaukonen, 1981

The Barbeque King, he's coming to town
With his shiny pants well he looks like a clown
And he'll cook your barbeque, any way you please
He's filling up your kettle now with every pound
The man can squeeze

That Barbeque King, he's having fun
He's putting the taste on your garlic bread bun
And he'll cook your barbeque, any way you please
He's filling up your kettle mama with every pound of meat the man
    can squeeze

The Barbeque King, he's got it made
With diamond stick pins and garlic pomade
Well he'll cook your barbecue any way you please
He's filling up your kettle with every pound the man can squeeze

The Barbeque King, he's coming to town
With his shiny pants well he looks like a clown
And he'll cook your barbecue, any way you please
He's filling up your kettle with every pound
The man can squeeze

BROKEN HIGHWAY

BY JORMA KAUKONEN

From *Too Hot to Handle*, Jorma Kaukonen, 1985

Broken highway, edge of town
Be my main street when that sun goes down
Broken highway, broken dream

Thieves and pimps, cheapest wine
Gamble game chance suits me fine
Broken highway, broken dream

Well wasted life, tortured soul
Close to madness without no goal
Broken highway, broken dream

Well at the mirror, behind my shade
Practice smiling but be on the rage
Broken highway, broken dream

TOO MANY YEARS

BY JORMA KAUKONEN

From *Too Hot to Handle*, Jorma Kaukonen, 1985

Well I opened the door and I found I was looking at danger
Well it's been so many years but we're hiding our faces like strangers
She says that she's got to go, but there ain't no way
I'm letting her walk while there's something to say
Too many years just to watch our hearts dying this way

She's feeling time for a seasonal change and she's yearning
To shake the trees of our lives in the streets here the leaves are for
*   burning*

All things on this earth, were made for the dying
And a look in my soul says there ain't much use trying
Too many years just to watch our hearts dying this way

In an unwritten time, I thought that life was for sharing
And that living together was simply a matter of caring
But things did not work out like I planned
And alienation has left me here damned
Too many years just to watch our hearts dying
Too many years just to hear our hearts crying
Well it's too many years just to watch our hearts dying this way

TOO HOT TO HANDLE

BY JORMA KAUKONEN AND MALLES MEJE
(ONE OF MARGARETA'S NOMS DE PLUME)

From *Too Hot to Handle*, Jorma Kaukonen, 1985

She's a woman that I cannot afford
Just look into her eyes a thousand bucks just roared
Into her vein
Into her vein
Into her vein she finds a reason to live

She's a woman with a habit that's too big
For a poor man like me to tamper with
Into her vein
Into her vein
Into her vein she finds reasons to live

Well I'm her deep loving man, stay while I can
If I hang out too long, I am a lost man
Inside her vein

Inside her vein
Inside her vein there lives a love that's all pain
I should not hang around
I know I should run
Inside her vein there lives a junkie insane
Inside her vein there lives a junkie insane

She's a high-class woman with a taste for number four
The only thing she craves is more and more and more
Into her vein
Into her vein
Into her vein she finds reason to live
She must have some more
She must have some more
She must have too much for me to afford
Inside her vein
Inside her vein
Inside her vein there lives a junkie in pain
See what I am
Alive and alone
Time just flees by soft as a moan
Inside her vein
Inside her vein
Inside her vein there lives a junkie insane
Was a sweet loving man
I couldn't run
Inside my vein there's a junkie insane
Inside my vein there's a junkie insane

SONG FOR OUR MOTHER

BY JORMA KAUKONEN

Written as Beatrice was dying

April 27, 1998
Fur Peace Ranch
Meigs County, Ohio

Mom would go beyond the stars on May 8, 1998.

Strength unto my life she was before I was a man
Daddy's off to fight a war in some far off distant land
He don't come around much just at special times of year
But Mama always holds our hands and puts away our fears

"Come and take a walk," she'd say, "down by that old Pierce Mill
And listen to the water passing by the rocks and rills.
That old gray goose will bite you, but you can feed the ducks,
Trust your heart in all you do, you won't have to trust in luck."

Chorus:
Mama tried to teach us to be strong
And keep walking against the wind even though your hope is gone
It don't matter how alone you are today
'Cause if you keep on walking hard, you'll find a better way

Many years have come and gone, now that I'm a man
My bro and I are all that's left in this part of our clan
Daddy won't be coming back, he's fought his final war
And Mama's eyes look far away, for some distant shore

She wanders in her mind now to that old tobacco farm
When she was just a girl at play in my grandfather's arms

He strokes her hair with loving hands and sends her on her way
To walk across this century, which brings us to today

Chorus

My brother sits beside her bed and holds her hand so tight
He looks upon her shuttered eyes, will she make it through the night?
The what she is remains today, the who she is, is gone,
But what she's done in both our lives I know will linger on

Her favorite books are closed now, her favorite song's been sung
For her boys who stay behind her, she's done all that can be done
She's going to see her friends now that have vanished for so long
She's on the road beyond the stars . . .

She's going . . . going . . . gone

HEART TEMPORARY

BY JORMA KAUKONEN

From *Stars in My Crown*, Jorma Kaukonen, 2007

Blue skies in the morning,
Stars they fill the night
Fall wind rustling through the trees,
Sings a song of great delight
On such a day, you think you'd say,
Exactly what you mean . . .
But in G-d's perfection, things ain't always
Just the way they seem

Chorus:

When the best you have to offer
Falls short of the mark

Self-inflicted holes are piercing
Deep within your heart

Blue skies in the afternoon
Breeze it starts to still
Two dogs sleeping, in the sun
They lie upon that grassy hill
At such a time, you think you'd find
The way to show your heart
But though you're reaching for her hand
Still you walk apart

Chorus

Sun upon that old barn roof, celebrates the day
I hold this moment in my hand
And follow it, along my way
The future flows, this feeling grows
Outside my windowsill
By letting go, I might escape . . . the prison of my will

Chorus

When the best you have to offer
Is all you have to give
Enjoy the moment, G-d has granted
One more day to live

Blue skies out my window
Say goodbye to early morning rain

RIVER OF TIME

BY JORMA KAUKONEN

From *River of Time*, Jorma Kaukonen, 2009

The river of time, it marks our line
From birth to death there is no rhyme
A chance to meet along the way
Will we go or will we stay
There is no sound of tolling bells
Our task on earth is living well

I dreamt my grandma held my hand
I felt a stranger in this land
Her ancient voice called out to me
You have your choice it's plain to see
It's time to move on down the line
We're all here floating in a river of time

The banks were shrouded in the fog
From the shore a barking dog
Recalled a time I'd long forgot
The flowers there forget-me-nots
I saw a wave from friends of mine
As I rolled down that river of time

It might be nice I could have said
To speak to loved ones long since dead
While I still flow they're on the shore
And I shan't see them anymore
Not on this side but in dreams
And dreams aren't always what they seem

The river flows it's just begun
My daughter follows and my son
When my time ends I'll rest on land
And while I slumber they'll still stand
They're a part of that endless line
We're all still floating in a river of time

As I float through another day
There are no waves to rock my way
The water lifts my spirits high
And in this moment you and I
Feel the current flow so fine
As we float down the river of time

SIMPLER THAN I THOUGHT

BY JORMA KAUKONEN

From *River of Time*, Jorma Kaukonen, 2009

I never thought that I would ever feel this way
Your tiny hand would press to mine as we would spin
Circles round the day
Each day would seem to hold a promise based in light
And when the evening brings its shadows home you
Sleep without a fight

Chorus:
What goes through your mind?
I'm looking for a sign
For common ground, where we can share
The things that fill our time

It's simpler than I thought
Your smile unties the knot
There is no time like now to learn
The lessons we forgot

Your world it grows so fast I cannot match the pace
Your spirit flowing deep within you leaves a smile
Of wonder on your face
I can't remember how it was before you came
Your tiny footsteps in the hall can sound like cracks
Of thunder in the rain

Chorus

You bring a gift of life to us that feels grand
I know these moments they will pass before I
Hold them in my hand
My window lets me look out on the summer rain
Will you remember of this day gone by as you
Grow older in your plan

Chorus

The river carries us into tomorrow's day
The people on the shore they wave us on our way
As we wind our way back home
The journey that you follow will be yours alone
May many years be yours to travel as you
Find your way back home

Chorus

EASY NOW REVISITED

WORDS BY JORMA KAUKONEN

MUSIC BY JORMA KAUKONEN AND LARRY CAMPBELL

From *Steady as She Goes*, Hot Tuna, 2011

Chorus:

I got the ridin' pneumonia today
And the weather's too fine to stay
Well I want to go, down to Mexico
Got a feeling I'll be heading that way

Follow the horizon, decades down the road
Living life, the way it comes, ain't such a heavy load
There's still time, to ride the line, I'll find a song to sing
The echo of my engine, its sound makes freedom ring

Chorus

Flying down the Dragon, you'll never see his lair
Taillights flash, around the turns, salvation's in the air
There's more to life, than paying bills and things aren't what they seem
So shiny side, up to the sky, and don't forget your dream

Chorus

Bridge:

When I was young I tried to learn to feel
The body slows but not so chrome and steel
No second-guess about the path you chose
So just ride on as daylight starts to close

Chorus

THINGS THAT MIGHT HAVE BEEN

BY JORMA KAUKONEN

From *Steady as She Goes,* Hot Tuna, 2011

When I was young, on the street where I lived
My brother and I were two distant kids
We shared the same house, we shared the same name
But out in the street we played two different games
Momma and Daddy were fighting wars of their own
They left their two boys to go it alone
We looked for a harbor, safe for the heart
Like ships in the night, our lives drifted apart
Sometimes I think of things that might have been

In the garden of life nothing blooms on its own
And nothing is gained by living alone
This plain little truth lay hidden in time
I wasted so much trying to find what was mine
Years float behind us, we mourned for the dead
And never took notice of things left unsaid
But life's for the living as the river flows on
There's time for our kids, and the moment is gone
Sometimes I think of things that might have been

We grew into men, we went our own ways
What happened in years began with a day
The days fell like leaves, till the branches were bare
A wound in the chest just like the tip of a spear
If I could go back, I might find a new road
An untraveled path, I missed long ago
But the arrow of time goes only one way
The past is the night, and it's gone in the day
Sometimes I think of things that might have been
Sometimes I think of things that might have been

SECOND CHANCES

BY JORMA KAUKONEN AND BARRY MITTERHOFF

From *Steady as She Goes*, Hot Tuna, 2011

We all want second chances, a chance at being free
A chance to take our measure here and see what we can be
The dancing isn't over till the last note has been played
We bow with thanks; we walk back home, to see what we have made

The mirror shows the message, you can't deny the time
Whose tracks you trace upon your face while waiting for a sign
If chances were like highways, a map would bring you home
There'd never be a detour sign as you drive on alone

Chances are like crystal, they shatter when they fall
You cannot bend the hands of time; you'll never save them all
You juggle aspiration, and balance it with pain
No matter how the drought drags on, there'll always come a rain

For life is but a highway, beneath tomorrow's skies
The winds of time will wash away the ache of old goodbyes
Our chances live in children, they'll grow beyond our reach
Our purpose grows from self to all, our mission is to teach

MOURNING INTERRUPTED

BY JORMA KAUKONEN

From *Steady as She Goes*, Hot Tuna, 2011

Went out early this morning, took a walk in the street
The silence was broken by the sound of my feet
There was no one before me, no one waiting at home
There was no one around, I faced the future alone

This ain't the way I want the future to go
Going down fast, or going down slow
I was counting on something
There was nothing to show
It was all smoke and mirrors, the things that I saw
You're born in the spring and you die in the fall
And that's all

I wanted the profit, I hated the loss
I wanted the shade, to hell with the moss
Life was a lottery, just to be one
The shadows of night replaced by the sun

The dreams that I had were alone in my head
As they turned to dust I might be better off dead
I tried to remember
All the books that I read
It was all smoke and mirrors and something you said
'Cause you're born in the spring and you die in the fall
And that's all

I thought that my life would be a walk in the park
Staying up late, alone in the dark
Nothing good happens after midnight has come
I'm lost in the silence, alone with a gun
The chances before me were fading out fast
The future was sliding right into the past
This wasn't the way
And things weren't so grand
It was all smoke and mirrors, the things I had planned
You're born in the spring and you die in the fall
And that's all

There's no chance of deserving, no chance of reward
There's nothing but chance, so shuffle the cards
I'm getting a car; I'm going on the run
No one said life would be nothing but fun
Silent as night the clock raced towards the dawn
I was wrapped in the morning though the curtains were drawn

A chance for redemption
I thought it would be
It was all smoke and mirrors, a bird in a tree
You're born in the spring and you die in the fall
And that's all

ANGEL OF DARKNESS

WORDS BY LARRY CAMPBELL AND JORMA KAUKONEN
MUSIC BY LARRY CAMPBELL

From *Steady as She Goes*, Hot Tuna, 2011

What kind of evil baby
I don't wanna know
Would poison pure waters
Just when they begin to flow

Nothin' you did baby
Nothing you said
Could call up the demons
That dance inside your head

Chorus:
Innocent light, trapped in the night
Angel of darkness
You've got it wrong, you don't belong

On the cold streets you roam
Sweet runaway, there's no debt to pay
Angel of darkness
Find your star, that's who you are
And follow it home

When you were a child, baby
Your were lost in the wild
With no one to save you
No shelter for your sky

Those sworn to protect you . . .
They brokered your pain
They nurtured neglect, girl
And left you standing in the rain

Chorus

Bridge:
Your fate's in your hand, darlin'
So grace it with pride
The color of night, will shade to the light
You're looking at an angel's ride

Chorus

SMOKERISE JOURNEY

WORDS BY JORMA KAUKONEN
MUSIC BY JACK CASADY AND LARRY CAMPBELL

From *Steady as She Goes*, Hot Tuna, 2011

Morning thoughts, and mist on these hills
The sounds of song, in rivers and rills

Begins my day, wrapped in the gray
Smokerise highway, take me home
Carry me home today

The road I ride runs to the stars
Living wraps me in blessing and scars
Time might pass, with nothing to say
Smokerise highway, take me home
Carry me home today

Chorus:

It's hard to see when the forest's so deep
With not much time to rest or sleep
You do your best, take time to pray
Carry me home today

Lonely sound, a train whistle blows
A chill in the air from oncoming snows
I try to chase, these vanishing days
Smokerise highway, take me home
Carry me home today

Chorus

Bridge:

Trying to find a rhyme, I'm living on borrowed time
A river must flow, and you've got to go
Carry me home today

I still recall, those chances to give
With time to grow, and tomorrow to live
But daylight calls, and morning holds sway
Smokerise highway, take me home
Carry me home today

Chorus

Smokerise highway, carry me home
Smokerise highway, carry me home
Smokerise highway, carry me home

IN MY DREAMS

BY JORMA KAUKONEN

From *Ain't in No Hurry,* Jorma Kaukonen, 2015

Well, won't you come with me
We'll go running through mountains
Just in time to set the morning free
Our hearts are young and strong
You're moving like an angel
We never seem to age in my dreams

I never took my time
I took it all for granted
The gift of life is never what it seems
Let's run like we did then
Like spirits in the morning
We never seem to age in my dreams

These precious moments fly
Like pages in the wind
Flying to a place beyond the stars
Memories fade with grace
Cast away like rust
And leave us wondering who and what we are

That sunrise shown like gold
I thought I'd live forever

But living well was way beyond my means
This moment breathes like fire
We watch the dawn together
We never seem to age in my dreams
This morning as I woke
As the midnight spell was broken
I looked around with nothing left to need
The world around us turns
I hold each passing moment
We never seem to age in my dream . . .
We never seem to age in my dream
You never seem to age in my dream

SEASONS IN THE FIELD

BY JORMA KAUKONEN AND LARRY CAMPBELL

We thought we had it all, all grown up inside our skin
A tank of gas and my guitar . . . bring it on, let life begin today
Life was no more simpler then it was just another time
We tried to find conviction without losing peace of mind

I measured time that summer with songs and sets of strings
Duty seemed so far away, one more song before the summer ends
Seasons keep measuring, the time we spend on earth
None of that made sense back then and no one saw the worth

Friendships come and lifetimes flow, and we're all made of dust
A momentary vision, am I sure it's what I really saw
The years began to change like seasons in the field
The crops of life that gave so much would soon deny their yield

Bridge:
A time won't last forever, no matter what we thought
Youthful wages never last, and freedom can't be bought

Looking in the mirror, we did the best we could
A bargain with the devil is always paid in blood

Nothing was so real then as waking up each day
The tasks that laid before me were scattered thoughts that circled round
   my mind
I had no vision that didn't live inside the cloud
The fire that burned inside me then was more than G-d allowed

And then one day when all had passed I wakened to myself
A thousand days had come and gone and outside there was autumn
   in the trees
Each precious moment was a blessing in disguise
I never saw so clearly, it was right before my eyes

Bridge

I still see a moment that keeps living in my heart
I can't turn my back on memories; they open all the doors that shield
   today
On a foundation we've been building since our youth
I draw it close, an ancient friend, and wrap myself in truth

Index